THE AMERICAN DISSENT

Books by Jeffrey Hart

THE AMERICAN DISSENT

VISCOUNT BOLINGBROKE: TORY HUMANIST

POLITICAL WRITERS OF EIGHTEENTH-CENTURY ENGLAND

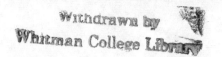
The American Dissent

★ ★ ★

A DECADE OF MODERN CONSERVATISM

BY

JEFFREY HART

1966

DOUBLEDAY & COMPANY, INC.

GARDEN CITY, NEW YORK

We gratefully acknowledge the following for permission to quote from copyrighted material.

HARCOURT, BRACE & WORLD, INC. From "Little Gidding" from the book *Four Quartets* by T. S. Eliot. Reprinted by permission of Harcourt, Brace & World, Inc., and Faber and Faber Ltd.

HARPER & ROW, PUBLISHERS. From *Protracted Conflict* by Robert Strausz-Hupé, *et al*. Reprinted by permission of the publisher.

THE JOHN DAY COMPANY INC., PUBLISHERS. From *Suicide of the West* by James Burnham. Copyright © 1964 by James Burnham. Reprinted by permission of the publisher.

NATIONAL REVIEW. For material from articles which have been printed in *National Review*. Reprinted by permission of *National Review*.

NEW YORK HERALD TRIBUNE. From columns by Rowland Evans and Robert Novak which were printed in the *New York Herald Tribune*. Reprinted by permission of the authors from the *New York Herald Tribune*.

IVAN OBOLENSKY, INC. From *Up From Liberalism* by William F. Buckley, Jr. Copyright © 1959 by William F. Buckley, Jr. Reprinted by permission of the publisher.

RANDOM HOUSE, INC. From *The Liberal Mind* by Kenneth R. Minogue. Reprinted by permission of the publisher.

HENRY REGNERY COMPANY. From *The Conservative Affirmation* by Willmoore Kendall; from *In Defense of Freedom* by Frank S. Meyer; from *Economics of the Free Society* by Wilhelm Röpke. All reprinted by permission of the publisher.

To John Murray Cuddihy

Contents

Posterity may know we have not loosely, through silence, permitted things to pass away as in a dream.

RICHARD HOOKER

We sit by and watch the Barbarian, we tolerate him; in the long stretches of peace we are not afraid. We are tickled by his irreverence, his comic inversion of our old certitudes and our fixed creeds refreshes us; we laugh. But as we laugh we are watched by large and awful faces from beyond; and on these faces there is no smile.

HILAIRE BELLOC

Preface

One fall afternoon, half-way through the 1964 election campaign, as we sat talking about one thing or another on the terrace outside his house, a colleague of mine—he is a political liberal, a fair-minded man, and a first-rate teacher—asked me a question he had evidently been saving for some time. "What is it you conservatives want?" he asked. "What's really bothering you? Does the growth of government really *hurt* you in any significant way? What would you do in Viet Nam? It's a *complex* world." His attitude was not at all unfriendly; his tone was that of a man who simply wanted to know. Yet his curiosity really centered, I think, on the question of why *I* was a conservative. The conservative position itself he thought he knew, from his general reading of the ordinary newspapers and the usual journals of opinion, and now he was confessing his bewilderment that a colleague should identify himself with such a position.

In fact, he had received virtually no information about the serious political positions of the American Right from the publications on which he quite naturally depended. Everyone knows, for example, that it is to say the least unlikely for a conservative book to get an open-minded review in the *New York Times*. More often than not, such books are not noticed at all; or if noticed, they are consigned to irrelevance. In journals of loftier intellectual ambition the situation is, paradoxically, even worse: the political Right is caricatured and sociologized rather than met on its substantive positions. The following sentences in *Commonweal* are representative:

[13]

"The ideology of the radical right is the ideology of those groups who have lost power and status in an industrialized, pluralistic America: the small businessman, the Southern white, the believer in an America identical with white Anglo-Saxon Protestantdom. But *strangely* [my italics], and dangerously, this ideology has caught hold with a group increasingly important in American society: the college-educated, suburban-dwelling, upper-middle class."[1] This author was not moved to reflect on the irony present in his use of the word "strangely"; though the situation he describes is strange indeed if the conservative position is now appropriate only to the neurotic, the threatened, or the freshly dispossessed.

The failure of the usual organs of opinion to communicate to the reading public the serious positions that have been generated during the last decade or so by the American conservative movement has in part been the result of intellectual sloth. To find out what the intelligent conservatives have been saying would involve looking up their books and articles and reading them: it is infinitely easier to handle the Right as the literary critic Jack Ludwig did recently in *Partisan Review*: they are a collection of "tax-nuts, Roosevelt-haters, TVA-haters . . . fluoridophobes, and old maids afraid of rape by a Negro."[2] But if laziness explains part of the failure, it may also be due to the perfectly understandable do-we-have-to-go-over-it-all-again attitude of those who feel that American conservatism suffered a definitive intellectual defeat during the twenties and thirties.

But whatever the cause, the failure in communication has been virtually total; and so my inquisitive colleague, while reluctantly prepared to admit that a significant segment of the populace does, for obscure and probably pathological reasons, incline to the political Right, could not begin to imagine why any moderately reflective man—myself, for instance, who am not, as far as he could observe, either an oil millionaire or in

[14]

a hazardous social situation—should voluntarily align himself with the conservatives. The phenomenon seemed to him eccentric and even irrational—and therefore disturbing. I sought to touch on a few of the concerns that have been central to recent conservative thought; but then, as usually happens in conversations of this sort, seeking the point of least resistance we passed on to other matters.

But the moment has remained in my memory—as symbolic, yes; but also as sad. For if liberals and conservatives are to reach even the point of informed *disagreement*, liberals will have to find out just why it is people quite as intelligent and learned as themselves do not, these days, necessarily end up as liberals. And unless they do this, my friend and his fellow liberals are very likely to be surprised, not to say stunned, by the political events of the next decade.

I do not conceive of this book as a Primer on Conservatism. None such exists, and for the best of reasons: it cannot be written. Rather, it is about what has happened to the conservative movement during, roughly, the past ten years. I have asked myself whether the conservative movement during the past decade has thought responsibly on such matters as the crisis in Viet Nam, the recent decisions of the Supreme Court, the situation of the American Negro, the United Nations, and so forth. My answer, which I propose to elaborate in this book, is, Yes. For my purposes, I decided to turn primarily to the performance of *National Review*, since it has been there primarily that conservative intellectuals have expressed themselves, day by day, since 1955. My concern is by no means exclusively with *National Review*, for there are distinguished conservatives who have not, for various reasons, played an active part in the journal; but I believe it is accurate to say that no important contribution by conservatives, from any country, writing in any discipline, has gone unremarked or unassimilated by the contributors to *National Review:* with the result that it has emerged as an authentic voice of conservatism. Not in the sense that it presumes to lay down "the" conservative position apodictically; its pages in fact boil with controversy as different elements of the conservative world seek to express their own emphases. It has, however, shown itself to be sensitive to the best in contemporary conservative thought—to Oakeshott deploring the effronteries of rationalism, to Voegelin disparaging the millenarists, to Leo Strauss counterrevolutionizing against the behaviorists.

Though this book is, indeed, sympathetic to American conservatism, its author—as will be seen—is by no means always in complete agreement with the positions taken by the conservative writers or by *National Review* on the various issues before us. Nevertheless, the editor of *National Review* —I have met with him twice in connection with this project —proved friendly and helpful, and was able to supply various kinds of information when I requested them. As a result, this is a better book than it otherwise would have been.

Goodrich–Four-Corners, Vermont
1965

THE AMERICAN DISSENT

I

The Emergence of Conservatism

In the Preface to *The Liberal Imagination* (1950), Lionel Trilling observed with an air of regret that "nowadays there are no conservative or reactionary ideas in general circulation," and that, as a result, "liberalism is not only the dominant but even the sole intellectual tradition." The observation that liberalism is our "sole intellectual tradition" has provided, indeed, the basis for his operations as a literary critic. If there *are* no conservative ideas in general circulation, liberal ideas meet with no resistance, and so tend to lose their subtlety and vitality, and consequently their relevance to human experience. It follows that liberals must provide their *own* resistance, their own criticism of liberal ideas; and this Trilling undertakes to do, using literature, with its awareness of complexity, difficulty and variousness as a kind of substitute for a conservative tradition. He undertakes these tasks (with an air of *noblesse oblige*) even while regretting that he has to do so, because there is no genuine conservative tradition; he enters upon them, indeed, stoically—knowing that such elegant operations will arouse the resentment of his simpler liberal brethren.

Growing up in America, at least in the secure, middle-class America in which ideas do actually "circulate," one sees that there is a good deal of force to the observation that liberalism constitutes our "sole intellectual tradition." The ideas one is likely to encounter—in school, as a magazine and newspaper

[19]

reader, in political speeches, in the college classroom, in television symposia—are almost universally liberal ones. Yet it
may happen—does, I think, increasingly happen these days—
that a certain disparity is noted between liberal idea and felt
experience. The young American knows, as a certainty, that
his high-school civics teacher would turn blue rather than say
anything against the principle of free speech; yet he knows
with equal certainty that in his own family, or the community
he grew up in, some things are *not* said, or, more subtly, that
there are certain modes, certain tones of voice, appropriate to
various subjects, suggesting a spectrum of attitudes and assumptions; and he senses that the very identity of the family
or community is inextricable from those attitudes and assumptions. The liberal principle (part of our "sole intellectual
tradition") then acquires for him, increasingly, a ghostly
quality. No, the world is *not* like that.

Back at the civics class, perhaps only because he is required
to be there, the young middle-class American encounters another liberal axiom, derived, like the first one, from the eighteenth-century Enlightenment: that the various nations, cultures, religions, groups are *equal*, that is, of equal value. It is
a pleasant thought; and again his teacher would turn blue
rather than proclaim that one culture, in point of fact, is inferior to another. Yet again, this does not seem to correspond
to experience. Observably, groups behave differently. Is it impossible to evaluate such behavior? Evidently not. One does
so every day. Once again it is seen that the liberal idea is a sort
of pious wish.

It may be that the young American develops the habit of
comparing liberal idea and assumption with observed actuality, and that the acid of skepticism spreads, eating in everywhere. Liberals, he understands, condemn "guilt by association," but he remembers the adage, "Birds of a feather flock
together." He begins to develop some sensitivity to language,

noting the abstract quality of "guilt by association," and the concrete quality of "birds of a feather"—the very phraseology refined by experience. His alertness to language leads him on. He notices that the *New York Times* refers to Spain ("Franco Spain") in tones quite different from those it uses when writing about just plain Poland or Yugoslavia (never "Tito Yugoslavia"), and he wonders whether life in Yugoslavia is really freer or pleasanter than it is in Spain (if he *goes* to Spain he finds that it is crowded with American liberal pundits, among others, having a marvelous time). What is more, Spain being on *our* side, he notices the curious, and ominous, liberal indifference to that fact.

If liberal doctrine and assumption violate his sense of fact, liberal attitudes tend to trouble his moral feelings. Enthusiasm for easy divorce, and moral hospitality to premarital intercourse, homosexuality, and abortion repel him at first glance, and upon reflection prove to be informed by a profoundly antidomestic ethos: the family is to be weakened vis-à-vis outer society, and the individual isolated with his desires. Who is so obtuse as not to know the liberal attitude on these matters? By this time, our young American may be somewhat loosened from our "sole intellectual tradition."

If he is of a scholarly bent, and goes on with his education, some surprising things turn up. Reading around, and not merely going to lectures, he finds that, in point of fact, there is more historical evidence for some traditional beliefs—the resurrection of Christ, say—than there is for such liberal certitudes as progress and human goodness. Declining to buy that sociology textbook, price twelve dollars, and monstrous in its official banality, he finds, on his own, that there really have been masters in the field. Georg Simmel, for example, shows that a person's *identity* is inextricable from the "pattern of his group affiliation." That is to say, each person belongs to a wide variety of groups, both organized and informal. One might be, for example, a Protestant of German descent, a family man, an alumnus of the University of Wisconsin, a member of the S.A.E. fraternity, an Elk, an angler, a resident of Oak Park, Illinois, a member of the local golf club, and so on. This complex obviously could be varied, subtly or drastically, by changing one or more of the groups. Another person might move in the same pattern, except that he is a Catholic, or perhaps a regular army man, or not an Elk but a Mason. According to Simmel, individuality is established and maintained by such variation in the pattern of group affiliation. The more groups there are—distinctive regions, neighborhoods, clubs, professional associations, and so on—and *the more independent they are*, the more various will be the patterns of individual affiliation, and the wider, in consequence, will be the possibilities of individuality. Simmel also observes that it is the exclusiveness of a group that makes for its strength and distinctiveness.

Now, Simmel's analysis is susceptible of wide application. It is the group, after all, that has always given meaning and a sense of continuity to the individual life, and as the integrity of groups is broken down—as is happening now in the case of the family, the privately controlled business, the club, the private school, the neighborhood school, and the college fraternity—the individual's sense of his own identity will be broken down as well. An entire literature has accumulated dealing with the phenomenon of the "identity crisis" in modern society, with alienation, with the loss of a sense of the self. Simmel's analysis points to one of the causes of this phenomenon, and the implications of his analysis plainly run counter to the liberal impulse to break down the power and destroy the exclusiveness of groups within the society. Simmel gives form and articulation to the suspicion that a serious contradiction exists between "equality" as conceived by liberals and their proclaimed desire for variety and individuality.

Nor can it be doubted that an assault upon the natural formation of groups is going forward at the present time under the auspices of liberal ideology, for virtually any day's newspaper can be called in evidence.*

Everywhere the truly inquisitive student turns, in the best modern thought, he finds liberal assumptions challenged. One important liberal tradition in ethics is the utilitarian (Locke-Bentham-Mill), which holds that pleasure is good and pain evil and attempts to construct an ethical philosophy on that basis. Yet Kenneth Minogue, an English liberal philosopher, has no trouble at all in exposing the weakness at the core of the utilitarian position: it offers no ground for moral obligation. Speaking of the "moral emptiness" of Benthamism, Minogue writes:

The individual, faced with some sort of moral choice, must [in the utilitarian view] simply decide what he and others want; but the utility of competing courses of action does not *determine* our choice, for the simple reason that it *depends* on our choice. Yet all manner of fascinating possibilities arise. Why not establish sadomasochistic cooperatives, in which those whose greatest happiness lies in inflicting

* For example, Arnold Toynbee's recent attack on local school boards: "The sovereign local school board is, in fact," he wrote in the *New York Herald Tribune*, "a fortress of McCarthyism that has not yet fallen, and the American people can hardly afford to leave this fortress permanently standing." See also the following note in *National Review*: "Yale University, recognizing that our age will let nothing be simultaneously valuable and inheritable, has for a generation been tending to convert its undergraduate body into a demographic replica of a federal prison—with students drawn from every social and economic class, every geographical region, race, religion and color, and no preferences, if you please, for sons of Yale men. And now Yale, which wouldn't be caught dead less levelled than any place else, is considering admitting new students from every—well, both, sexes. The dean who thought up the idea, and supplied the needed rationalizations (it will raise scholastic standards, keep the boys in New Haven for weekends, etc.), took a moment, in passing, to compose the perfect epitaph for our civilization: 'Any form of exclusiveness,' he ruled in exquisitely levelled prose, 'is bad.'" (*National Review*, II, xxi, p. 3.)

pain meet up with those whose greatest happiness consists in enduring it? Why not cooperation between those afflicted with blood-lust and those about to commit suicide? Such disruptive possibilities could be plausibly defended in utilitarian terms.[3]

The other principal liberal tradition in ethics, derived from Kant, is a much more elegant thing, but scarcely more plausible than utilitarianism. Viewing ethical behavior as, so to speak, self-validating, Kant dispensed with "the hypothesis of God" in his autonomous ethical system. Yet Kant's system, as has often been pointed out, was actually a form of secularized deism—and not entirely secularized at that, for, though Kant dispensed with the hypothesis of God in accounting for the moral law, he smuggled Him back in as a kind of *deus ex machina* to account for the coincidence of virtue and happiness. Kant's moral idealism was subsisting on a hidden religious capital, and such capital is quickly used up. In Tillich's words, "autonomy is able to live as long as it can draw from the religious tradition of the past. . . . But more and more it loses this spiritual foundation. It becomes emptier, more formalistic."

II

So far, I have been suggesting in a rather impressionistic way the sort of response a young American growing up in the forties and fifties might make to the pervasive liberal atmosphere. He resists its pressure and is skeptical of its claims. Intellectually, liberalism seems to him thin, and, at best, even in its intellectual virtues, derivative. Emotionally, it troubles him. He is not yet a conservative, for he lacks a coherent and principled alternative position, and his culture does not provide one—for, as Trilling remarked, there are "no conservative ideas in general circulation." Yet Trilling's re-

mark was truer in 1950 than it is today. During the thirties
and forties, resistance to liberalism had very largely been reduced to a defense of free-enterprise economics. Informed as
it was at its best by the thought of such scholars as Von Mises
and Hayek, such a defense was commendable enough; yet it
scarcely constituted a comprehensive conservative position. In
other areas, resistance to liberalism was peculiarly arid: the
journalism of John T. Flynn and of the later Mencken was
scarcely of the sort to put conservative ideas, or for that matter any ideas, in general circulation. As the decade of the
fifties began, however, there were indications that this state
of affairs was due to change. In *God and Man at Yale* (1951),
William Buckley, then a recent Yale graduate, launched an
attack upon the hegemony of liberal ideas and attitudes in
the Academy, and he called attention to the existence of conservative alternatives. In 1952, Whittaker Chambers' auto-
biographical *Witness*, appearing against a background of espionage revelations, helped to dramatize the fact that we are
in the midst of a world revolution—a revolution involving the
profoundest of intellectual and spiritual issues, as well as political ones. But perhaps Russell Kirk's *The Conservative
Mind* (1953) should be taken as marking the beginning of the
conservative intellectual resurgence. The appearance of this
book was an event of great importance, for Kirk succeeded in
demonstrating the existence of a conservative intellectual tradition "from Burke to Santayana," and one saw that such
a tradition might be drawn upon to give intellectual form to
the intuition of liberalism's weakness. Examining and expounding the thought most importantly of Burke, but also
of John Adams, Walter Scott, Coleridge, John Randolph,
Calhoun, Tocqueville, More and Santayana, Kirk showed
that the traditional culture of the West, with its habits and
assumptions, beliefs and moral imperatives, had been defended in the past with powerful intellectual weapons, and

he suggested that it might be possible so to defend it in the present and the future. In addition, *The Conservative Mind* performed for many a valuable secondary function. For some time, no doubt for several generations, the assumption had been widespread among students, and not only among students, that conservatives are vulgar—that they are merely Rotarians, Babbitts and (to use David Riesman's term) Homeguardists, and therefore both incapable of thought and untouched by the ideal.† Wilhelm Röpke, one of the most civilized of European economists, has recounted an anecdote about his reception by American students which nicely illustrates the point. They told him that they were familiar with his work on the free market economy and with his critique of socialism, and that they were aware of his conservative views generally, but they pointed out that they were accustomed to associate such opinions with bankers and members of the chamber of commerce and so were astounded to find them espoused disinterestedly by a man of urbanity and immense erudition.[4] Russell Kirk's evocation of a conservative intellectual tradition from Burke to Santayana, though raising many more questions than at that point one could expect to have answered, showed beyond dispute that the conservative position could be articulated with graceful intensity.

It is quite natural, of course, that the conservative intellectual position should have begun to emerge only recently, and in response to liberal intellectual hegemony. Conservatism does not normally exhibit itself as a "position" or as a system of ideas, but remains implicit, unarticulated, relying on the various understandings and intuitions upon which

† Such sociological essays as those collected by Daniel Bell in *The New American Right* (1955) and *The Radical Right* (1963) represent an attempt to sustain this myth.

an actual civilization is based. Conservative theory does not originate in a tract or a manifesto, but is written, as de Maistre put it, "in the hearts of all countrymen." It becomes articulate under attack. Much as Burke, facing the abstractions of the French *philosophes*, so destructive in their implications for the actual English nation, found himself "alarmed into reflection," so modern conservatives, in Gerhart Niemeyer's words, have felt "the need for a specific conservative way of thinking . . . only as a reaction against a certain type of political ideology which seemed to know no commitment to the living community." Thus, under pressure from liberal abstractions—and the pressure has increased daily—conservative ideas have more and more exhibited themselves, emerging from habits of behavior, from actual experience, and from historic pieties, to become available *as ideas*; for implicit in the civilization of the West are ideas and assumptions that prefer, so to speak, to remain latent, exhibiting themselves as propositions only under attack, much as the images on a photographic plate become visible only when subjected to the acids of the developing bath.

If the appearance of *The Conservative Mind* in 1953 may conveniently be thought of as marking the beginning of the conservative intellectual resurgence, the weekly magazine *National Review*, launched in 1955 by a group including William Buckley, Brent Bozell, James Burnham, John Chamberlain, Willmoore Kendall, Russell Kirk, Suzanne LaFollette, Frank S. Meyer, Erik von Kuehnelt-Leddihn and William Schlamm, sought to give the movement direction and coherence. In background and temperament these people had little enough in common, yet they seem to have been able to function together surprisingly well. The moving spirit, William Buckley, then twenty-eight years old, had had a flashy personal success with his first book, *God and Man at Yale*, and this had opened the way for him to demonstrate a formidable debating skill on radio and TV, and in college auditoriums across the country. In these public appearances, Buckley was quick-witted and elegant, behaving with a good deal of hauteur and taking a genuine delight in his own rhetorical resources. In a way he seemed a figure more suited to the atmosphere of the Oxford Union than to that of the American campus. Indeed, his emergence in the early 1950s actually had a touch of the Byronic about it—in part because of the astounding variety of his talents: not only a writer and a masterful public debater, he speaks several languages, is an excellent pianist, both rides and skis expertly, and delights in hazardous journeys in his ocean-going sailboat; but also because of his deliberately outrageous challenge to constituted cultural authority. I myself did not see a Buckley performance until he had become something of a scandal, and the occasion was quite characteristic. He was at Harvard in 1954 debating with James Wechsler on the question of whether the conservative or the liberal is in fact the "nonconformist." The situation, of course, was preposterous, and nothing could have been more ludicrous than the sight of Wechsler at once fawning on his Harvard audience and maintaining that the liberal is the true nonconformist. Talking past Wechsler, Buckley proved his point by cracking jokes about the liberal notables crowding the hall in front of him.

Like Buckley himself, his brother-in-law Brent Bozell established a reputation at Yale as a debater and campus *enfant terrible*, but his temperament is essentially more meditative and scholarly. He writes slowly, and his essays characteristically reflect a deeply pondered effort to get at the roots of things. He is a good polemicist, but his forthcoming two-volume study of the Supreme Court seems really the more characteristic expression of his spirit. Willmoore Kendall, a brilliant professional political scientist and a superb prose stylist—but also an intense and therefore sometimes thorny character—taught both Buckley and Bozell at Yale, and then joined forces with them on the magazine, both as book editor and columnist. Russell Kirk, culturally and temperamentally a traditionalist, found *National Review* a natural place for him to write a column called "From the Academy"; Suzanne LaFollette had been managing editor to Albert Jay Nock when he edited the famous *Freeman* during the twenties, and had become a dedicated anti-Communist as a result of her experience as secretary to the committee set up under John Dewey to investigate Stalin's great purge of the 1930s. Some of the other originating spirits had had a radical past. James Burnham at one time had been known as Trotsky's literary executioner, so sharp were his skills as a polemicist, and he also had served as an editor of *Partisan Review*, meanwhile teaching philosophy at New York University. After the war he moved to the Right, and became perhaps the nation's most acute anti-Communist strategist. John Chamberlain had been a fellow-traveling socialist and daily book-review editor of the *New York Times*. Submerging into *Time*, Inc., for a number of years, and moving to the Right politically, he found himself a member of the hard anti-Communist faction at *Time*, along with Whittaker Chambers and William Schlamm; more recently, he has appeared in the *Wall Street Journal* and *Barron's*, as well as *National Review*. Both Schlamm and Frank Meyer had been members of the Communist Party, Meyer holding positions of considerable responsibility in the Party hierarchy. He left the Party in 1949, emerging as a conservative after a period of intense and searching philosophical meditation.

Proceeding from the insight that we live in a period of wide-ranging revolution—political, moral, theological; a revolution, moreover, whose effects will increasingly be felt in every American city and village—the editors concluded that a "natural conservatism," the "continuing piety of men living in untroubled times . . . that universal human tendency to hold by the accustomed, to maintain existing modes of life," would be "radically inadequate," and that circumstances today call for a "conscious conservatism"—in effect, a counter-revolutionary conservatism—which would "take as its standards concepts founded in truth and in the traditions of the West, but scorned today by the 'enlightened.'" Such a conscious conservatism would be

a reaction to the rude breach the revolution has made in the continuity of human wisdom. It is called forth by a sense of the deep loss that such a cutting off brings about. It [would] now, perforce, be the natural conservatism toward which it yearns. The world in which it exists is the revolutionary world.[5]

Necessarily, the concerns of the magazine have been broad. As Frank Meyer says, "it has not been limited in its perspectives to the arena of the purely political. It looks toward nothing less than a deep-going renewal of American life in the spirit of the Western and American tradition—a renewal at every level of existence: social, intellectual, philosophical, spiritual, as well as political."[6] In its efforts toward this end, the magazine naturally depends upon the consistent contributions of its editors, but it also has published a large number of other writers, including Evelyn Waugh, Roy Campbell, John Dos Passos, Donald Davidson, Max Eastman, Alistair Horne, Whittaker Chambers, Raymond English, Ross Hoffman, Francis Graham Wilson, Thomas Molnar, Ezra Pound, Colm Brogan, Ernest van den Haag, Eliseo Vivas, Richard Weaver, Francis Russell, Hugh Kenner, and Will Herberg (Kenner and Herberg eventually were added to the masthead). Among younger writers, *National Review* has made some striking discoveries: Joan Didion, Garry Wills, Guy Davenport, William Rickenbacker, M. Stanton Evans, Richard Whalen. One result has been that the magazine has proved to be journalistically and intellectually (if not commercially) successful to an impressive degree. Its circulation, also, has been a pleasant surprise. Beginning with eight thousand subscribers, it now has about one hundred thousand, and about three hundred thousand readers.‡

Since 1955, moreover, writers associated with *National Review* have published a number of books, many of them growing out of articles and controversies within the magazine. Among such books are Buckley's *Up From Liberalism* and *Rumbles Left and Right*, Burnham's *Congress and the American Tradition* and *Suicide of the West*, Meyer's *The Moulding of Communists* and *In Defense of Freedom*, Kirk's *A Program for Conservatives*, and Kendall's *The Conservative Affirmation*.

‡ The circulation figures are not without interest. The magazine began in November, 1955. At the end of succeeding years, subscribers numbered as follows: 1956, 20,000; 1957, 20,000; 1958, 27,000; 1959, 29,000; 1960, 34,000; 1961, 54,000; 1962, 60,000; 1963, 61,000; 1964, 90,000. Up to a point, it can be assumed that the rise in circulation was simply the result of a new commodity finding its natural market. But the magazine went on to pass the general level of opinion journals over the years, roughly 30,000–50,000, figures within which almost all the journals of opinion in this country have remained during the last decade. *National Review's* plunge past the upper limit has presumably been caused by a number of factors: a) unlike the other journals of opinion, it has no real competition, i.e., there is no other weekly edited for a well-educated audience, whose views are anything like *National Review's*; b) there has been a considerable commotion during the past years associated with the rise of the Far Right, on whose impetus *National Review* undoubtedly rode, particularly in 1964; c) the magazine's managers have no doubt improved their promotional techniques; and d) the journal, which even in the early days Clinton Rossiter described as "alternately enraging, entertaining, and provocative—what more can I ask of a magazine" is intrinsically interesting. Beginning in September, 1961, the editors, in recognition of growing circulation, adopted a cover design employing color, and a better grade of paper, which, they explained, "tends to lift a magazine out of the butcher-paper sectarianism which no longer suits our circulation explosion." No doubt the changes had something to do with increasing the journal's newsstand appeal.

III

To exist as an imaginative force, a magazine must have a distinctive style, a special voice of its own; and that style must express something valid. This remains true whatever the mode. The *New Yorker* speaks with its own voice—urbane, knowing, surprised by nothing, contemptuous of the solecism, imaginatively involved with money and with social class. *Partisan Review*, probably the best of the quarterlies, gains its power from the fact that it too speaks in special tones: Jewish, at once scholarly and political (but not really literary), serious, and in a general way Marxian and Freudian. In comparison with *Partisan Review*, the other quarterlies, *Kenyon Review*, *Hudson Review*, *Sewanee Review*, seem diffuse and arbitrary—and, therefore, dull.

The imaginative appeal of *National Review* is due in no small part to the fact that it has been able to evolve its own special tone, not difficult to describe, but composed of elements that at first glance one would suppose difficult to bring into effective combination. First, a kind of gaiety and insouciance that might be called "Ivy League," and which is reminiscent of some things in the early Scott Fitzgerald, most notably in the way ease combines with lightheartedness to produce a genuine liberation: great puffy balloons collapse. In addition to the gaiety, there is a dedicated "hard" anti-Communism, shared by all the writers but gaining added authority from men who, to use Whitman's expression, were *there*—who were Communists, and experienced the profound appeal of Communism, but rejected it, and so know deeply what both acceptance and rejection of Communism entail. Less definite than either of these, but pervasive nevertheless, is a voice that is "naturally" traditional, expressive of high regard for "a way of life," for the amenities, for the values implicit in politeness. Buckley himself has written disparagingly of "rhetorical totalism," of a tone that is "hard, schematic, implacable," and thus suggestive of "unyielding dogmatism that is in itself intrinsically objectionable, whether it comes from the mouth of Ehrenburg, or Savonarola, or Ayn Rand."[7] Buckley's own tone, and that of the magazine, represents the antithesis of "rhetorical totalism." It is worth noting that the section devoted to books, movies, the theater and so forth is called "Books-Arts-Manners"; and though the word "manners" as used here means more than "politeness"—means, more neutrally, the various imaginative signals by which we communicate our feelings and intentions (what Sir Harold Nicholson wrote about in his *Good Behaviour*)—still, its presence turns out to be significant. Buckley himself, for example, exhibits what I would characterize as a "social" intelligence of a very high order: from the surfaces of things, from the language people use and from their intellectual manners, and from their often half-conscious behavior, he is able to move to the profoundest political and moral conclusions. The word "manners" appearing in *The Nation* or *New Republic*, for example, would somehow strike a discordant note: not that they necessarily have *bad* manners; just that their concerns tend to be so abstract.

At first glance these voices—lighthearted, toughly anti-Communist, traditional—might seem disparate indeed. As a matter of fact, it seems to me, they have not turned out to be so, and upon reflection one sees why. Gaiety—civilized fun—not only is compatible with the others but intellectually, today, presupposes them. The capacity to laugh about a thing, a thing you also care deeply about, implies the ability to step back from it, to *place* it, to recognize that it does not constitute the only actuality. As far as the Communist is concerned, politics is the ultimate category, and not at all something to be humorous about; human history *is* the history of class struggle, and that is that. It is in the political arena that man must work out his salvation. Laughter is the mode that refuses to take the world quite that seriously. Recognizing the inherent contradictions and absurdities of man's existence, it steps back and allows the world to *be* the world. Thus Kierkegaard could say profoundly that the earnestness of one's faith is tested by one's "sensitivity to the comical"; and Malraux, writing on the history of art, could take the appearance of the "archaic smile" in sculpture as a sign that man had become aware of his soul. Serious as they are about politics, the conservatives who write for *National Review* do not seem to consider it the ultimate category; and humor, as they employ it, is the sign of a proper distance—of temporary removal; of the willingness to step back, and, in the higher sense of the word, play with the subject at hand.

One might wonder, indeed, why so many organs of political opinion seldom say *anything* funny. Though often intelligent and well-informed, they are uniformly solemn. *The Nation, New Republic, New Leader, The Reporter:* so rare is wit that when it does put in an appearance, as in Murray Kempton and Jules Feiffer, the conservatives are so surprised that they tend to overrate it. Why are these magazines so solemn? For them too, one gathers, politics is the ultimate category. Though they are far from bringing to it the millennial hopes of the Communist, there is nothing, for them, that transcends a political issue. Politics is where one works out one's destiny, and defines one's quality—if one has any. And there is nothing funny about *that*. (Probably, some of their writers have extra-political "beliefs"; but surfaces do not always lie; they are, oddly enough, often profound.) The cheerfulness of *National Review*, in contrast, seems to come from its ability to loosen its relation to politics, to recognize the ironies, incongruities, and absurdities of political life. The magazine has thus recovered a spirit more characteristic of an older journalism. "When I first came to New York, in the mid-twenties," recalls John Chamberlain, "the controversies raged quite as they do now. But intellectual warfare in those days was waged gaily. . . . The sectarian impulse had not yet triumphed, and parties were stimulating gatherings instead of mutual admiration societies."[8] Such gaiety, indeed, is inextricable from freedom of spirit; solemnity, on the other hand, accords with a sour intolerance of other men's opinions.§

§ Such Catholic magazines as *Commonweal* and *America* might be expected to recognize categories that transcend politics; and of course they do. Their excessive solemnity, however, proceeds from the extreme importance political *respectability* has for them. We may see that for upwardly-mobile Catholics, eager to assimilate to the Establishment, political liberalism is no joking matter; nor is conservatism. Of the two magazines, it seems to me that *Commonweal* is the grimmer. *America* is also capable of transcendence of liberalism when a religious issue is at stake. In 1964, for example, Rolf Hochhuth's play *The Deputy* was creating an international stir, for in it he condemned Pope Pius XII for "silence" on German treatment of the Jews. In an editorial published two days after the New York opening of the play, the *New York Times* backed Hochhuth. The editorial was called "Silence," and, embracing the Pope in its indictment, concluded: "The facts may be in dispute; the history imperfect; the indictment too severe. But the philosophical issue is ever alive. In a word, it is silence. Specifically applied to the years of Hitlerism, there were many governments, and many political, religious and other leaders, who failed to speak up, let alone act. . . . Those who merely remained silent contributed in different degrees to the downfall of man and his conscience in the twentieth century." Quoting this condemnation, *America* appealed with devastating but wholly implicit irony from the *Times* present to the *Times* past; for on December 25, 1942, the *Times* had not characterized as "silence" the Pope's appeal on behalf of the "hundreds of thousands of persons who, without any fault on their own part, sometimes only because of their nationality or race, have been consigned to death or a slow decline." Observed the *Times* editorially in 1942: "This Christmas, more than ever, the Pope is a lonely voice crying out of the silence of a continent." It went on: "Because the

[35]

Certainly humor is one of the most difficult subjects for literary criticism (we may suppose it no accident that Aristotle's treatise on comedy has been "lost"). Even so, the wit of *National Review* accounts for a considerable part of its charm, and its charm is part of its power. A comment or two on its characteristic modes is therefore in order.‖

Often the fun is nonpolitical, as in this opening paragraph of a review of Heinrich Boll's *The Clown* by Guy Davenport, in which he provides a short but more or less definitive account of German humor:

German humor, like French modesty and the Eskimo cuisine, is one of those perplexities so resistant to understanding that our anguish when we encounter it is more like suffering than mere dumb-

---

Pope speaks to and in some sense for all the peoples at war, the clear stand he takes on the fundamental issues of the conflict has greater weight and authority. When a leader bound to impartiality to nations on both sides condemns as 'heresy' the new form of national state which subordinates everything to itself, when he assails the exile and persecution of human beings 'for no other reason than their race or political opinion' . . . the impartial judgment is like a verdict in a high court of justice. Pope Pius expresses as passionately as any leader on our side the war aims of the struggle for freedom." (See *America*, April 18, 1964, pp. 534–35.) *The Deputy*, of course, was entirely a political act, and without interest as a work of art. It received the approval of the Left, and was attacked from the Right: and the *Times* is never out of step with liberal opinion, even when it has to contradict itself. But *America*, when its own deepest concerns were at issue, proved capable of transcending its workaday liberalism.

‖ Dwight Macdonald has attempted to solemnize the odd idea that conservatives are characteristically humorless. "Culturally," he writes, "a conservative is someone like Irving Babbitt or Paul Elmer More, not always the liveliest company in the world but a respecter and defender of tradition." ("Scrambled Eggheads on the Right," *Commentary*, April, 1956, p. 389.) There is something astonishingly provincial about this. Babbitt and More *were* conservatives, but so were Aristophanes and the best Roman satirists; and, of course, the most conservative writers in English are also, it happens, the wittiest—Dryden, Pope, Swift, Gay, Johnson. For that matter, the conservative T. S. Eliot reintroduced wit into English poetry. I don't want to press the point, but the great *liberal* literary critic Matthew Arnold (was he the *only* great liberal critic?) dismissed Chaucer as not serious enough.

foundment. The blindest worshipper of Mozart is stopped cold by the jokes in his letters; about half of Wilhelm Busch is understandable. One has a paralyzing suspicion that Goethe meant, from time to time, to be funny; Immanuel Kant used to roar over a cartoon depicting a boy pulling a brick by a string ("*Ach!* a dog you expected, *nein?*"), and Hitler used to break up his *Generalstabversammlungen* with his little pleasantry about the Parisian flower-seller who, on seeing him emerge early one morning from his Mercedes Benz to admire the Opera, threw her bouquets into the air and screamed, "*Merde alors, c'est le diable!*" So when Heinrich Boll is said to be a great German comic novelist and we sit down to inspect his work, our eyes glaze over and our feet ache, but humor, savage (as the publishers claim) or other, never arrives, even with string and brick.[9]

The humor can also be verbal, even typographical. Here is the way *National Review* handled one of those all-too-familiar groups whose pomposity is embodied in their ludicrous titles ("The First National Conference of the Congress on Survival Has Come And—oops, the title's over—gone, having spent three days and some dollars at the Biltmore in New York City . . ."). Sometimes the humor is ironic, and depends on the reader's awareness of the predictable: you have to know how monotonously certain liberals are honored in order to relish the treatment *National Review*, in a short paragraph, gave the news of yet another testimonial dinner. ("From a news dispatch: 'Dr. Harold Taylor, who is retiring as President of Sarah Lawrence College, will be the guest of honor at a dinner to be held in the Hotel Waldorf Astoria on Thursday, May 21. The theme of the dinner will be The Liberal Spirit in American Life. Edward R. Murrow will preside. Speakers will include Dr. Robert Oppenheimer, Archibald MacLeish, and Mrs. Eleanor Roosevelt.' Tickets can be reserved through NATIONAL REVIEW.")

Irony may also be used to expose the gap between moral pretension and actual behavior, and for this reason it has proved to be the peculiarly appropriate, and effective, mode

[37]

of comment upon liberals, whose grandiose and generally very abstract moral claims almost automatically generate ironies when brought into conjunction with their actual behavior. Consider this episode involving the American Civil Liberties Union. In 1958, Brent Bozell, an editor of *National Review*, campaigned successfully for the Republican nomination to the state legislature of Maryland, and was, unexpectedly, supported by one Irving Ferman, Washington representative of the liberal American Civil Liberties Union. As Ferman explained, "Mr. Bozell has an extremely sober, keen, and well-trained mind, and his election would add much to the state legislature." There followed a major flap at Civil Liberties Union headquarters, and a demand for the expulsion of Ferman. Over the years, as a columnist on the *New York Post*, Murray Kempton had specialized in defending dissident figures. Over and over again he had made the point that all men are different, and that generalizations are therefore useless. The Smith Act, he said, would not have been passed had the legislators looked Elizabeth Gurley Flynn "in the face" and seen her as a human being—a woman getting on in years, a dreamer, a crusading type. Nevertheless, Kempton came out for the expulsion of Ferman from the *civil liberties* union. Asking "Who Promoted Ferman?", *National Review* explained that in Kempton's view, evidently, Ferman was "a security risk within the ACLU," and commented that "in a word, one is free, where Mr. Kempton is concerned, to advocate the violent overthrow of the government. Only don't advocate Bozell for public office."[10]

Quite effectively, sometimes, the irony operates *within* a sentence. Concentration of this sort is a distinctive characteristic of Buckley's style, where an "outrageous" (but *true*) statement is relegated to a subordinate clause. The truth therefore acquires the status of a thing assumed, noticed merely in passing. ("Even the *New York Times* seems a little nostalgic for the days when the Supreme Court, not yet having converted itself into a perpetual constitutional convention, could be regarded as a-political. Justice Minton's seat, it declares in a headline that no desk man seems to have regarded as too odd to run, 'May Go To A Judge.'" Or again: "Just after Mr. Kennedy's inauguration, I met with Professor Arthur Schlesinger Jr., historian and dogmatic theologian for Americans for Democratic Action, in public debate in Boston. . . .") Sometimes, Buckley's wit is a matter of ingenious comparison, the extravagance of which, surprising us at first, reminds us that the reality itself is pretty surprising:

Then, in 1948, poor Mr. Henry Wallace permitted himself to be run for the Presidency of the United States by a group of pros who hugged the Communist Party line even as you and I, edging our way across the peak of the Matterhorn, would hug a defile.[11]

Or:

Many people are not satisfied to be unique merely in the eyes of God, and spend considerable time in flight from any orthodoxy. Some make a profession of it, and end up, as for instance the critic Dwight Macdonald has, with a political career that might have been painted by Jackson Pollock.[12]

Buckley's wit also expresses itself in elaboration, bordering on the rococo, but which can, if necessary, instantly strike a hard blow. Or else the fun is in the juxtaposition of different modes of speech, the colloquial with the esoteric, or the archaic with slang. The following passage comes from a speech to the Conservative Party of New York on its second anniversary. Its concluding sentence unwinds slowly, full of sound political advice, but playfully bringing together words as disparate as "asymptotic" and "homeruns," and ending with a fine touch of fantasy:

[39]

As you prepare for the forthcoming engagement, you are also preparing for the one after that, and the one after that. I do strongly urge you, then, to bear always in mind the twin conservative concerns for advance and prudence. A conservative is concerned simultaneously with two things, the first being the shape of the visionary or paradigmatic society towards which we should labor; the second, the speed with which it is thinkable to advance towards that ideal society; and he possesses the fore-knowledge that any advance upon it is necessarily asymptotic, that is, that we cannot hope for ideological homeruns; not, at least, until the successful completion of the work of the Society for the Abolition of Original Sin.

Thus one is aware at all time in reading *National Review* of the attitude defined in an early issue: "No one would be more resentful than *National Review* of any effort to drain the fun out of politics, that being, we feel, one of its major justifications."

IV

Yet with all this activity, which has now been going on for over a decade, very little communication—as I pointed out earlier—has taken place between conservative and liberal intellectuals. For all his concern, in the Preface to *The Liberal Imagination*, over the scarcity of conservative ideas in circulation, despite, indeed, his show of distress over that fact, Lionel Trilling has not reviewed one book of conservative tendency that has appeared during the last ten years—notwithstanding the appearance of books by Buckley, Kenner, Kendall, Kirk, Burnham and Meyer; or, moving outside the immediate ambience of *National Review*, by Strausz-Hupé, Kissinger, Leo Strauss, Voegelin, Oakeshott, and Waugh. He has, of course, found time to review any number of books of radical tendency, by such writers as James Baldwin, C. P. Snow and Norman O. Brown. And *this* has been the performance of a critic who has claimed to have at the center of his work a special awareness of the "inevitable intimate, if not always obvious connection between literature and politics."

As everyone knows, the official position of the liberal intellectual community is that truths are likely to emerge from a confrontation of opposing ideas; and there is much to be said for this position. An opponent is likely to spot the contradictions and weaknesses that one conceals from oneself. On this basis, it might have been expected that liberal intellectuals would have welcomed the appearance of a magazine like *National Review*. Though they certainly would find its position on the whole unacceptable, they might have been expected—if only as liberals—to recognize the value of another perspective. The initial response of the liberal community, however, was savage. The magazine had been out for only a short time when Dwight Macdonald, Murray Kempton, and John Fischer (the editor of *Harper's*) each produced lengthy essays writing it off as a total failure. Of the three, Macdonald is by far the ablest writer, a gifted phrasemaker who is brought in—much as an Outside Gun is brought in by, say, a beleaguered loan shark—when a special job is required. He has, in fact, done "jobs" on Mortimer Adler, James Gould Cozzens, Ernest Hemingway, Thornton Wilder, etc. Brought in for the *National Review* job by *Commentary*, Macdonald characteristically pulled social rank—an odd tactic, though, one feels, when employed by a writer of the Left in a liberal, and, officially, egalitarian magazine. "Here," said Macdonald, "are the ideas, here is the style of the *lumpen*-bourgeoisie, the half-educated, half-successful provincials.¶ . . . Anxious, embittered, resentful, they feel that the main stream of American politics since

¶ He means people who live outside of New York.

[41]

1932 has passed them by." He opined that William Buckley would be a good journalist "if he had a little more humor"** and "if he knew how to write." And he concluded—he has not, I think, reminded anyone of this prophecy—that *National Review* had a dim future.[13] For his part, Murray Kempton devoted an essay to "Buckley's National Bore," describing "the swamp to which *National Review* has come so soon."[14] John Fischer used what amounted to the entire editorial section of the March, 1956, *Harper's* to attack *National Review*, charging that the magazine is "dedicated to the Conspiracy Theory of Politics," and is "dreadfully earnest," its editorial tone being "almost indistinguishable from that of the *Daily Worker*," besides which, it is "Utopian" and "would like to leap back to 1928." All these statements are patently false.

Well, ten years went by, and, as far as *Commentary* was concerned, nothing at all had changed—though this time they brought in Richard Rovere instead of Macdonald, perhaps for the sake of introducing some variety. Conservatives are mindless, Rovere reassured the evidently anxious *Commentary* readership: they espouse "pre-industrial domestic policies" and "pre-nuclear foreign policies." (Curiously, Rovere didn't hesitate to cite Buckley's advocacy of continued nuclear testing as an illustration of a "pre-nuclear" policy— *bring back Macdonald!*) He charged that conservative intellectuals concern themselves not with "what our relationship with the Soviet Union ought to be, but [with] whether it was right to have any relationship at all." From writers of this stripe, he concluded, "we have had, so far as I am able to tell, almost nothing but insults to the intelligence."[15]

** While we are considering matters of wit and style, one might notice that the title of Macdonald's article, "Scrambled Eggheads on the Right," is something less than Chesterfieldian.

Richard Rovere's importance is entirely due to the representative character of his mind, not to anything intrinsic; yet for this very reason it seems to me worth saying that in this article he entirely deserted his responsibilities as a journalist—and it should be easy, as well as entertaining, as we move through a variety of important matters, to show, in passing, to how alarming a degree he has here been guilty of *la trahison des clercs.*††

†† One of the more engaging features of our public life is the presence in it of two political journalists named Richard Rovere. In contrast to the Rovere quoted above, the other one, who wrote *Senator Joe McCarthy*, informed us that "for a while [McCarthy] tried statesmanship. He was led to this by some of the Rightist eggheads . . . most notably L. Brent Bozell. . . . In one period, early in 1956, McCarthy had Bozell write some meaty speeches on foreign and military policy, and some of these were quite good. One, on April 25, *described with remarkable prescience our lag in missile development and the diplomatic consequences of that lag; it may well have been the year's most prophetic speech.* . . . Under Bozell's tutelage, McCarthy voted to give the Air Force 960 million more than the President had thought necessary." (Page 241, italics added.)

Liberalism

No one can read far in contemporary conservative writing without understanding that "liberalism" is a principal opponent. Yet to many readers this must seem an odd combat. The word "liberal" itself has had a long and various history, and has accumulated favorable connotations. We speak of a "liberal education," meaning a broad one, an education not confined to vocational techniques or to the physical sciences. In a similar way, we speak of the "liberal arts," meaning many of the things we prize most. In another of its aspects, the word means "generous," as in "a liberal quantity," or in "a loan on liberal terms." The word, then, is part of our language; and it would be odd for any group to attack "liberalism" in the sense of broad learning, or generosity. Yet the conservative writers appear to have a quite different "liberalism" in mind. They agree that Arthur Schlesinger, Jr., for example, is a "liberal," and they do not mean that he is a generous spirit or distinguished by breadth of learning. They mean that his position is identifiable on the political spectrum, that it dictates some choices and not others, and that those choices are not determined by the "facts" but by the position. They also agree that the *New Republic*, the *New York Times*, *The Nation*, the League of Women Voters, the ADA, most college faculties, many newspaper reporters, most radio and TV commentators, the Foreign Policy Association, Hubert Humphrey, and Adlai Stevenson are "liberal" in just that sense. On the face of it, this is a sweeping charge, and one that would seem difficult to prove. Those whom the conservative writers call "liberals" protest that the positions they take are the result of simple common sense, honestly and flexibly applied to a variety of problems. Taking up a word, "pragmatism," that has also been used with a great many meanings in American philosophy, they apply it to their politics: it is "pragmatic"—that is, practical and not ideological. Complex problems have arisen, and reasonable men of good will have confronted them, pragmatically. There was the Depression, the Spanish Civil War, the Second World War, and the convulsions that accompanied them; there has been the slow conflict since the war, and the internal disturbances that have accompanied it: in response there has been offered the best possible answer that reasonable men, under the circumstances, could devise. Indeed, these "pragmatists" take on a heroic quality in the writings of Arthur Schlesinger, Jr. Beset by ideologues on the Right and the Left, the Fascists and quasi-Fascists on the one hand, and the doctrinaire socialists and Marxists on the other, they have confronted the problems of our time mercifully free from ideology, and have defended the "vital center."

Setting aside for the moment the question of whether or not it is true, an account of this sort has much about it that is appealing both emotionally and intellectually. Everyone knows from personal experience that simple solutions are likely to be deceptive, that reality is complex and recalcitrant. Since 1945, some of our most influential writers have been reminding us that this applies with particular force to politics. From Reinhold Niebuhr, Hannah Arendt, Leo Strauss, Hans Morgenthau, and Walter Lippmann we have heard that few problems have ideal solutions, that human reason itself is limited in its capacity to grasp all aspects of a problem, and that politics is therefore the art of the possible. There is no doubt that they are right. And Schlesinger's description of the people the conservatives call "liberals" is in harmony with this point of view. Skeptical of easy solutions, confronting reality without disabling presuppositions, and, for the most part, intelligent and honest men, they have—one is led to think—done the best they could. Furthermore, there does not seem to be, for example, any systematic "liberal" theory of the state, such as we find among the older classical liberals, or among the Marxists, or in Hegel or Burke. Perhaps it is true, then, that the answers of modern liberals really *are* pragmatic, arrived at in detail and as circumstances require.

Over among the conservative writers, an entirely different account prevails. James Burnham, in his book *Suicide of the West*, puts it with characteristic pungency: "The judgments that liberals render on public events, domestic and foreign, are as predictable as the salivation of Pavlovian dogs. Whether it's a matter of independence for Pogoland or school integration for some Southern backwater; the latest loyalty oath or a nuclear test ban; the closed shop or the most recent inquiry of the Committee on Un-American Activities; foreign aid or poll taxes; the United Nations or Fair Employment; whether it's X, Y or Z, you can know in advance with the same comforting assurance with which you expect the sun to rise tomorrow, what the response of the liberal community will be."[1]

The two descriptions cannot be true. Either the "liberals" are pragmatic, and respond to problems as circumstances demand, or they come to the problems with certain preconceptions which, as Burnham argues, make their response predictable, and renders them cohesive as a group.

A good deal of evidence in support of Burnham's contention is revealed, as it were, inadvertently. It comes in as ancillary to a discussion of some issue, or in a subordinate clause, or in the way an adjective is used. Nathan Glazer, for example, is one of our most intelligent sociologists. Writing a review of a book on urban renewal recently, he had occasion to mention, in passing, a book that opposes it, Jane Jacobs' *The Death and Life of Great American Cities*. He had to explain that Jane Jacobs, though *against* urban renewal, is no conservative; and he backed up his argument—cleansed Miss Jacobs so to speak—by citing the other positions she has taken:

A few years ago, while I was defending Jane Jacobs' *The Death and Life of Great American Cities* in an argument with one of the Federal officials who run our housing programs, I was told that in various cities right-wing reactionaries were making use of the book to mobilize votes against public housing and urban renewal. Now Jane Jacobs is no reactionary—she has publicly taken stands on such issues as civil defence and *de facto* school segregation, and allied herself with pacifists, socialists, and other radicals.[2]

To the innocent eye it is not obvious what a position on urban renewal has to do with civil defense (i.e., fallout shelters), or what either has to do with segregation, *de facto* or otherwise. If one wanted to help Negroes, one might also want to protect them with shelters. If shelters, *simply on practical grounds*, are really foolish, why cite Jane Jacobs' position on them to prove her virtue? There would seem to be an inner logic operating here, and not a mere "pragmatic" confrontation with the issues as they arise.

In an unguarded moment, the *ADA World*, official organ of the Americans for Democratic Action, provided a similar sort of evidence that "liberalism" exists as a cohesive body of opinion, and indeed as a kind of culture within a culture. Willmoore Kendall picked up the passage, and cited it in *National Review*:

"Mrs. Foster"—and Mrs. Foster, believe it or not, is ADA's Trips Abroad Director, which is something us conservatives don't have— "points out that . . . ADA's *unique contacts* in Europe and Israel . . . enable you to meet the *people who count* in each country, and *particularly your fellow liberals.* They are delighted to welcome us, as ambassadors of what they call 'the other America.' . . . You meet the *leaders*—but you also meet people just like yourselves."[3] [Italics Kendall's.]

Allowing for excesses understandable in writing of this sort— the claim that the ADA traveler will meet "the leaders" and the "people who count"—it nevertheless does appear that the liberals recognize themselves, just as they are recognized by conservatives, as a body of opinion that is not simply commonsensical, and indeed, as an identifiable subculture: notice the phrase "the other America" in the above quotation.

Meditating upon phenomena of this sort, and trying to find a vocabulary capable of describing them, *National Review* and the writers associated with it are then charged with dedication to the "Conspiracy Theory of Politics." *National Review,* for its part, has denied repeatedly that it considers the cohesiveness of liberal opinion to be explicable by any such theory. "*National Review's* position," wrote Buckley in an early issue, "is that our society behaves the way it does because the majority of its opinion makers, for various reasons, respond to social stimuli in a particular way —spontaneously, not in compliance with a continuously imposed discipline; there is no conspiracy involved."[4] Still, in Buckley's statement there is an ambiguity, and perhaps a qualification: his word "continuously" takes something away from the force of "spontaneously" (i.e., is there some *discontinuous* discipline?). The ambiguity suggests that Buckley has the impression that "spontaneously" does not quite do justice to the facts of experience. Liberal opinion does not *feel* spontaneous. "The editorials in the *Washington Post, New York Times, New Republic,*" Burnham observes, "or indeed Paris' *Le Monde* or London's *Sunday Observer* . . . the discussions of the Foreign Policy Association [and] the League of Women Voters" are more or less identical: "the small flourishes of special rhetoric in their commentaries are like the minor decorations permitted on a rigorously fixed style of painting, architecture or music."[5] Holding as they do that liberal opinion is thus identifiable and cohesive, these conservative writers argue that such cohesiveness is traceable not to some superior intelligence of the liberals which allows them to arrive, independently, at the same correct conclusions, nor to any comprehensive conspiracy, a conscious collaboration of liberals across the country, and indeed across the world, but rather to shared underlying assumptions which, though seldom articulated, are decisive in their effect. To quote James Burnham once again: "Liberals differ, or may differ, among themselves on application, timing, method and other details, but these differences revolve within a common framework of more basic ideas. . . . This does not mean that every liberal is clearly aware of this common framework; on the contrary, most liberals will take it for granted as automatically as breathing. If brought to light, it is likely to seem as self-evident and unquestionable as Euclid's set of axioms once seemed to mathematicians."[6]

One of the most interesting tasks performed by contemporary conservative intellectuals has been the attempt to analyze such assumptions, to raise them to conscious awareness. *National Review* has contributed to this enterprise, and also, through its weekly examination of events, attempted to show in a continuous way the effect those assumptions have had on political and cultural behavior. It was in the nature of this enterprise, no doubt, that it should have offended, and even outraged, some of the pleasantest people around, people of taste, respectable temper, and social power. As Michael Oakeshott has written, liberalism "has ceased to be merely one style in politics and has become the stylistic criterion of all respectable politics."[7] And to raise liberal assumptions to awareness, as the conservative intellectuals have done, is to confer upon them the status of the debatable; it is to open the question of the truth of those assumptions, and to require that evidence be mustered in their support. This is an especially painful situation when such assumptions are connected with "all respectable politics." In this chapter I will try to show how conservative intellectuals have brought key liberal assumptions to awareness and criticized them, and how, in this connection, the magazine *National Review* has played its own distinctive role through its scrutiny of the events of the last decade.

II

Basic to the liberal attitude, according to a number of recent writers on the subject, is a distinctive attitude toward *time*. As K. R. Minogue, an English liberal, puts it, liberals exhibit "a special kind of hope." To them, he writes, "'the present' means not only everything that is happening now; it also carries a further meaning that the present is only what *ought* to be happening now."[8] Thus a government, or a mode of consciousness, can exist at this very moment, and still not be "modern" in the liberal lexicon, for to the liberal, "time, like everything else . . . is simultaneously a fact and an aspiration."[9] The words "progressive" and "reactionary" as used by the liberal depend upon this *linear* imagination of time, and to the liberal the future, simply by virtue of its futurity, is good. The "modern" man, that is to say the liberal, represents the future insofar as it can manifest itself within a chronological present, where, indeed, it would manifest itself completely and at once were it not for the irrational obstacles erected by reactionaries—by vested interests, by the prejudiced, the superstitious and the ignorant. From this imagination of his situation spring both the optimism and the fury of the liberal. He is optimistic (the title of the most recent book by Arthur Schlesinger, Jr., is *The Politics of Hope*) because he thinks that the "obstacles" can be removed by "enlightenment" (by education and by pedagogically conceived legislation), but he is angry because these things seem to work so slowly.

Because of the liberal's optimism, observes Michael Oakeshott, an English conservative, and Professor of Political Science at the London School of Economics, "the past is significant to him only as an encumbrance." The "evanescence of imperfection" may be said to be the first item of his creed.[10] Experience presents itself to him as a series of "problems" to be solved. "He is not devoid of humility; he can imagine a problem which would remain impervious to the onslaught of his own reason. But what he cannot imagine is politics which do not consist in solving problems, or a political problem of which there is no 'rational' solution at all. Such a problem must be counterfeit."[11] To a conservative like Buckley, for example, the situation in South Africa may admit of *no* solution:

It is at this point exactly that one needs to remind oneself that the situation is as it is, and not as it might have been if, let us say, the white community had accommodatingly volunteered to march into the sea and let the waves curl up over their hair. Or if the Bantu witchdoctors during the eighteenth century had warned their people never to cross the Limpopo river, else their skins would turn white. . . . Someday, when you have nothing else to do, come up with a solution for South Africa, won't you?[12]

The liberal, in contrast, supposes that only the stubbornness of the South African whites blocks a "rational solution." He therefore supports manifestoes, parliamentary motions, and embargoes directed at reducing their "stubbornness"—only to find that such measures increase it. The view that all problems admit of rational solution, moreover, constitutes a rejection of the possibility of tragedy, and therefore of an insight into the human condition that has been a part of the Western tradition since at least the time of Homer.

Because the liberal is an optimist, the word "change" has a hopeful sound to him. He *likes* to say that "we live in a world of change"—for, as James Burnham has pointed out, the expectation is that change will bring about improvement. Remembering that men in the past have not, for the most part, celebrated change, that, indeed, Plato regarded it as the *defect* of the phenomenal world, and that the experience of mutability has at all times been the source of melancholy reflection, one may agree with Oakeshott in finding a kind of unworldliness in the liberal attitude, an eerie lack of attachment to the concrete actualities of the world. Like Faust, the liberal cannot say to the moment: "Linger, thou art so fair." And we remember that the mainspring of Faust's conduct was boredom. As Oakeshott puts it, if "we glance below the surface, we may, perhaps, see in the temperament [of the liberal] . . . an impatient hunger for eternity and an irritable nervousness in the face of everything topical and transitory."[13]

Because of his abiding hospitality to change, the liberal, writes Burnham, "tends not merely to accept change that happens to come his way, but to foster innovation." In Burnham's view, this aspect of the liberal's position has had momentous consequences in our epoch of world revolution. Liberals

are prepared, in fact, if . . . reforms are slow in coming, to accept revolution, if the revolution in question or in prospect can be thought of as in some way "popular" or "democratic," and against "reactionary forces." Nearly all liberals have looked kindly on, have often actively supported, at least in the early stages, all revolutions from the Left that have occurred during this century; and there have been a lot of revolutions. This was as true in the case of the Russian revolution of 1917 as of Castro's revolution in 1960; of the Algerian Arabs' revolt against France as of the Indonesians' revolt against the Netherlands. If a goodly percentage of these revolutions has gone sour, this does not in the least affect the liberal's optimistic attitude toward the next one.[14]

If the liberal can be active and zealous in attacking a *status quo*, he is, in contrast, likely to lapse into total passivity before what he considers the direction of inevitable change. Senator Paul Douglas, a liberal on most matters but heterodox on the issue of Red China's admission to the U.N., and indeed in his overall anti-Communism, criticized just such passivity in a speech made in 1961. "There is all too great a tendency in modern life," he said, as quoted in *National Review*, "to go along with the procession in order to feel part of the wave of history. Sometimes the wave of history reverses itself, and I believe that one should stand for what one believes to be right even though one is in a minority. I certainly do not grant that the forces in favor of admission are going to get the necessary two-thirds or that they will wear us down within the Security Council itself."[15]

Inextricable from the liberal's optimistic view of history is his optimistic view of human nature. He believes, as Burnham says, that "human nature is changing and plastic," with enormous if not infinite potentiality for improvement. He knows, of course, that evils exist, and in fact is exceptionally acute in detecting them, but he does not consider them to proceed from any innate defect in human nature. Men's evil deeds are due to inorganic causes: defective social institutions, ignorance, and so forth. Eleanor Roosevelt had the ability to express this doctrine in its purest form, and as a received certainty. "I was shocked," she once wrote, "to hear that not long ago, in one of our schools, some older boys beat up their teacher. When this happens, you can be sure that the blame does not lie with the young people. . . ." The doctrine appears on loftier intellectual levels as well. In the speech in which he accepted the Sidney Hillman Award in 1959, Robert Maynard Hutchins, admitting that the doctrine is a matter of "faith," observed: "The democratic [i.e., liberal] faith is faith in man, faith in every man, faith that men, if they are well enough educated and well enough informed, can solve the problems raised by their own aggregation."[16] Even such sophisticated liberals as Arthur Schlesinger, Jr., Sidney Hook, and Charles Frankel, tend to return, as Burnham observes, to this fundamental faith, though they do so, more frequently these days, in an embarrassed manner. Burnham quotes Charles Frankel: "Can we, amidst the collapse of our hopes, still maintain the essential elements of the liberal outlook on history? I think we can."[17] Thus the "essential elements" cannot be abandoned, despite the collapse of hopes. This is not the language of empirical inquiry. The sophisticated liberal reaffirms the optimistic view, even if more tentatively than his eighteenth- and nineteenth-century predecessors or his less perceptive contemporaries. He must do so, for it is the foundation of his position.

A profound, if controversial, historical analysis of the roots of liberalism has been provided by Eric Voegelin, a philosopher of history who has influenced the views of a number of the more important conservative writers—Gerhart Niemeyer, Russell Kirk, Willmoore Kendall, and, in particular, Brent Bozell. A professor of government and a man of staggering erudition, Voegelin has projected a four-volume magnum opus, *Order and History*, three volumes of which have already appeared. In it he explores the various ways in which civilizations since antiquity have experienced and dealt with the tension between order and meaning on the one hand and the experience of arbitrary event on the other. The work is a monumental and pioneering one, bringing together the results of modern scholarship in a wide variety of fields, and Voegelin, in the volumes that have already appeared, makes a great contribution to our understanding of Greek and Jewish thought; yet because the enterprise is incomplete, it has yet to make its full force felt. The book of Voegelin's that so far has had most influence is a short but concentrated one, *The New Science of Politics*, a series of lectures he delivered at the University of Chicago in 1951. The power of Voegelin's position in this book proceeds from the fact that, using his immense scholarship, he is able to argue plausibly that the *passion* attached to the liberal "politics of hope" has deep and ancient religious roots, though heretical ones. His historical argument, if it is valid, would help to account for the profound feelings liberals bring to otherwise uninteresting causes. (He does not mean to suggest, of course, that one cannot legitimately "hope" for limited and particular improvements, but rather that liberal *feeling* cannot be explained on the basis of that kind of "hope.")

According to Voegelin, modern liberalism is only one mode, and indeed a senescent one, of an "immanentism" that has been present in the Western religious tradition since its very earliest days. The term "immanentism" is a key one, and it can be defined by referring to its orthodox opposite. For the Church Fathers, for St. Augustine, and for St. Thomas Aquinas, for the central Christian tradition since the time of the primitive Church, time and history point to something beyond themselves, and derive their final meaning from sources outside of time. Beyond worldly success and failure lies the supernatural destiny of man, perfection through grace in eternity. Yet from the very beginnings of Christianity, even from the time of St. Paul and St. John, an alternative tradition has existed, attempting to put final significance *into* history. Voegelin identifies the earliest representatives of this tendency as the gnostics, early heretics, against whom Irenaeus directed his famous polemic *Adversus Haereses* (ca. 180). In Voegelin's account, "gnostic speculation overcame the uncertainty of faith by receding from transcendence and endowing man and his intramundane range of action with eschatological [final] fulfillment."[18] Voegelin makes it clear that a tremendous amount of specialized scholarship on the gnostics has been completed during the past generation, and that the movement and its philosophical significance are only now beginning to be appreciated. He traces the gnostic tendency to endow history with final meaning through the Middle Ages and Joachim of Flora, who "immanentized" the Trinity into three epochs of history, culminating in the "third realm," that of the Holy Spirit, and concludes his account with a virtuoso application to modern history:

The miracle [immanentization of final meaning] was worked successively through the literary and artistic achievement which secured the immortality of fame for the humanistic intellectual, through the discipline and economic success which certified salvation to the Puritan saint, through the civilizational contributions of the liberals and progressives, and, finally, through the revolutionary action that will establish the Communist or some other Gnostic millennium. Gnosticism, thus, released human forces for the building of a civilization because on their fervent application to intramundane activity was put the premium of salvation. . . . [But on this course of history] falls a shadow: for the brilliant expansion is accompanied by a danger that grows apace with progress. The nature of this danger became apparent in the form which the idea of immanent salvation assumed in the gnosticism of Comte. The founder of positivism institutionalized the premium on civilizational contributions in so far as he guaranteed immortality through preservation of the contributor and his deeds in the memory of mankind. . . . But what should in this order of things become of men who would rather follow God than the new Augustus Comte? Such miscreants who were not inclined to make their contributions according to Comtean standards would simply be committed to the hell of social oblivion. The idea deserves attention.[19]

Among contemporary conservative writers, Brent Bozell has made perhaps the most direct use of Voegelin's analysis, applying it to what he understands to be the *despair* of modern liberals. Certainly liberals at the middle of the twentieth century are less sanguine than their predecessors were, and one cannot compare the writings, say, of W. W. Rostow, Reinhold Niebuhr, Lionel Trilling, and Walter Lippmann, with those of earlier liberals such as John Dewey, Robert La Follette, Parrington, or Woodrow Wilson, without being aware of a sharp change in tone. The older joy in the liberal hope has evaporated; it is available only to the less sensitive and intelligent now. Addressing himself to this mood in an article on the foreign policy of John F. Kennedy, Bozell singles out a figure of speech Kennedy used in November, 1961, to characterize our current protracted struggle with Communism. Kennedy called it a "twilight struggle." It may easily be supposed that Kennedy meant by this that in such a struggle clear choices are hard to define, and the enemy difficult to isolate; and further, that it is an ambiguous struggle, neither war nor peace. But Bozell sees that the metaphor has other possibilities: "Whether he expected the twilight to go on forever, or, eventually to lengthen into night, the President did not say—though he did make clear there was no third alternative. A careless metaphor? I think not. How better portray the paralysis that grips modern liberalism—the mood and conviction of *despair?*" Bozell proceeds to analyze this despair in Voegelinian terms:

Why should Liberals despair? Because at the deepest philosophical depths—as Eric Voegelin has compellingly demonstrated—Liberalism is anchored to the ancient heresy of gnosticism with its belief that the salvation of man and of society can be accomplished on this earth; and because gnosticism, in its moderate, Liberal expression is at the end of the rope. The Liberals' hope of perfecting man through the agency of man is collapsing, in part, because Liberals recognize that all of the Western experiments in this kind of thing, reaching back to the heady days of the Enlightenment, have tragically foundered; but more important, because Liberals are coming to understand, even if darkly, that the logic of their analysis and ambition points them down the road they cannot follow: that the gnostic dream of an earthly paradise can be realized (as Khrushchev knows), not by changing society, *but by changing man,* by transmutative surgery on the soul. *It follows that if gnosticism is ever to triumph it will triumph in the Communist form.* Yet Liberals instinctively recoil from that prospect: their sense of humanity, their residual attachment to the values and forms of the West, forbid the Communist solution. What a pickle—to be possessed by a world view that demands the victory of your enemy! Men afflicted by such a neurosis go mad, and civilizations do also. And in the meantime they fight—stubbornly—but aimlessly, without hope and without purpose: a "twilight struggle."[20]

As Bozell says, and as we have seen from the thrust of their own statements as cited earlier in this section, the liberals do depend on "history" to give meaning to their lives. But if one has placed one's faith on "change" to bring about peace, freedom and well-being, and if change seems more and more to bring about their opposites; if one has counted on "history" to justify one's existence; and if history, on a sober view, seems to adumbrate mainly the darker implications—what is one to do, as a liberal? And even if history did *not*, on the whole, appear to be a slaughterhouse, but rather the developing and cheerful thing some nine-teenth-century optimists thought it—even then, how could one be sure of its meaning, its pattern? The most sensitive and intelligent liberals have faced this problem, and the great liberals have faced it publicly. One recalls the famous question John Stuart Mill asked himself, just before his nervous collapse:

> I was in a dull state of nerves, such as everybody is occasionally liable to; unsusceptible to enjoyment or pleasurable excitement. . . . In this frame of mind it occurred to me to put the question directly to myself: "Suppose that all your objects in life were realized; that all the changes in institutions and opinions which you are looking forward to, could be completely effected at this very instant: would this be a great joy and happiness to you?" And the irrepressible self-consciousness distinctly answered, "No!" At this my heart sank within me: the whole foundation on which my life was constructed fell down. All my happiness was to have been contained in the continual pursuit of this end. The end had ceased to charm, and how could there ever again be any interest in the means? I seemed to have nothing left to live for.[21]

Mill had the force of mind and imagination to see the sterility of the "historical" hope. W. W. Rostow, one of the most gifted of modern liberals, has also faced the question of eschatology, of final meaning, and in terms reminiscent of Mill. In his most popular book, *Stages of Economic Growth*, and in his major work, *The United States in the World Arena* (1960), he traces the process by which nations move from preindustrial to modern and post-modern conditions: the "take-off," the "drive to maturity," and the final stage of "high mass consumption." Like Mill, Rostow has the imagination to know that in its last historical development the liberal hope will not satisfy. In the stage of "high mass consumption" a kind of malaise will set in, which Rostow calls "secular spiritual stagnation."

In the long run, however, the problem of increasing wealth and leisure—the threat of secular spiritual stagnation—surely becomes central to organized societies which have internalized growth.[22]

Rostow even speaks of "the horrors of universal plenty and excessive leisure." Having raised the problem, the last liberal "problem" to be solved, he can only postpone it. Just as the domestic proletariat provided a cause for the liberal during the earlier part of the twentieth century, so he envisions a world proletariat providing an analogous cause during the second half. But he is too intelligent to be able to recreate the earlier enthusiasm. To such a pass has the liberal linear imagination of history come.

III

The cover of the 1964 Christmas issue of *National Review*, using the sort of illuminated gothic script usually associated with Christmas greetings, reproduces the text of an exhortation to school administrators by the American Association of School Administrators as set forth in the November issue of their bulletin: *"To school administrators confronting problems involving religion and the public schools. Delete the religious orientation of school Christmas observances. Present Christmas as one of many contributions made by different religions to America's heritage."* The appearance of this text on the cover may be taken as symbolic of the concern virtually all conservative writers have shown over a tendency they find deeply rooted in liberalism. Because it assumes, either implicitly or openly, that man's destiny is entirely temporal, liberalism has been a powerful force working toward the secularization of society. Between conservatives and liberals, to use Kendall's metaphor, there runs a line of battle, "and that line stretches from the bottom of the chart of American

[61]

politics all the way to the top, passing through pretty much every issue that enters into our politics."[23] The sector on that battle line in which the issue of secularization is being contested has been an especially active one of late, and so conservative writers, in addition to their more theoretical reflections upon religion and its relation to morals and to politics, have had a good deal to say about its role in the news of the day.

Frederick D. Wilhelmsen, author of, among other books, *The Metaphysics of Love* (1962), a fine essay in existentialist theology, asserts in unqualified terms this aspect of liberalism:

> Liberalism and Communism are different things, but they do have a common ancestor. . . . That common ancestor is rationalism. Both liberalism and Marxism have grown out of an urge to desacramentalize and thus disenchant the world; both represent a compulsion, itself irrational in origin, to eliminate every non-rational and transcendent aspect of human experience.[24]

Clearly, this resembles Voegelin's account, noticed earlier, in which liberalism is one mode of "immanentization," of assuming that meaning is historical rather than derived, as in the sacramental system, from beyond history. Another frequent contributor to *National Review*, M. Stanton Evans, finds that the "key political difference between conservatives and liberals of all kinds lies here—in their conflicting views of man." The conservatives do not "share the secular humanism" which is "characteristic of liberal thought, classical and collectivist." Significantly, William Buckley's first book has as one of its central concerns the secularizing tendencies he observed in operation at Yale. By and large, conservative writers, in *National Review* and in their various books and articles, agree that religious faith is integral to the constitution of man's being and fundamental to an intelligible ethics. "In the absence of a teleology arising out of knowledge not merely descriptive," says Richard Weaver, "nothing can be done."[25]

In view of such an analysis, it is not at all surprising that conservatives have fought secularizing tendencies wherever they have made their appearance in our society. Conservatives have not, furthermore, been receptive to the argument that religion is a strictly "private" thing, having no role to play in the public sphere. In a recent *National Review* article, "Religion and Public Life," Will Herberg, the religion editor of the magazine and the author of *Protestant-Catholic-Jew* (1955), shed a good deal of light on the issues at stake. Observing that "the Supreme Court actions outlawing the New York State Regents' prayer a year ago, and enjoining Bible readings and the Lord's Prayer in public schools earlier this year, were greeted with approval by a number of Protestant theologians, and by some Catholic publicists, mostly laymen," Herberg went on to explain carefully the form taken by such approval:

> Their argument . . . is essentially a *religious* one. Whatever may have been the case some centuries ago, they say, religious symbols and ceremonies in public life today, considering the advance of secularism in our culture, are becoming a mockery, a travesty of religion, a superficial routinization that, in its tendency to trivialize faith, is worse than an honest and outright secularism. Let the movement toward the "de-religionization" of our public life, so powerfully promoted by the recent Supreme Court decisions, go on, they say, and go on to the bitter end. Then, perhaps, the real religious situation in this country will become apparent; and seriously concerned men and women will turn in the only direction in which a renascence of authentic faith could be expected—to the home and the church.[26]

Herberg finds "some truth" in this view, but he concludes that it is, at its heart, "profoundly and dangerously wrong," for, as our theological and political traditions should lead us to realize,

[63]

a society, and the state through which it is organized politically, remain "legitimate," "righteous," and "lawful" *only insofar as they recognize a higher majesty beyond themselves,* limiting and judging their pretensions. Once the state forgets or denies this . . . it divinizes itself, and thereby ceases to be a "legitimate" state in the theological understanding of the term. Therefore the "established order," the state, above all, ought to include within itself signs, symbols, and ceremonials constantly reminding itself and the people that it *is* subject to a majesty beyond all earthly majesties. That is the indispensable function of religious symbols and ceremonials in public life, one that no responsible theologian, however resentful he may be of trivialization and superficiality in religion, can afford to forget.[27]

Thus Herberg argues, with a good deal of force, that the child who takes the pledge of allegiance including the words *under God,* "if he is encouraged to pay attention to what he is saying, will know that the American state and nation are not absolute; that they stand under the scrutiny and judgment of a higher power."[28]*

* In his essay "The Oxford Movement, a Reconsideration," in *The Reinterpretation of Victorian Literature,* ed. J. Baker (Princeton, 1950), Charles Frederick Harrold, perhaps the best modern Newman scholar, makes a similar point: the transcendence of history is a political necessity because "if we believe, with the secularists, that the Kingdom of Heaven can be established by political and economic programs, then we have no right to object to the claims of the state to embrace the whole of life in order to produce and distribute its secular goods, even though it demands—as it logically will, in time—the absolute submission of the individual will and conscience. The realization of this fact drove the religious conscience of the Victorian age to disapprove of unrestricted liberal doctrine" (p. 50). In contrast to the progressives, Harrold points out, the members of the Oxford Movement "were not social idealists. On the other hand, they were blessed with a sophistication far more profound and far more profitable than that of the hard-headed social reformer: a religious sophistication, by which they realized man's dilemma more intensely than the most fervid secular idealist, since they saw it as an inner, 'inherited' burden of evil which could never be lifted by any political or economic program, but which required, for its eradication, a turning to a frame of reference transcending the flux of history" (p. 48).

In another essay on the same subject, Herberg analyzes the assumptions concealed in the phraseology of Justice Tom Clark's majority opinion in the *Schempp and Murray* (Lord's Prayer and Bible reading) cases. According to Justice Clark, public activity, to satisfy the strictures of the First Amendment, must have "a secular legislative purpose and a primary effect that neither enhances nor inhibits religion." In this statement Herberg finds a "strange incoherence," for the second part of Justice Clark's test of constitutionality does not follow from the first, but rather contradicts it: "for the promotion of religion may well be seen as a major 'secular' purpose of the state in its furtherance of the common good of the *civil* order." This view of religion's value to the civil order, Herberg argues, "was the almost universal conviction of Americans at the time of the adoption of the federal Constitution; and it has remained the conviction of the American people, and the practice of federal and state government to this very day, despite the confusion introduced by recent Court decisions."[29] After providing a good deal of historical documentation in support of his contention that such a view of religion *has* been a part of the American tradition, he concludes that

within the meaning of our political tradition and political practice, the promotion [of religion] has been, and continues to be, a part of the very legitimate "secular" purpose of the state. Whatever the "neutrality" of the state in matters of religion may be, it cannot be a neutrality between religion and no-religion, any more than (to recall the language of the Northwest Ordinance) it could be a neutrality between morality and no-morality, knowledge and no-knowledge. All three, in our American conviction, are necessary to "good government" and "national prosperity"; and all three fall within the scope of the friendly assistance of the state.[30]

In opposing the secularizing tendencies of liberalism, other *National Review* writers have made, like Herberg, a strong case for their claim that they are in accord with American traditions. In an article that may be taken as representative of the historical position of the magazine in this matter, "Lowest Common Denominator," which appeared in April, 1959, Willmoore Kendall traces the history of the public schools from 1639, when the town of Dorchester, Massachusetts, levied a land tax for the support of a "free school," through various other early provisions for schools, such as the 1647 provision by the Massachusetts General Court that every township must "after the Lord hath increased them to the number of fifty householders," name a teacher and furnish a school for him to teach in, "it being," the Court opined, "one chief object of that old deluder, Satan, to keep men from the knowledge of the Scriptures." Even as late as 1837, Kendall shows, "when Horace Mann became secretary of the Massachusetts Board of Education, everybody understood the Court's mandate to mean, quite simply, that the public schools were to instruct their charges in the Christian religion." As Mann himself put it, twelve years after he became secretary:

I could not avoid regarding the man, who should oppose the religious education of the young in the public schools, as an insane man: and were it proposed to debate the question between us, I should desire to restore him to his reason, before entering upon the discussion.

"The record," Kendall concludes, "is clear: Through the first two centuries of our history Americans thought of themselves as building, and handing down to their descendents, a *Christian* society. They intended their public schools to provide the religious and moral training appropriate to such a society."[31] Quite capable themselves of reading the language of the First Amendment, it never occurred to them that there would come a moment when Christianity, let alone religion in general, would be barred constitutionally from the public schools. The conservatives' conviction that in opposing such secularizing moves they are in harmony not only with American tradition but with the wishes of the overwhelming majority of the people received support from a 1962 Gallup poll. As an editorial noted in August: "If there was ever any doubt that the Supreme Court's prayer decision was unpopular with the American people, Dr. Gallup has now dispelled it. His latest poll shows that an astonishing 80 percent of those questioned approve religious observances in public schools, while only 14 percent oppose them."[32]

From its earliest issues, it has been a principal concern of *National Review* to publicize the activities of the secularizers, and to resist them. Particularly vigorous recently has been the secularist campaign to eliminate religious symbols from public life. The American Civil Liberties Union, notes the November 30, 1957, issue, for example, "is up in arms this week over a) Minnesota's intention of including a cross in the state's centennial emblem and b) the decision by the Chicago Lake View High School to have Christmas decorations this year."[33] An editorial written in January, 1958, reads in part:

Our boiling point is, admittedly, low. As with Napoleon's tomb, you have to look down to see it. And now we confess to having had, even in this season of good cheer, the most *uncharitable* thoughts about some of our fellow men.

What has driven us to this position has been a series of news stories that remind us that Christmas is, among other things, open season for attacks on Christmas. A town in Illinois, for instance, was attacked by the American Civil Liberties Union for using Christmas decorations this year. . . . A Judge enjoined a New Jersey town from playing Christmas carols over a public address system in the Town Square. . . . In many towns teachers instructed the children to sing "Deck the Hall" and other songs without religious connotations, rather than "Silent Night" or "O Little Town of Bethlehem." We were about to reflect that if Mary and Joseph were to knock on the door of the typical American bureaucrat today they would be refused shelter on the grounds of the First Amendment. . . .[34]

[67]

The bizarre lengths to which the campaign against religious symbols is being carried provoked Buckley to write a column in 1962 on the attempt to have the Christmas tree banned from the Boston Common, where one has stood each year for generations. "In Boston (of all places)," Buckley began, "a secularist has cranked up a campaign to deny the municipality the right to erect and maintain a lighted Christmas tree: on the grounds that to do so is officially to celebrate, at public expense, a feast day in the calendar of a single religion." Asking "What is the answer to these arguments?", Buckley concluded that, indeed, under the interpretation of the First Amendment favored by the current Supreme Court, the Christmas tree on Boston Common probably *is* illegal, but drew the second conclusion that if "a minority can prevent a majority from publicly celebrating its feast days in a public manner . . . [the] time has come for this civil right, so recently discovered by the Supreme Court, to be re-defined. We must hang on to religious liberty, while recognizing that religious liberty, when used to deny religious liberty, is not very useful at all. What we need is to loosen up the Constitution (I should say Mr. Warren's Constitution) enough to allow us a prudent and fair-minded approach to the problem."[35] Other columns have spoken out vigorously on this theme. "Instead of dismissing their complaints as sophistical drivel," commented one editorial, "the courts have given aid and comfort to the secularist fanatics. They are treated as though they had rational grounds for fearing that the State is in the process of establishing a State Church— something which not a single religious sect in America espouses."[36] Another editorial concluded that soon the schools may put up signs reading "No Spitting or Praying."[37]

In another respect, as a number of conservative writers have pointed out, it is part of the economic logic of our time that interpretation of the First Amendment to mean strict separation of church and state will work in the direction of secularization. If, on the one hand, government is to play an increasing role in the life of the community, and if, on the other, government can have nothing to do with religion, then the result will be that more and more of the life of the community will be secularized. A larger tax on the individual's income, for example, seems likely to be levied for government aid to education. If none of that money can go to private religious schools, it follows that those schools will suffer relatively to the subsidized public schools. The parent who sends his child to the private school—as far as liberal opinion is concerned—is yet to be taxed more and more for the public school, limiting his ability to support the private one, and limiting his freedom, therefore, to give his child a religious education. Thus the growth of federal influence can be wedded effectively to secularization: and, as a matter of fact, the two are advocated very frequently by the same people.[38] Ironically enough, the liberal position on this matter will penalize the poor man first and most heavily: the wealthy parent will always have the option of sending his children to private schools. Thus when the liberal's ideology comes into conflict with his ostensible "democratic" and "humanitarian" attitudes, it is the ideology that wins out.†

Turning to the religious situation in Europe, we get varying reports from different conservative writers. According to both Russell Kirk and F. A. Voigt, English author and editor who was *National Review's* London correspondent until his death in 1957, religious indifference has spread depressingly among the European masses. In a moving arti-

† Even the very small amount of federal aid allowed to private religious schools under the 1965 aid-to-education bill has been greeted by the Left with varying degrees of dismay. See the *New York Times's* editorial, etc.

cle, "Empty Churches," written in August, 1961, Kirk finds Christian practice at a low ebb both in western Europe and England. In Denmark and Sweden, he says, less than one per cent of the population retains any active church membership, and in England the "Church of England, though by law established, obtains the active participation of only five percent of the English population; the English dissenting churches are in worse plight. . . . The Theological Revival of the twentieth century affects cultured people—always a small minority—but it has almost no influence upon the apathetic modern masses."[39] While admitting that the masses are indifferent, Voigt, a few years earlier, spoke of the high quality of Christian *intellectual* life. "There is a steady and, it would seem, increasing production of books that combine true piety with severely critical scholarship. . . . Some are concerned with the history of the Church. . . . There are numerous commentaries on separate books of the Bible. . . . Many are concerned with the 'rediscovery' of . . . the early (no longer called 'primitive') Church." Such modern scholarship, he noted, has "tended to confirm, rather than confute, the Bible's relevance and veracity." Nevertheless, he said, ominously, "there is a strange foreboding, which is unrelated to politics or to the menace of Communism, that a time of persecution lies ahead. In common with so much of the deeper religious life of England, this foreboding is strongest in the flock and among the humbler clergy."[40]

National Review's correspondent in Munich, Erik von Kuehnelt-Leddihn, gives a more mixed picture of the religious situation on the Continent, and, if anything, it seems more hopeful—perhaps as a result of the fact that ominous contrasts to Western culture are geographically so much closer. The countries on the Continent are much closer to the East, to the Wall, than England is, and also to the Moslem culture of North Africa. "Many of us," Kuehnelt-Leddihn writes, "listen in the evening to strange voices and songs coming on short-wave across the Mediterranean. There is something menacing in these wailing and screaming sounds which must have been familiar to our ancestors who defended Europe against the Moslems."[41] As in this case, one frequently finds something personal in Kuehnelt-Leddihn's writing that goes beyond cultural relativism, and in a concrete way: no, those sounds are not ours, do not belong to Europe or to the West—whatever else they may be. The picture he draws of the religious situation in Europe is a complicated but not pessimistic one. He defines three main trends: the urbanization of the faith, the return of the intellectuals to institutionalized religion, and "the new and friendly relationship between Catholics and Protestants, especially between Catholics and Lutherans."[42] The experience of the war, he says, has caused a revolution in the spiritual and intellectual life of the cities, which have replaced the countryside as sources of Christian vitality, and as a result "religion has become less sentimental and more intellectual." "Thirty or fifty years ago," writes Kuehnelt-Leddihn, "a religiously inspired essay or article never found its way into the secular press. The Unholy Liberal Inquisition saw to it that nothing 'dogmatic' ever got into print, outside of the Protestant or Catholic ghetto. . . . Today, Protestants and Catholics have a strong position in Europe's learned societies, the periodicals and the daily press. As far as periodicals are concerned, some of the very best are in the hands of active Christian laymen." On the other hand, recent years have seen the rise of "a new, lower-class anti-Christianism," which might have "fatal consequences in a democratic framework where mass-whims count for more than the convictions of an elite."[43]

In a sense, of course, what this section of the present chapter has been demonstrating is a truism. Despite the presence on the liberal side of theologians like Reinhold Niebuhr, many clergymen, and many Christian laymen, the conservatives would seem to be correct in their view that one of the ways in which they differ from the broad drift of liberal opinion is in the explicitness and the firmness of their religious commitment, and in their will to resist the secularizers.‡ To be sure, though liberalism has fostered the process of secularization, there are many modes of Western hostility to Christianity. John Courtney Murray speaks in *The Problem of God* (1964) of aristocratic skepticism (Voltaire, Hume), the materialist indifference of the market place, and the deliberate, willed atheism of the Marxist or the Sartrian existentialist, who view religious belief not so much as untrue as immoral. All of these are prominent in our cultural landscape; all of them participate to some degree, amorphously, in liberal feeling; and to them might be added the sort of hostility that grows out of resentment, the hatred felt for something high and admirable precisely be-

---

‡ A few right-wing intellectuals are not believers. James Burnham and Ernest van den Haag recognize the value of religion historically and psychologically to a humane society. Like the others, they are opposed to secularization. In 1959, however, Max Eastman—a political conservative and a militant atheist—resigned from the masthead of *National Review* in protest against its religious sympathies. "Can you," asked William Buckley, "be a conservative and believe in God? Obviously. Can you be a conservative and not believe in God? This is an empirical essay, and so the answer is as obviously, yes. . . . The pro-religious conservative can therefore welcome the atheist as a full-fledged member of the conservative community, even while feeling that at the very bottom the roots do not interlace. . . . Can you be a conservative and despise God, and feel contempt for those who believe in him? I would say no." (William Buckley, "Notes Towards an Empirical Definition of Conservatism," *What Is Conservatism?*, ed. Frank S. Meyer [New York, 1964], pp. 222–24.)

[72]

cause it *is* high and admirable, the hatred Iago feels for
the handsome and virtuous Cassio: "He has a daily beauty
in his life,/That makes me ugly."

IV

It is consistent with the liberal's optimistic rejection of the
past and of custom, and also with his rejection of the metaphysical sanctions that have traditionally obtained in the
West, that his attitudes on practical moral questions should
have a revolutionary character. Liberals, according to Minogue, "have rejected the patriarchal order which Europe
has inherited," and, in his phrase, tend to be "tolerant" on
most of the traditional moral questions.[44] This aspect of
liberalism has received extensive treatment from American
conservative writers. From the standpoint of the liberal, according to James Burnham, for example, "it is difficult to
justify the strong attachments so often found in the past to
such non-rational groupings as the family or the nation, or
indeed to any groupings more parochial than mankind. Not
surprisingly, we find that most liberals favor easy divorce
laws—indeed, these are ordinarily called 'liberal' divorce
laws. Liberals and their forebears have carried the brunt of the
campaigns that over the past hundred and fifty years have
so greatly loosened the bonds of matrimony."[45] In this, as
in so much else, the liberal idea is at variance with the common sense and the settled opinion of mankind. As far as
marriage is concerned, observes G. K. Chesterton, with his
splendid ability to articulate a widespread and ordinary feeling, "the overwhelming mass of mankind has not believed
in freedom in this matter, but in a more or less lasting tie."[46]
Disapproval of easy divorce, he argues, is based upon a sure
instinct: "In everything worth having, even in every pleasure,

[73]

there is a point of pain or tedium that must be survived, so that the pleasure may revive and endure. . . . All human vows, laws, and contracts are so many ways of surviving this breaking point, this instant of potential surrender. . . . Coercion is a kind of encouragement."[47] Such an expression of the common feelings of man is seldom met with among intellectuals. Indeed, *National Review* has noticed how frequently what must, I suppose, be called "educated" opinion comes out against such ordinary sentiment. "A recent issue of the London *Economist*," observes a 1959 editorial, "comes out in favor of 1) repeal of all sabbatarian legislation now on Britain's statute books, 2) repeal of the Labouchere amendment (which makes homosexuality unlawful), and 3) removal of the existing legal barriers to the performance of abortions ('the matter [should be] left absolutely at the doctor's discretion'). 'Let the list lengthen,' the *Economist* proclaims, for 'Britons are not as free as they think.' "[48] That last sentence is worth thinking about. The *Economist* admits that Britons "think" they are free, but proposes another definition of freedom—"real" freedom perhaps—which evidently is not dependent for its valuation upon the opinion of those who experience it.

Another editorial, entitled *Forward, Day By Day, with John Dollard, Professor of Psychology, Yale University*, cites his bizarre opinions as delivered in the *New York Times Book Review* of July 14, 1957: "*Infanticide should be dealt with as a psychiatric and social problem and not as a problem for the criminal law; means of birth control should be freely available; both the eugenic and sociological arguments for sterilization are excellent; the legal hazards surrounding artificial insemination should be removed; since abortion seems inevitable, it should be legalized for safety's sake . . . the legal taint should be removed from suicide; . . . the strictures against euthanasia should be removed for a patient*

[74]

desiring it, and the physician who cooperates in unselfish exercise of his professional judgment should be absolved from blame."[49] From the "humanitarian" point of view, one gathers, murder is not murder as long as the victim is young and helpless enough ("infanticide"). Another of Dollard's sentiments is almost unbelievably callous: "both the eugenic and sociological arguments for sterilization are excellent." Translated, that means that inferior specimens (the "eugenic" argument) and the poor (the "sociological" argument) ought to be sterilized. One recalls that, as Hannah Arendt points out, the first Nazi gas chambers were in operation long before their use against the Jews; they were designed to be used on mentally retarded individuals, for "eugenic" purposes—and were abandoned for the time being only because of a general outcry. All the rest of Dollard's statement goes equally against the grain of civilized feeling: artificial insemination, abortion, suicide. The list presents a bleak impression of his view of human nature, and if he had set out to define himself as outside the consensus of the West he could not have done it more completely.

A particularly interesting *National Review* editorial was evoked by a controversy that raged at Harvard over the refusal of Dean Monro to liberalize the regulations governing the hours within which girls may visit Harvard dormitory rooms. The Dean refused, on the grounds that some students had been abusing the current rules by holding sex orgies and wild drinking parties. In a letter to the Harvard *Crimson* he quoted a statistic to the effect that 50 per cent of the women who graduate from American colleges have lost their chastity, and said that under the circumstances of an increasing sexual intemperance and personal indiscipline he was not disposed to liberalize the existing hours. Rather, he was thinking of constricting them. Naturally, he immediately found himself at the center of controversy. The *Crimson*, reported *National Review*, "editorialized by poohpoohing the scandals, insisting that they were merely isolated incidents—involving, presumably, no more than 50 percent of college girls," and also gave room to a former *Crimson* editor to express his opinion that what a student does in his room is his own business and no one else's. Commented *National Review*: the ex-editor's article "has had the disquieting effect on the Harvard campus of the voice whose counsels you intuitively reject, but whose words, for lack of ground on which to stand, you know not how to resist." There is no liberal principle whatsoever, observes *National Review*, to which Dean Monro can refer in support of his feelings of disapproval. The civil law is ambiguous, and almost entirely lacking in deterrent force. The sanction of community feeling is itself a kind of residue of the older religious sanction, and in any case is not persuasive to a liberal. As *National Review* concludes, "What Dean Monro faces is the Problem of the Evanescing Sanction."[50] Or, as Frank Meyer, a few years earlier, described the situation of the liberal who instinctively dislikes certain kinds of behavior but can find nothing in his own set of consciously held principles which can be invoked against them: "liberals . . . are still living on inherited moral capital, so that, happily, their actions often do not rigorously follow the logic of their beliefs."[51] A notable Harvard alumnus, George Santayana, put the matter even more bluntly in an essay that appeared after his death: "Isn't this looseness in everything in so far as it may not be useful, this blankness of will in respect to ultimates, an evident application of the principles of liberalism dominant in the nineteenth century? . . . The question at once arises, how long, if all moral codes are tolerated, those who hold those views can be restrained from putting them in practice? And what authority can the dominant morality

[76]

retain? Evidently none: yet it is wonderful how long it has taken the liberal world to discover that it has deliberately abandoned mankind to moral anarchy."[52]

Of unusual interest in this connection is a strange and complicated case to which the magazine devoted considerable space in its third issue, the case of Dr. James Dooley. *National Review*, alone, recognized the importance of the case, and showed enterprise in assembling the facts and presenting them in a careful and responsible way. The case itself, because of the issues it raised, deserved far more attention than it received in the press, and in journals of opinion; and one suspects that, in time, it will come to be recognized as one of the classics of legal history.

James Dooley, a doctor of outstanding professional qualifications, and a specialist in treating seriously disturbed children, had treated some of his patients, it was established, by engaging with them in homosexual acts. Brought to trial, Dr. Dooley contended that such treatments were an integral part of a pioneering technique of psychotherapy, and that by means of it he had succeeded in improving the condition of many of his patients. The prosecution, for its part, argued that the letter of the law was clear, and that Dooley had been guilty of "indecent assault and risk of injury to a child." It further argued that not all of the "treatments" had been therapeutic, but that, in point of fact, Dr. Dooley was gratifying his own unnatural desires.

Plainly, there are a number of issues involved here, and, as *National Review* reports, opinion in the Connecticut community in which Dr. Dooley practiced was sharply divided. The greater number of ordinary citizens—"the farmers, artisans, merchants, laborers and some part of the teachers, lawyers, writers, artists and the wealthy who are scattered here and there through the hills"—agreed with the eventual verdict in the case. Found guilty, Dr. Dooley was sentenced to from one to six years in the penitentiary. On the day of the trial, however, about fifty spectators appeared in the courtroom to demonstrate their support for the doctor, and their rejection of the verdict the court was expected to hand down. "These were not the farmers, artisans, merchants and laborers; nor, except for a marginal few, were they were idlers. More than fifty of them, well dressed and assured in manner, were a selection of the region's intellectual elite. Most of them were women, the women recognized as community leaders, who head charity drives, belong to clubs, run the Parent-Teacher-Association, the Association for the United Nations, the League of Women Voters. Almost without exception they were liberals, by their own classification—though of course many who think of themselves as liberals were not there, and would not have agreed with those who were."[53] To these people Dooley was a martyr in the cause of science, and the columns of the local paper filled with letters in his behalf. One admirer wrote that "a truly great, pioneering physician" had been subjected to a "grave ordeal": "It makes one feel that society has not gone too many steps forward since the trials of Giordano Bruno, if a physician, using unorthodox methods in his studies to help mankind, can be incarcerated for doing so."

While admitting the complexity of the issues, and throughout the article treating respectfully and seriously the "powerful" defense made by Dooley, *National Review* nevertheless agreed with the verdict of the court, and carefully explained its reasons for doing so, pointing out that the justifications offered for Dooley depended upon assumptions whose potential consequences are far-reaching and dangerous. The doctor and his defenders, it argued, failed to make the basic

distinction between "the unfolding world of scientific inquiry and the unchanging world of moral absolutes," and it
pointed to the implications of such confusion: "Those who
believe that scientific progress is not subject to the re-
straints of traditional morality cannot at their convenience,
for reasons of sentimentality, taste or tactical usefulness,
draw back from the consequences of such a position. . . .
These principles accept a total experimental attitude toward
the human personality provided only a) the experiment
works, and b) the person conducting the experiment is motivated by a concern for the 'welfare' of the object upon which
the experiment is being made." In the opinion of his defenders, Dooley had satisfied both criteria. Addressing itself
to the first criterion, *National Review* asked whether "the
Nazi doctors who experimented with human victims in order to benefit society—and, in a sense, the wretched victims
who were thereby put out of their misery—[would] have
been heroes rather than brutes, 'the most creative' rather
than 'the most destructive,' had they come up with a cure
for cancer?" The magazine also viewed as dangerous the
desire of Dr. Dooley's defenders to rest their case on the
question of motivation.

Dr. Dooley's defenders argue, in effect, that only man's subjective
motivations (which modern psychologists themselves tell us may be
only a bundle of self-serving rationalizations) determine whether an
act is socially objectionable. Whereas a lie is a lie, they would say, it
is reprehensible only if the person who commits it means to do harm.
A theft is a theft, but not punishable if the thief steals for exalted
motives. Espionage is espionage, but not censorable when the spy
(as with Klaus Fuchs) claims he acted in the higher interests of
mankind. The sexual violation of children is the sexual violation of
children, but is not evil if one intends good for the children.[54]

Certainly it is true that the law has traditionally taken motivation into account in its judgment of a man's act, but

from the foregoing argument it can be seen that *National Review* is concerned lest the objective nature of the act be lost sight of altogether. Liberalism, it argues, hostile, in Santayana's words, "to any fixity in human morals, in institutions, or in ideas,"[55] contains no principle which would rule out behavior that even the liberal would find intolerable.

The stand of *National Review* in the case of Dr. Dooley is in accord with its judgment of the mindless scientism of Dr. Alfred Kinsey, who, it argued editorially, equated love with sex and reduced sex itself "to the single act of the physical orgasm." Viewing Kinsey's attitude as offering us "a crude and cruel parody" of the nature of a human being, the magazine observed that "in man the physical acts of sex are part of an immensely wider psychological whole, which is in turn fused into and ultimately subordinated to a love that is moral and metaphysical in its essence." The reductive "science" of Kinsey "destroys the real man, and plunges into the desolate materialism of our time, for which man is nothing more than motion and appetite." Even worse, if possible, was Kinsey's attitude toward the law:

His researches proved, he believed, that marital infidelity, premarital sexual intercourse, and sexual aberrations are widespread—though it is hard to see why he regarded as a startling discovery what has been known to every poet and prophet since the beginning of time. Therefore, *therefore*, he argued, and many have argued after him, the strict social attitudes and laws covering such behavior are, as an anthropologist put it, a "censorious insistence on an outworn code." They should be brought up to date and liberalized in order to be "in accord with the facts."

A flatter confusion, commented the magazine, much as it did in the Dooley case, "between the moral and the empirical order, between values and facts, could hardly be imagined."[56]

[80]

V

So far this chapter has been showing that, in the view of the principal conservative writers, certain liberal attitudes differ markedly from those of most men, past and present. Perhaps in no connection is this more marked than in regard to the idea of the nation. In the liberal, the idea of the nation, or, as he often calls it, the "nation-state," arouses little affection. As K. R. Minogue observes, liberals deplore the "competing gangs called nation states," and feel a powerful allegiance to "human brotherhood."[57]

For most other men, in contrast, the idea, say, of "England" or "France" or "Spain" calls up a greater number of concrete associations, and is a more compelling thing than "human brotherhood" or "Mankind," which seem too remote and abstract. It is the smaller unit, as Burke saw, that first engages the affections, and it is through the smaller that we may move naturally to an awareness of the larger. "To be attached to the subdivision," wrote Burke, "to love the little platoon we belong to in society, is the first principle (the germ as it were) of public affections. It is the first link in the series by which we proceed towards a love to our country, and to mankind." And indeed we do not have to be reminded that both the region and the nation have moved the poets, sensitive to the natural feeling of men, to write some of their most memorable passages. Thinking only of England, the idea of the nation has inspired the greatest poets—from John of Gaunt's famous description in *Richard II* —"this scept'red isle,/This earth of majesty, this seat of Mars,/This other Eden, demi-paradise,/This fortress built by Nature for herself/Against infection and the hand of war,/This happy breed of men, this little world,/This precious stone set in the silver sea . . . This blessed plot, this earth, this realm, this England"—to Eliot's lines in *Little Gidding*— "So, while the light fails/On a winter's afternoon, in a secluded chapel/History is now and England." But the liberal, so contend the conservative writers, tends to start with the largest and most abstract entity, rather than with the smaller, more concrete one: he speaks of "humanity," not, say, of "England." As the poets know, however, the word "England" has a power of its own—"Great Britain" does not have it—that is part of our speech and of the Western heritage.

Burnham has been particularly circumstantial in his consideration of this aspect of liberalism. In a *National Review* article on the *Americans for Democratic Action* which appeared in 1963, he pointed to the "thoroughgoing internationalism" of that liberal organization, and called in evidence both its charter and its platform. "The 1961–62 version of the platform," he observes, "declares that 'support of the principles of the United Nations'—not the national interest of the United States—'is the cornerstone of our policy.'" Concludes Burnham: "Granted the ADA's dedicated internationalism, it is not surprising that in its periodicals and other literature we never come across any words, articles or symbols that could be called 'patriotic.' No flag ever appears; no patriotic quotations or slogans; no reference to patriotic memories, holidays or observances. This is natural enough, for ADAers regard themselves as citizens of humanity and the world, bound to a higher loyalty than any mere patriotic ties."[58] In his book *Suicide of the West*, Burnham went into greater detail on this matter, noting that "unless they are professional politicians needing votes in the hinterland," liberals

are likely to feel uneasy at patriotic ceremonies. These, like the organizations in whose conduct they are still manifest, are dismissed by liberals rather scornfully as "flag-waving" and "100 percent Americanism." The national anthem is not customarily sung or the flag shown, unless prescribed by law, at meetings of liberal associations. When a liberal journalist uses the phrase "patriotic organization," the adjective is equivalent in meaning to "stupid, reactionary, and rather ludicrous." The rise of liberalism to predominance in the controlling sectors of American opinion is in almost exact correlation with the decline in the ceremonial celebration of the Fourth of July, traditionally regarded as the nation's major holiday. To the liberal mind, the patriotic oratory is not only banal but subversive of rational ideals; and judged by liberalism's humanitarian morality, the enthusiasm and pleasures that simple souls might have got from the fireworks could not compensate the occasional damage to the eye or finger of an unwary youngster.[59]

Burnham also notes a survey of history textbooks used in the public schools, which found that this antinational tendency has produced a marked change in content as compared with older textbooks. Patrick Henry's "Give me liberty or give me death," for example, was cited in twelve of fourteen older texts, but in only two of forty-five newer ones. Nathan Hale's alleged last words, "I only regret that I have but one life to lose for my country," appeared in eleven of the older books, and in only one of the newer: John Paul Jones's "I have not yet begun to fight" in nine of the older, none of the newer.[60]

Elsewhere in the same book, Burnham points out that the liberal feels no sense of outrage when "bearded young men say they will not fight for their country," and is not offended when "a mob in an underdeveloped land smashes the consulate or embassy of his nation," and "quite probably finds pledges to the flag or oaths of allegiance actively distasteful." The liberal is "likely to have an opinion more lenient than that of non-liberals concerning the deviation from earlier norms of patriotic citizenship by men like Robert Oppenheimer or Alger Hiss, particularly if their actions can appear to be motivated by humanitarian or universalistic goals."[61]

Not infrequently, such liberal attitudes reveal themselves with startling frankness, usually in passing—in an aside or a casual remark. As far as Justice William O. Douglas is concerned, it should be easy for men to shake off their national attachments. "Each of us is a citizen of the world," he writes, "and the nation-state is obsolete."[62] Another example: Reviewing Douglas MacArthur's memoirs for *Commentary*, and indeed making a point of reviewing them on the whole *sympathetically*, Marcus Cunliffe, an English liberal, remarked that MacArthur "lived in and for the Army: for the abstractions in the West Point motto—Duty, Honor, Country—*that make us wince*" [italics added].[63] Those words do not really make most people wince. It is the liberal attitude that seems odd and suspect—indeed, that makes *us* wince, because it is so remote from ordinary human feeling.

The abstraction of the liberal from particular nations and cultures doubtless has its remote origin in the belief of the Enlightenment that men, regardless of origin, have in common a universal rationality. Assuming men to possess such a common reason—and it *was* a pure assumption: they did not bother to collect evidence for it—the philosophers of the Enlightenment could look forward to the not very distant time when mankind, "liberated" from the "accidental" effects attributable to race, religion and nation, would employ universal reason to create a harmonious world civilization. "Patriotism and nationalism," as James Burnham observes, "are non-rational and discriminatory. They invidiously divide, segregate, one group of men ('my group') from humanity, and do so not in accord with objective merits determined by deliberate reason but as the result of habits, customs, traditions and feelings inherited from the past."[64] These things, then, supported by no rational principle, and despite the "residual" attachment to them that the majority of men feel, must fade from the scene, inaugurating the reign of universal humanity. Interestingly enough, however, as the older belief in a universal reason has faded—sophisticated liberals, indeed, no longer really *believe* in human rationality; they have read their Freud—the liberal symbolization of human brotherhood has been revised, so to speak, downward. Thus, in Edward Steichen's popular collection of photographs, a liberal classic entitled *The Family of Man*, the pictures, as Jacques Barzun has pointed out, place an extraordinary emphasis on man's "animal needs and sensual pleasures." "The book opens," writes Barzun, "with a rather tendentious female nude, prone amid the ferns of a forest glade. This is followed by episodes of kissing and caresses in public places. Next, in the middle of a black page, is a small square transom through which one sees a shoulder, face, and hand belonging to a couple making love. The vignette is printed horizontally so that there shall be no mistaking the subject. The theme of copulation is frequently repeated, notably as a restorative after the half dozen pages devoted to schoolwork. The only other image of man that receives comparable insistence is that of suffering, as shown by faces of misery, worn limbs and postures of dejection."[65] Pity the poor *philosophe!* looking among Noble Savages for the universal rationality that would transcend differences of culture. His modern descendants have found such transcendence in man's animal needs and his capacity for suffering. Summing up his view of Steichen's photographs, Barzun says that they express a spirit hostile to "whatever is formed and constituted . . . whatever is adult, whatever exerts power, whatever is characteristically Western, whatever is unique or has a name, or embodies the complexity of thought." They celebrate what is "common and sensual; what is weak and confused; what is unhappy, anonymous, and elemental."[66] In a later section of this chap-

[85]

ter, we will examine some of the deeper meanings of the liberal preoccupation with suffering; but for now it will suffice to point out that the impulse in this collection of photographs is the same as in the belief of the Enlightenment in a universal "reason," except that it has been transposed to another category: all men have bodies. Yet now, as then, the liberal wishes to transcend cultural differences, and so powerful is his wish to do so that he ends up merely ignoring them. He neglects, as Frank Meyer points out in one of his *National Review* columns, "not only the chasm which separates Western civilization from Communist neo-barbarism, but also the profoundly different moral concepts that underlie Western, as distinguished from Indian or Chinese or Islamic, civilization, or from African pre-civilization—to say nothing of the lesser but still profound differences of *ethos* that separate one nation from another within the West."[67] In Meyer's view, moreover, the liberal's attachment to the large abstraction of a global "mankind" is really one mode of the recurrent desire to escape from history. A world state, the liberal seems implicitly to believe, "will abolish all tension and remove all responsibility from our shoulders, while everyone lives happily ever after in peace and prosperity." It is "the myth that emerges as the final solution to all problems."[68] Much as Marx dreamed of a classless society as constituting the end of history (all history, he said, is the history of class struggle), and other nineteenth-century figures sought an end of conflict through imaginative participation in the idea of childhood, or of death (Spengler), and responding to the same impulse as Nietzsche, who said that history is a nightmare from which we must awaken, the liberal seeks in his abstract, transcendent dream of a universal humanity relief from the actual conflicts of historical experience.

Some of the conservative writers have not been slow in

pointing to the practical consequences of the liberal's universalism, especially when that is brought into conjunction with
his egalitarianism. On what principle, for example, would the
liberal resist a world-wide progressive income tax? "From the
theoretical point of view," as James Burnham writes, "there
is no reason why democratic centralization should stop with
the single nation. Modern liberal doctrine tends naturally
toward internationalist conceptions and the ideal of a democratic order based through one mode or another on the majority will of all mankind."[69] Willmoore Kendall has called
attention to "the increasing tendency of liberals to appeal, if
I do not misunderstand them, to the principle of equality in
its crudest form. I for one seem to sense such an appeal in
much of the current argument in favor of foreign aid, where
the idea seems to be that *because* we are rich and they are
poor, it is our duty to share our riches with them . . . [and
that] if anybody enjoys privileges everybody else doesn't
have then something ought to be done about it. I seem
to sense such an appeal in the current propaganda in favor of
a United Nations Bill of Rights, each draft of which seems
to come closer to saying: nothing will do except a world-
wide cooperative commonwealth of equal men."[70]

VI

One liberal impulse that figures prominently as a target of
conservative attack has become so familiar that it will be
dealt with here only briefly. Indeed, it is deducible as a
practical application of liberal universalism. The liberal tends,
according to the conservatives, to refer all problems to the
largest available political authority, and he deeply distrusts all
smaller centers of power that in fact, or in potentiality, resist
such authority. Just as the nation stands, irrationally, in the

way of world government, so regional government stands, irrationally, in the way of national, and private authority in the way of public. For the liberal, says Minogue, "all widespread problems turn into political problems, inviting a solution by state activity," and as other writers point out, the more comprehensive the public authority employed, and the more uniform its application, the more satisfactory it will be in liberal eyes.

Now, this tendency in liberalism is too manifest and consistent to be accidental, and in effect it favors some values over others, though the liberal is not always explicit or frank about this. G. K. Chesterton, reminding us, as ever, of the obvious thing we very likely had forgotten, pointed to the connection between privacy and freedom. In a chapter of his *What's Wrong With the World* called "The Wildness of Domesticity," he observed that the home "is the only place of liberty. Nay, it is the only place of anarchy. It is the only spot on earth where a man can alter arrangements suddenly, make an experiment, or indulge in a whim. . . . The home is the one place where he can put the carpet on the ceiling or the slates on the floor if he wants to." This smallest social unit Chesterton viewed as a "small human omnipotence, a definite cell or chamber of liberty."[71] The more private a thing was, he thought, the *freer* it would be, and the more public the more regulation it would need. Of course, he knew all the observations that customarily are made on this subject, and certainly could have distinguished, as we have been instructed to do, "between 'positive' and 'negative' freedom, between the 'old' and the 'new' freedom, between 'social,' 'political,' 'civil,' 'economic,' and 'personal' freedom, the freedom that involves 'the recognition of necessity,' and the 'inner freedom' that some writers have identified with equality."[72] And he knew that only public authority could keep certain forms of private power from becoming monopolistic. But the freedom he was most concerned to protect was the sort that entailed the actual privileges suggested in what I have quoted from him above, and modern conservative writers tend to agree with him that privacy and such freedom are intimately connected; not necessarily privacy and equality; not even privacy and a certain kind of justice: but privacy and freedom. In the private school, conservatives point out, prayers may still be said if those who support the school so desire. The private club is free to choose those members it wants. The private business is free to sell what the owner wishes to sell (if no longer to whom he wishes to sell). Preoccupied as they are with certain other values, liberals, argue the conservatives, have been dangerously insensitive to the nexus between privacy and freedom.

The late F. A. Voigt, for example, noticed the singular absence from recent liberal declarations concerning "rights" of the familiar rights of private property. "In two world wars," he wrote, "and in the period between the wars, two Presidents of the greatest property-owning nation that ever existed proclaimed certain rights which they regarded as fundamental to all mankind. But although the American Constitution says that 'no person shall . . . be deprived of life, liberty, or property without due process of law,' neither President Wilson nor President Roosevelt found the respect shown for property in their country's Constitution worth recommending to mankind." Voigt goes on to point out that in the public statements of these two Presidents, and indeed of the vast majority of Western statesmen, we find "that almost every conceivable right acclaimed by the modern world was raised to a principle of universal application—with one exception." In a contradiction of tragic significance, "liberty was never so much extolled, property never so little."[73]

The British Labor Party, which most American liberals

much prefer to the somewhat more conservative Tory Party, has been unremitting in its attacks upon all subordinate and autonomous social entities. (*National Review:* "The latest political document of the Labor Party in England zeroes in on the residual inequalities that have obstinately survived the socialist steamroller and the conservative scalpel. There are, even, vestiges of social classes left to contend with! The evil in such a thing the authors do not feel the need to discuss. 'We take it as self-evident,' they write, 'that our society will be healthier and happier without social classes than it is with them.' They deplore the advantage that accrues to children 'whose family background was materially and culturally enriched.' They call for abolition of the inequality and nepotism that prevail in 'small and family businesses'; they rage over the fact that, by one means or another, there are those who continue to 'enjoy standards of living far higher than their incomes should permit after payment of tax.' They promise, in short, continued warfare against anyone who presumes to labor with extraordinary zeal or ingenuity in behalf of himself and his family. Let him labor, they say in effect, but let the State see to it that he labors in vain." *National Review*, II, xix, p. 3.) As far as private schools are concerned, Labor Party opinion is distinctly hostile, and the more leftward segments of the party have made destruction of the private school one of their special concerns. If this view prevails, observes *National Review*, "any future war that England may win, will not have been won on the playing fields of Eton because Eton, like the other famous British 'public' schools, will have been swept away in an orgy of 'democratization.' The 'Victory for Socialism' group . . . has come out for the immediate abolition of all private and independent schools."[74] The Labor Party "policy document" of 1956, as F. A. Voigt pointed out, makes the goals of party policy unmistakably clear. Individual families are not to be permitted to perpetuate their power: "Death duties are to be raised to 100 percent on all save the very smallest estates; no father should leave any wealth behind for his children," for that would constitute a violation of equality. (R. H. Tawney, the source of much ideological inspiration for the British Left, also advocated a 100 per cent death tax as a way of increasing public power at the expense of private.) The Labor Party, Voigt continues, pursuing equality at whatever cost to other values, holds that "education is a commodity," and advocates that "the schools of England . . . be 'democratized,' so that there may be no freedom of choice on the part of parents in selecting schools for their children."[75]

The transfer of power from individuals and from independent groups to the state, argues Frank Meyer in his latest book, *In Defense of Freedom,* has as its goal a great social transformation. "Those . . . who conceive that the nature of men can be changed to meet the specifications of a design of earthly perfection, need perforce some mechanism through which to act. That mechanism must be one suited to the exercise of power by men who are certain that they, and they alone, understand what must be done, and who are fired by the mission to force their understanding upon the great mass of other men who do not understand. The mechanism stands ready to hand. The state, which is the sole universally accepted repository of force, need only be captured, and that force extended beyond its natural purposes."[76]

Sensitive to the centripetal tendencies of liberalism, Michael Oakeshott argues that liberal politics are uniformitarian politics. "There may not be one universal remedy for all political ills," concedes the liberal, "but the remedy for any particular ill is as universal in its application as it is rational in its conception. If the rational solution for one of the problems of a society has been determined, to permit any relevant part of the society to escape from the solution is, *ex hypothesi,* to countenance irrationality. There can be no place for preference that is not rational preference, and all rational preference necessarily coincides. Political activity is recognized as the imposition of a uniform condition of perfection upon human conduct."[77] If equality of condition is good, and if, furthermore, public education promotes equality and private education does not, then no private schools should exist. If forced racial segregation is wrong in New York or Alabama, it is wrong in South Africa. The dislike of so-called accidental difference, which results in this uniformitarianism, found its first practical expression, argues James Burnham, "in the political field, with the liberal program for universal and equal suffrage unrestricted by property, race, color, religion, and ancestry. It then spread to the economic and social fields, where the egalitarianism takes the practical form of steeply progressive income and inheritance taxes (or direct expropriation when impatience spurs a more rapid approach to the ideal)."[78]

Interestingly, Burnham points out that liberals resent capital far more than income, for capital, "especially in the form of real property but in some degree all large accumulations of capital, usually is bound up with the past, with the family, even with local domicile and tradition. Thus capital, from the standpoint of liberal principles, seems more irrational and backward-looking than income, which may be thought to be the product of intellectual talents similar to those that enable a bright student to score well in examinations, therefore qualifying as rational—up to a point."[79]

One effect of this liberal attitude is a disinclination on the part of liberals to look for other than federal solutions to the problems that arise. We may take higher education as a paradigm. If it seems to be in need of funds, the liberal answer comes automatically: federal funds. Alternatives are available, however, and they occur to men who are not the prisoners of ideological preconceptions. Dr. John Howard, for example, president of Rockford College, has suggested an eminently workable one: allow every individual taxpayer to subtract up to one hundred dollars from his tax payment provided he has during the year made a gift of up to one hundred dollars to any college or university. As William Buckley observed, "It is the special genius of Dr. Howard's plan that it would transfer from the public sector to the private sector the right to distinguish among the various appeals or the various colleges, and to design appropriate educational programs. The plan would leave to the individual college the discretion to utilize the money acquired according to its own lights, rather than in pursuance of whatever objective the government has in mind for the moment. It has the advantage, moreover, of avoiding the whole church-state issue. Since it is not the government that is giving out the money, it is entirely your business which college you want to give to, even as you now give money to a church college and take a tax deduction. So that if you want to write out a check for $100 to good old Notre Dame, Earl Warren won't be there to snatch the pen from your hand and tell you you are destroying the First Amendment."[80] As Buckley points out, the plan also has the virtue of flexibility. If one hundred dollars turns out to be too high a figure, because too many taxpayers take advantage of it, then a lesser figure can be fixed by a simple vote of Congress. The plan would obviously protect individual choice—the taxpayer could support the college and the kind of education he *wanted* to support; and it would protect the independence of the colleges and universities—they would avoid the intrusion of federal power. But these are not values dear to the liberal: Dr. Howard has written no articles for the *New York Times* magazine section; he does not appear in TV symposia; and his plan has been discussed for the most part only in the conservative journals.

[93]

VII

One of the stranger effects of liberal assumptions is a double standard of judgment which pervades liberal statements on matters both domestic and foreign. Built into liberalism there appears to be what R. H. S. Crossman, a British Laborite, calls "moral asymmetry." "In the 1960's," writes Crossman in a recent *Partisan Review* article, "the area of moral asymmetry has changed; but its extent is just as great as ever . . . to the left of center it is no longer at the altar of Russian Communism that intellectual honesty is sacrificed. Yet I strongly suspect that in twenty years' time we shall look back with pained repugnance at the hypocrisy with which progressive-minded people in the sixties turned a blind eye to the racism prevalent in black Africa, while condemning South African *apartheid*. Nor will it be easy, when the sixties are seen in the perspective of history, to deny the existence on both sides of the Atlantic of a double standard in our attitude to racial minorities at home . . . which makes honorable newspaper men suppress irrefutable evidence that Negro rioters can commit crimes of violence, and tempts literary critics gravely to overpraise negro writers for books which they would have treated very differently if composed by people of their own color."[81]

As this section will show, Crossman may be premature in saying that the double standard no longer functions in regard to Communism, yet he is quite correct about its existence, and, as himself a man of the Left, deserves great praise for his intellectual honesty in pointing it out. Conservative writers, for their part, have seen that this built-in moral asymmetry generates ironies which may be exhibited simply by bringing separate liberal statements together. "The ADA," notes *Na-*

tional Review, for example, "has gone on record as supporting diplomatic recognition of the Communist Chinese government, and its admission to the UN, at the same time that it supports exclusion of Spain from the UN."[82] Liberal commentators and liberal groups like the Anti-Defamation League have been virtually unanimous in condemning boycotts of Communist-manufactured goods in American stores.[83] Yet few weeks go by without liberal appeals for boycotts directed against South Africa; Martin Luther King used the occasion of his Nobel Peace Prize to call for a boycott of Mississippi, and later demanded one against Alabama. In 1962, to give one more example, Chester Bowles, in a wild moment of ideological self-exposure, committed himself to the view that segregation in South Africa is "the worst situation in the world today." As *National Review* commented editorially: "Repeat: 'the worst situation in the world today.' End comment."[84]

The disparities and contradictions exhibited in liberal attitudes frequently are so drastic that they suggest, in James Burnham's words, that "behind the shiny values that are the nominal goals of liberal conduct there may lie impulses, drives and interests that are not given open recognition in the official ideology."[85] Yet despite the attention conservative writers have given to the phenomenon (and a few more striking examples of this will be provided in a moment), it has remained for a sophisticated and critical liberal philosopher, K. R. Minogue, to give the most persuasive analysis so far of its causes.

At the center of the liberal sensibility, Minogue argues, is a special sensitivity to *suffering.* The liberal is dissatisfied with the world, he says, not because it lacks variety, or because it is subject to mutability, or because it lacks aesthetic charm, or because it seems unheroic—but because it contains suffering. "The theme that progress in civilization

[95]

is bound up with a growing distaste for suffering in all its forms," writes Minogue, "is a common one in liberal histories of modern Europe, and we find it succinctly stated by Bentham: 'The French have already discovered that the blackness of the skin is no reason why a human being should be abandoned without redress to the caprice of a tormentor.' He is discussing—a theme dear to an English heart—the sufferings of animals, and hopes that the 'day may come when the rest of the animal creation may acquire those rights which never could have been withholden from them but by the hand of tyranny . . . the question is not, Can they reason? nor, Can they talk? but, Can they *suffer?*' "[86]

The liberal, accordingly, tends to be willing to sacrifice the myriad of other values that men and cultures have prized— heroism, beauty, individual freedom, chastity, piety—in favor of the grand project of eliminating suffering. The liberal, not unexpectedly, has developed a special acuteness in discerning what Minogue calls "suffering situations," such as the use of child labor in nineteenth-century Britain, or, more ambiguously, of slaves in nineteenth-century America. "The point of suffering situations," according to Minogue, "is that they convert politics into a crudely conceived moral battleground. On one side we find oppressors, and on the other, a class of victims."[87] This approach, Minogue says, may be carried a step further, and include the positing of what he calls "implied suffering" and "potential oppression." Thus the behavior of the juvenile delinquent is taken to *imply* a history of suffering, and the parents appear as potential oppressors. The most important assumption operating here, as Minogue observes, is that human virtue is natural and spontaneous, while vice is the result of the environment. The "delinquency, or even downright nastiness of the victims is an index of their suffering."[88]

Interestingly enough, this liberal environmentalism does

not include the oppressors, actual or potential. They are not, as Minogue says, "seen as the product of their environment, for that would incapacitate the indignation which partly fuels the impulse of reform."[89] Even though liberals tend to dislike violence, their disapproval of the violence of others varies according to the "victim status" of the person employing it. As Minogue observes, "All left-wing revolutions are carried out by groups who make out their own credentials as victims, and liberals are likely to dismiss such violence with gentle regret. The violence of a Mao Tse-tung is more acceptable than that of a Chiang Kai-shek, that of a Castro more than that of a Batista. The violence of left-wing revolutionaries is excused partly by the past and partly by the future—the past because violence is taken as an inevitable response to past oppressions, the future because revolutionary violence is conducted under the banner of hope: hope for the end of suffering, and the initiation of a new order."[90] Thus the liberal approaches the Cold War with a kind of social-worker mentality, imagining, as James Burnham says, "the entire globe . . . spread out like a gigantic slum eagerly awaiting the visit of an international legion of case workers."[91] Meanwhile, those who have "made out their own credentials as victims" find their violence excused and explained away. "Liberals the world over," observes Burnham, "have lately been very impassioned indeed in defence of the freedom of Negroes to attend universities in the Southern states of the United States; but few liberals have expended much feeling over, have even bothered to note, the daily and gross violations of the freedom of Christians in most Communist countries—in several of which, as it happens, known members of Christian churches are not, generally speaking, permitted to enter universities. Liberals everywhere . . . bestirred themselves in support of the rights and freedoms of Algeria's Moslem revolutionaries—including

[97]

the terrorist bands of the F.L.N.: but the liberal dismay over the lost freedoms and rights of a million Christians of European origin, whose only home was and for generations had been Algeria, was too faint to be heard in the passing journalistic breeze."[92] A great deal of the most effective conservative writing during the past ten years, in *National Review* and elsewhere, has been devoted to the exposure of this liberal double standard, and to the demonstration of how the liberal concern with suffering can transform itself, in Hegelian fashion, into its opposite, a peculiarly calloused *indifference* to suffering.

Sir Arnold Lunn, in an article called "The Flight From Pity" which appeared in *National Review* in 1960, pointed out that this calloused attitude has developed, ironically enough, along with the growth of "professional humanitarianism." He examines a pamphlet published by a group of very notable Christian Socialists, including Tom Driberg and Canon John Collins of the Committee for Nuclear Disarmament. The pamphlet, while admitting that the Soviet Union has been guilty of cruelty, mitigates it with the observation that Russia "has sometimes behaved as ruthlessly and unscrupulously as any capitalist government."

"I wonder," remarks Lunn, whether the authors of the pamphlet have "ever read *The Dark Side of the Moon*, to which T. S. Eliot wrote an introduction. The book describes the obscene horrors of the trainloads which carried innocent Polish citizens to Siberia . . . and in which many adults died of thirst and exhaustion. Mr. Driberg might perhaps reply that these horrors are no worse than the lack of charity of Notting Hill landlords who discriminate against lodgers on the ground of color, a subject on which Mr. Driberg, writing as a Christian, has been very eloquent in the columns of *The Tablet*."[93] In a similar vein, Eugene Lyons reported on a pamphlet published by the American Friends Service Committee under the title "Meeting the Russians: American Quakers Visit the Soviet Union," a joint report of a visit to that country by Clarence Pickett, secretary emeritus of the committee, some staff members, and some academic people. "The pamphlet is," Lyons says, "as cold-blooded and cynical a document as has come to my attention in many a year. . . . I searched its 94 pages for one word of compassion for the victims of the brutal totalitarian state: a soupçon of sympathy for the millions steeped (as is evident even in this account of conditions) in wretchedness and subjected to routinized injustice; a syllable of sharp criticism of the Communist despots. In vain . . . To make it even more nauseous, the report is utterly self-righteous, invoking religion, peace and other noble values on every page."[94]

As *National Review* commented on the massacre of 303 inhabitants of the Algerian village of Melouza by the FLN: "There were 303 victims. Before the eyes of the assembled mothers, wives and infants, the husbands, fathers and sons were tortured and sliced to death according to the unspeakable and unprintable practices in use by the North African terrorists." *National Review* pointed out that "not one prominent voice in the United States, official or unofficial, has been raised in horror or protest at this deed. . . . No editorial, that we have seen, appeared in any great paper or journal; no indignation was sounded from radio or TV; not even a passing comment came from the White House, from the Vice-President [Nixon] so lately returned from that region, or from the leaders of Congress. . . . Have we then at last reached a point where material complacency, 'reasons of state,' and a bloodless ideology of 'anti-imperialist' progressivism have quite dried up our consciences and our hearts?"[95]

Supreme Court Justice William O. Douglas exhibits the

liberal double standard in peculiarly pure form. Lecturing on the Bill of Rights at N.Y.U. in 1963, he deplored "precautionary arrests," "ex-post-facto law making," "suppression and persecution" of the press. "He deplored them," notes a *National Review* editorial, "in, respectively, Pakistan, South Korea, (Menderes) Turkey—all authoritarian right-wing regimes. He did *not* deplore them in Albania, Algeria, Bulgaria, Red China, Cuba, Czechoslovakia, Ghana, Guinea, Hungary, Indonesia, Mali, Outer Mongolia, Poland, Rumania, Ukraine, United Arab Republic, USSR, Yugoslavia— all authoritarian (or worse) left-wing regimes."[96]

Proving that callousness of this order does not exist only in the upper reaches of government, *National Review* devoted an editorial to the reactions of one Nina Landau to her visit to Red China. Miss Landau, a New York student, defied State Department regulations to take the trip to China, and upon her return told Mike Wallace all about it in a TV interview. In China, said *National Review*, "all the doors were held wide open. Miss Landau was even invited to witness the execution of three 'counter-revolutionaries' who had been condemned to death for leading an anti-government student riot. This kind of thing Miss Landau took in stride. She was 'more curious than shocked' by the prospect of witnessing an execution, but she turned down the opportunity. Not, she made it clear, from a maidenly squeamishness (how else deal with counter-revolutionaries?) about watching men die; she simply wasn't that 'interested' (executions, after all, are rather commonplace nowadays). Instead, said reporter Landau, 'I went to a marvellous ballet.' There is a lot to be said for going to the theater in China, where soundproofed walls keep out distracting noises of shots, and counter-revolutionary screams."[97]

Projected into attitudes on foreign policy, this liberal double standard often plays a weird role, as conservative writers have been quick to point out. Right-wing coups by army elements are greeted by universal liberal head-shaking. Left-wings coups, on the other hand, evoke a capacity for infinite hope. With regard to Castro and Cuba, for example, the role of the *New York Times* has been peculiarly ambiguous. As early as June, 1957, a *National Review* editorial observed that "the *New York Times* seems to be taking over sponsorship of the revolt against President Batista of Cuba that is being led by the ex-law student, Fidel Castro, and his miscellaneous dissidents, locally and internationally backed by the Communists." The editorial went on to comment on the role played by Herbert Matthews, the *Times'* Latin American "expert":

Two months ago *Times* correspondent Herbert L. Matthews, after spending a couple of days with Fidel in his Sierra Maestra camp, wrote an account that sounds like a public relations handout. Matthews is now back in Santiago, not far from the Sierra Maestra, wiring despatches that would qualify him as a member of Fidel's psychological warfare section. Already, in a quote attributed to "a graduate student," Matthews is displaying the Larger Vision: "Fidel has lifted Cuba out of the inertia that was engulfing us as it has the people of the Dominican Republic, Nicaragua and Venezuela."[98]

Perceptively, the editorial makes the connection between Matthews' role in Cuba and his position on the Spanish Civil War, with regard to which he called the largely Communist International Brigade "the finest group of men I ever knew or ever hoped to know." One senses, indeed, that the Left found in Cuba a way of refighting the lost Spanish war; and, surely, a large part of the passion Castro was able to enlist in support of his cause was derived from the cultural and religious analogies that could be found between Spain and Cuba. In his book *The Yoke and the Arrows* (1957), indeed, Herbert Matthews returns to the Spanish Civil War and does what he can to destroy the famous Nationalist

[101]

legend of the defense of the Alcazar—only to be devastatingly refuted by a Spanish historian.[99] Two years after the editorial on Matthews' Cuban opinions cited a moment ago, *National Review* took notice of another Matthews' pronouncement on Cuba:

> The Castro revolution in Cuba is not Communist in "any sense of the word" because 1) there are no Communists in positions of control, and 2) most Cubans don't regard it as Communist, and 3) Major Diaz, who says it *is* Communist, was sacked from his job for incompetence, and 4) Castro himself is "decidedly anti-Communist," and 5) what Communists there are in the regime are in "secondary positions" in "motion pictures, and culture" (which, by implication, don't matter much), and 6) Communists have aims and loyalties different from those of Castro, and 7) Castro isn't the man to share power with anyone, and 8) Castro's land reform isn't the kind of reform the Communists had demanded—so says *Timesman* Herbert Matthews after his first visit to the regime he helped to start in Cuba; proving once again that there is no offense against either reportorial accuracy or logic that Matthews is not willing to commit, in full public view, in behalf of any Leftist regime anywhere. He is, clearly, without shame.[100]

When, in 1962, Castro made his famous speech admitting that he was a "Marxist-Leninist," the *Times* could muster only "surprise" that he could dare to make such an announcement on the eve of a meeting of the Organization of American States: there was no comment on the mistaken evaluations of its Latin American "expert." As late as 1962, *National Review* observed that "the *New York Times* published maps in both its October 28 and November 18 issues that divided the world into Western, Communist, and 'Unaligned' countries. In both, Cuba, if you please, was shaded 'Unaligned.' A phone call to the maps section of the *Times*: Was this a misprint? 'No—We do not consider Cuba a part of the Communist bloc.'"[101] Such reluctance to say that something or someone *is* in fact Communist has not, of course, been confined to the *Times*. In October, 1961,

Eleanor Roosevelt answered a question this way: Q: "Khru-shchev said recently that Castro was not a Communist. Do you agree?" A: "I have never heard Mr. Khrushchev define what a Communist really is. I do not know Dr. Castro. If Khrushchev meant Castro is not well versed in Marxism, he might be right; but I cannot assess a man to whom I have never spoken."[102]

VIII

In reading the liberal writers and their conservative critics, one finds that, perhaps not unexpectedly, some of the most intelligent and sophisticated of the liberals have criticized, and criticized severely, one or another of the aspects of liberalism which we have been examining. In *The Liberal Imagination*, Lionel Trilling confronts the fact that liberalism has generated no great literature in our time. Not one of the classic twentieth-century writers—Yeats, Eliot, Pound, Frost, Tate, Ransom, Proust, Joyce, Mann, Rilke, Gide, Lawrence, Faulkner, Hemingway—has produced work informed by liberal ideas. But though Trilling has a great many things to say about the deficiencies of liberal ideas, he treats those deficiencies as accidental, rather than intrinsic; he does not draw what would seem to be the obvious conclusion, that liberal ideas have been unable to inform a great literature because of their essential abstractness, because they are so far removed from concrete circumstance and from the emotions that men actually do feel. It is part of the very nature of liberal ideas that they are critical of most of the emotions that do conduce to great literature. In reading through his essays, one sees that Trilling indeed is capable of putting very sharply a good many of the criticisms of liberalism that we have found in Oakeshott, Burnham, Buckley, Meyer, Kendall and the other conservative writers. In "Kipling" he criticizes liberal contempt for the idea of the nation, and for physical courage. In "The Kinsey Report" he annihilates Kinsey's mindless scientism. Nevertheless, he seems inhibited by some sentimental attachment to the liberal milieu, and, politically speaking, never strays very far off the reservation.

Similarly, W. W. Rostow has discerned the imaginative void at the center of liberalism, has seen that it promises only a "secular spiritual stagnation." Nathan Glazer, a fine sociologist, recognizes in a recent article called "The Asphalt Bungle" the validity of the criticisms conservatives have been making of federally planned "urban renewal": very expensively and inefficiently, it mainly succeeds in effecting a sterile evisceration of our cities. The states, he says, find it hard to turn down that federal money, even when the project it pays for has been disastrously misconceived.[103] In another important article, "The Negroes and the Jews," Glazer points out that the aggressive egalitarianism of the "Negro revolution," carrying to an extreme one of the main tendencies of liberalism, threatens to destroy many of the things Americans have always valued highly, including the independence of private institutions and the identity of separate groups within the society.[104] Again, Minogue ridicules the sentimentality of liberal assumptions about supposed victims, and further demonstrates that liberalism provides no plausible sanctions for ethical imperatives. R. H. S. Crossman is pained by the intellectual dishonesty of the liberal double standard. If most liberals are inclined to dissolve the idea of nationality in the emotion of Human Brotherhood, Irving Kristol has his doubts. Observing that twenty years ago the idea of a distinctive "national character" was in scholarly disrepute, and was even thought to have a good deal in common with a mischievous racism, he goes on to point out that observable national differences do seem to persist: "We are keenly aware that two decades of 'Americanization' have made the Japanese different from what they were, but have not made them significantly less different from what we are. And whereas it used to be thought that the 'underdeveloped' countries needed nothing but money to catapult them into modernity, it is now clear that what goes on in the conscious and subconscious minds of the peoples of these countries is far more important than what goes into their pockets in the form of foreign aid. How else explain the fact that, in Latin America, the immigrant—whether German, Italian, Japanese or Jew—usually manages to achieve a varying degree of affluence, while the indigenous population seems incapable of doing so?"[105] The pure liberalism of the ADA sometimes proves too much for some, as it did for Richard Neustadt: "Neustadt's first brush with liberal intellectuals," writes Arnold Beichman, "came shortly after he had joined Americans for Democratic Action. A few months later, he read how ADA leaders had denounced President Truman for his announced determination in 1947 to prevent Stalin from seizing Greece and Turkey by guerilla activity and military intervention. Neustadt resigned."[106]

The list of liberals who have been skeptical about one or another aspect of liberalism could be lengthened. Nevertheless such critics habitually surround their skeptical observations with elaborate rituals of purification, protesting that on all other issues except the one under discussion they are in fact orthodox liberals. Nathan Glazer, estimable though he is, has been particularly conscientious in this respect. Nor, at least in public, do these skeptical liberals bring the various criticisms of liberalism together. To do so would be to risk demonstrating the inevitability of William Buckley's conclusion: "Liberalism cannot sustain our civilization on the little it has to offer. It is sustaining the majority of our intellectuals, but that proves to be easier than holding together the world."[107] Nevertheless, under the pressure of the world revolution, as contradictions and evasions are exposed to an ever greater extent, liberalism most certainly will undergo fragmentation. Many liberals will move to the Left, jettisoning their remaining Western cultural attachments. Others, just as inevitably, will move to the Right, becoming more conservative.

III

The Negro Problem

To so various a phenomenon as the Negro civil-rights movement no simple response would seem possible. Its goals range
from the limited ones of the Montgomery, Alabama, bus boycott of 1955 to the unlimited ones projected by James Baldwin and some of the younger and more radical Negro leaders,
who talk in terms of a total restructuring of American society.
Its tactics include the demonstrations organized by leaders
like Martin Luther King, the legal and political strategies of
Roy Wilkins' NAACP, as well as economic pressure, school
boycotts, and, in the case of fringe groups, premeditated
violence. As we will see in the next chapter, various civil-rights
groups and leaders have become involved with revolutionary
movements abroad. Negro demands, furthermore, have raised
all kinds of legal and moral problems which might have been
expected to provoke careful, not to say philosophical, reflection. Just where, for example, should the line be drawn beyond which public authority ought not to coerce individual
choice? What, that is to say, are the *political* implications of
our high valuation of privacy? Or again, when a conflict occurs
between school integration and quality of instruction, which
ought to take precedence? Should children be "bussed" to
other neighborhoods, or does the neighborhood school embody competing values that should be taken into consideration? Some spokesmen have demanded that Negroes, in com-
pensation for past wrongs, receive *preferential* treatment in,

say, hiring practices or civil service advancement; but does this take sufficient account of the white employee's right to fair treatment? Again, though some states have in fact abused their responsibilities, is the federal system, with its history of state jurisdiction in well-defined areas, of so negligible a value as not to enter into our calculations when Negro "rights" are in question?

By and large, moreover, discussion of the Negro problem has been carried on in terms which neglect some of the realities of the Negro's predicament, which is by no means entirely due to discrimination or segregation. As a number of social scientists have shown, certain distinctive features of Negro life itself have played an important part in keeping the Negroes at the bottom of the social ladder. In New York, for example, the Puerto Ricans, later arrivals than the Negroes, and also subject to discrimination, have moved up much more quickly. For one thing, the Negroes—unlike the other ethnic minorities, who owned candy stores, small restaurants, grocery stores, and the like—have not gone into shopkeeping and small business in any appreciable numbers, even though such ventures, providing experience with credit and saving, and with local politics, as well as affording opportunities to employ members of one's own family or community, have traditionally been one road to advancement.[1] How "different matters would be," remarks Nathan Glazer, "if Negroes owned the grocery stores they patronized . . . , as most groups in the past have, and as Puerto Ricans today do."[2]

Another factor contributing to the predicament of the Negro has been the instability of his family pattern. In contrast to other ethnic minorities, which have created extended family groups, useful in the accumulation of savings, and able to help advance gifted members, the Negro family has been chronically unstable. In a disproportionate number of cases, no father lives at home, and the rate of illegitimacy is high. Thus, prejudice and deficient education can explain much, but not all, about the plight of the Negro.[3] Discrimination, often of a brutal kind, does indeed exist, yet other groups have been discriminated against and have responded differently. Before World War II, both the Japanese in California and the Jews in New York found the most desirable jobs closed to them, and of course met social discrimination of all kinds, yet an astonishingly high proportion of them attended college. "Graduate Jewish chemists," writes Glazer, "peddled cosmetics that they had concocted and bottled, graduate Japanese technicians worked as busboys. But this overtraining also meant that when the barriers came down these groups were ready and waiting. The Negro today is not."[4]

Both the moral and political problems raised by the pressure of the Negro movement, and the distinctive features of Negro life that have contributed to the Negro predicament, would seem to call for careful analysis, lest, as Garry Wills remarks in *National Review*, "while sympathizing with Negro urgency, and making every effort to understand even the wilder gestures arising out of this urgency, we . . . allow these immediate pressures to bend the permanent structure of our society permanently out of shape . . . [and] sacrifice the peace of us all to the demands (even legitimate demands) of some."[5] Nevertheless, public discussion of the Negro problem has been of extremely low quality. Despite the complexity of the issues involved, and despite the fact that competing values are often at stake, the overall response of our usual organs of opinion has been what can only be called tragically simple-minded. Though social scientists have indeed shed light on all sides of the question, not much has yet penetrated to the level of public discussion. For the most part, whether out of bad conscience or habitual sentimentality, the molders of public opinion have viewed the Negro purely as a victim, all of whose demands are therefore valid. Among intellectuals, a peculiar variant of this approach has become prominent, and the Negro has been pressed into service as a kind of surrogate for the "worker" or "proletarian" of the 1930s. The idea then was that the ills of society derived from the existence of class barriers, which alienated man from man, and the political Left, with varying degrees of intensity, looked forward to the day when the victimized classes, rising to political power and economic security, would put an end to class barriers and consequently to alienation. As the prospective savior of society, the proletariat was sentimentalized into a kind of crusading brotherhood, and its members were imagined to possess all the wholesome virtues. Now that the masses have actually risen to power, the old romantic vision has faded; it is no longer plausible even to the political Left to imagine that the teamsters or even the steelworkers are going to save us all from bourgeois corruption. The Negroes have become the heirs of that old emotion. Like the old working class, they *have* been victimized; and therefore— "therefore" is the illogical step—they are the repositories of virtue and their claims are absolute. The Negro has even inherited some of the mythic-sentimental attributes of the proletariat: warmhearted spontaneity, solidarity outside the law, superior sexuality, natural generosity. We have been asked by Norman Mailer, for example, to become "white Negroes." In Richard Avedon's collection of photographs, *Nothing Personal,* to which James Baldwin wrote the accompanying text, representative groups of Americans and well-known public figures are photographed in such a way as to make them look corrupt, diseased, effete or weary; only a single picture shows a healthy-looking, dignified group—a group of civil-rights workers. This book is an extreme example*; yet it remains true that, out of a sentimentality similar in kind, if different in degree, serious discussion of the issues raised by the pressure of the Negro revolution has all but been foregone by the usual organs of liberal opinion, from the *New York Times* leftward to *New Republic*, the *New York Post*, *The Nation*, and beyond. Negro demands, sometimes legitimate, but often questionable, are usually granted an absolute validity, and other claims are reduced to nullity. The liberals, as James Burnham observes, are morally disarmed before those whom they regard as less well off than themselves.

One of the valuable services performed by conservative writers has been the introduction of mind, of the ability to make intellectual and political distinctions, into the discussion of this problem. They have not been the only ones to do so; but the conservatives have certainly been the principal ones to do so, and also the most public in their role. It should not be supposed that the conservative analysis is based on an insensitivity to the predicament in which the Negro finds himself, or a lack of awareness concerning the genuine wrongs he has suffered. Garry Wills, reflecting on American history, observes that "the wrong done to the Negro— or to the American Indian—is so unmanageably large a debt that even those with the best will in the world try to evade

---

* But perhaps not so exceptional after all. Writing in *Partisan Review*, Martin Duberman said this of the Student Nonviolent Coordinating Committee workers: "In their depth of feeling for each other and for their cause, in their simplicity and courage, they stand out against a purposeless, sterile backdrop in something truly like heroic outline, showing us what might be hoped for when the barriers that artificially separate people are broken down . . . Intimacy among them has been allowed to ripen through constant contact and mutual reliance, and has been further intensified by common dangers and goals." (*Partisan Review*, Winter, 1965, pp. 150–51.) This is vintage stuff, and could not have been better expressed by a WPA muralist.

the logarithmic ordeal of itemizing these accounts," and John Chamberlain, writing on segregation, points out that it is "totally at variance with the spirit of the Constitution to tax a Negro to pay for publicly owned property (such as schools) and then deny him the equal use of such property."[6] Conservatives have differed from liberals in their writings on the Negro problem not because they are insensitive, let alone anti-Negro, but because they have been able to achieve a certain perspective, a perspective that derives from their concern to prevent the drive for Negro equality from eclipsing those rights which are valuable to all Americans. As will be seen, it does not seem to me that they have as yet addressed themselves to all aspects of this difficult problem. Nevertheless, they have brought into the discussion of it vital considerations that have been almost universally neglected in other quarters.

In 1957, for example, Richard M. Weaver called attention to the number of previously customary "rights" that had been infringed by the pressure for racial equality. "There was a time," he noted, when ownership of property gave the owner the right to say to whom he would and would not sell and rent. But now, with the outlawing of restrictive covenants by the Supreme Court (especially in *Shelley* v. *Kraemer*), this right has been invaded, if not effectually taken away. There was a time when owners had complete discretion as to whom they would or would not hire to work in their private businesses. . . . There was a time when private educational institutions had the right to set up any standards they chose for the admission of students. Now at least one state has a law which forbids any institution even to accept applications with data relating to the race and religion of the student applying. Just recently there has come the decision of the Supreme Court in the Girard College case, in which the terms of a will which had stood for more than one hundred years were set aside because the charity it provided had been limited to white orphan boys." Certainly it would be unjust to Weaver to suppose that his concern derives from insensitivity or even bigotry; rather, it proceeds from a perception of the nexus between private property and personal freedom which is thoroughly familiar in the political philosophy of the West. Locke associated ownership of property with individual freedom and personal dignity, and Burke agreed, as does Michael Oakeshott: "Of the many species of liberty which compose the freedom we enjoy, each amplifying and making more secure the whole, we have long recognized the importance of two: the freedom of association, and the freedom enjoyed in the right to own private property."[7] In an effort to secure fair treatment of Negroes and other minorities seeking to buy or rent homes, liberals have been anything but sensitive to the rights of ownership. Judge James W. Hodson, of the Washington (State) Superior Court made the crucial distinction in declaring unconstitutional a state anti-discrimination law under which a homeowner had been ordered to sell his house to a Negro; the Fourteenth Amendment, he pointed out, secured for the individual equal treatment before the law: the *State*, that is, could not treat individuals unequally. He added: "This court concludes that it is palpable sophistry to argue that [the defendant], in endeavoring to sell his home, is acting by, for or as the State. A private individual acting in his private capacity is perfectly free to discriminate as he pleases."[8] Of course, the debate is not over, as controversy over "fair housing laws" in various states indicates. "Before our generation," comments *National Review* editorially, "it never occurred to any court or magistrate that a man could not decline to sell or rent his property to anyone, for any or no reason; or that if he declined to sell to someone by reason of race, color or creed, it followed that he 'hated' that race, color or creed. It should not be surprising if it takes some citizens a few years to swallow the new set of rules."[9]

[113]

How far the ideologues of equality are prepared to go is shown by the response of the New York Commission on Intergroup Relations to the refusal of the West Side Tennis Club to accept Ralph Bunche, a prominent Negro. Alfred J. Marrow, the Commission's chairman, announced that "he was going to investigate *all* New York clubs, and would seek a new law prohibiting discrimination in any club of any kind."[10] (*National Review:* "As things are now going, it looks like a good precaution to clear the guest list for your next cocktail party with the Anti-Defamation League and the NAACP."[11]) Though most people would admit that the government—state or federal, as the case may be—has the duty to ensure that public housing is free from discriminatory renting practices, it gives many people pause to find that such control has been established over totally private housing: "New York's City Council," a 1957 *National Review* editorial pointed out, "has forbidden 'discrimination' in the sale or rental of a) apartments in buildings that house more than two families, and b) houses in developments consisting of eleven or more units. 'Historic'—the term certain councilmen have applied to the relevant ordinance—seems to us too mild a word by half. In the past such measures have applied to public buildings or buildings at least partially financed with public funds. This measure by contrast, governs owners of private rental property, and deprives them of freedom of choice among prospective tenants. Measures that diminish individual freedom are, in America, the historic ones. We started in 1788 with just about every freedom in the world, and have been having a lot of history ever since."[12] In contrast to liberals, who structure the problem in terms of "human rights"—the outcome of the clash being implicit in the description of it: how can one give second place to a *human* right?—the conservatives regard the freedom connected with property to *be* a human right. It is not, after all, a vegetable or a mineral right. They feel that erosion of the privacy of private property will erode freedom generally. It is banal to object that some property owners use their freedom in ways one may disapprove of: for freedom, by definition, opens up precisely that possibility. Conservatives, in the main, agree that although such freedom may indeed be used at present to discriminate against the Negro, the society as a whole will nevertheless be better off if we maintain it; and indeed the Negro will, in the end, be better off, as a part of that still free society.

II

As far as segregationist laws are concerned, the position of *National Review* has been clear and consistent. It has held that the force of law should be employed neither to compel segregation nor to force integration. The law, that is, should treat people as individuals and not as members of ethnic groups—it should, in short, continue to act as it normally has in America. In *Brown* v. *the Board of Education*, an editorial pointed out, the Supreme Court made only the "negative finding that laws enforcing the segregation of public schools are unconstitutional. The Supreme Court did *not* proclaim enforced integration the law of the land."[13] Yet only two years later, the "difference between forbidding segregation and forcing desegregation" had already been set aside."[14] The New York Board of Education had adopted integration as its considered policy, and was using its legal power to compel it. "In New York, the issue is Johnny's *duty* to be integrated even if no children of another race live within miles of him, and he has to go halfway across the city to find a 'mixed' school to attend."[15] Parents who have resisted the "bussing" of their children to distant and often hostile neighborhoods have found the force of law arrayed against them: that is, the law had begun to "discriminate" against white children. Sometimes the concern over "racial balance" leads to situations as absurd as they are pathetic. "In the integrated Village Creek development [Norwalk, Connecticut], a Negro electronics technician has been prevented from buying a home by his would-be *Negro* neighbors, with the tacit backing of the NAACP. The resident Negroes argued that for Charles Vaught to buy a home on Split Rock Road would be to undermine the racial balance of the neighborhood. (Nine Negro home-owners on Split Rock Road are all right; ten are too many.) And they kept Mr. Vaught out. They were forced, as *The Reporter* magazine so aptly summed it up, 'to discriminate in order to keep from segregating.' "[16]

At the same time, *National Review* opposes racial injustice, and approved of the economic pressure the Negroes were able to bring to bear in Montgomery, Alabama, by means of a bus boycott. "There doesn't seem to be any doubt about the fact that the forty Negro leaders in Montgomery, Alabama, have conspired to boycott the bus company, and evidently there is a law against that kind of thing in Alabama. It is a bad law, in our opinion; it is difficult, in these days of centralized political power, to make effective protest. In free societies, change should be brought about as a result of social, not legal pressure; and that is the kind of pressure the Negroes are in the process of exerting."[17] The magazine pointed out editorially that in other regions of the South "the boycott the Negroes have instituted against business concerns which discriminate against Negroes in one quarter of their operations is a wholly defensible—we go so far as to say wholly commendable—form of protest; it is a form of social asservativeness which we must understand, and can sympathize with. . . . We frown on any effort of the Ne-

groes to attain social equality by bending the instrument of
the state to their purposes. But we applaud the efforts to define their rights by the lawful and nonviolent use of social
and economic sanctions. . . . That way is legitimate, organic
progress."[18] Furthermore, the magazine sharply rebuked
those Southerners who invoke the doctrine of states' rights in
connection with the Negro problem, but forget about it when
federal jurisdiction in other matters is in question—thus defining their states'-rights position not as principled but as self-
serving.[19]

III

Ironically enough, in view of the fact that the conservative
position has sometimes been interpreted, incorrectly, as being anti-Negro, conservative writers have consistently treated
the Negro as an equal, applying to such figures as James
Baldwin, Adam Clayton Powell, and Martin Luther King
the same standards of probity, intellectual and moral con-
sistency, and personal style that they customarily apply to
white men. They make none of those subtle, and sometimes
not so subtle, "allowances" that one may find in the liberal
journals, and which consist of embarrassed silence, conde-
scending explanations, or excessive praise. As R. H. S. Crossman observed, in an article previously quoted in this book,
the liberal "double standard," really a form of condescension,
makes otherwise honest reporters suppress comment on
Negro violence or malfeasance, and "tempts literary critics
gravely to overpraise Negro writers for books which they
would have treated very differently if composed by people of
their own color."[20] The conservatives, in contrast, have be-
stowed praise or blame regardless of color. Most recently, for
example, it called attention to the fatuity of Martin Luther

King's remarks on the murder of Malcolm X: " 'It revealed,' said King, 'that our society [note the guilty party: not the Black Muslims, but you and I, all of us: Dallas] is still sick enough [note again the cocktail-clinician diction] to express dissent through murder.' There's a fine formulation for you. The murder of Malcolm X, a gangland operation like that of Albert Anastasia, was an expression of dissent."[21] Such moments constitute part of the liveliness of the magazine. Undeterred either by King's Nobel Peace Prize, or by his status as a victim, it exhibited him in all his intellectual glory.

Or take the case of James Baldwin. Until very recently, Baldwin's extravagances have been virtually immune to criticism. When *The Fire Next Time* appeared, first in the *New Yorker*—scorning society among the Lanvin ads—then between hard covers, few reviewers called attention to its errors and contradictions. With the exception of F. W. Dupee in the *New York Review of Books*, who quietly, and in his own way, placed Baldwin as a "virtuoso of ethnic suffering," reviewers either praised his "style," or talked about the plight of Harlem Negroes, or about how bad the conditions in Mississippi are. They did so, as Garry Wills points out, even though Baldwin made assertions—*deliberately* made them, in Wills's view—that are obviously preposterous.

In *The Fire Next Time*, says Wills, Baldwin asserts first that "it is too late for us to convince the Negro of our good faith, since the growth of black power in the world makes any gesture on our part look like an effort to buy off our future conquerors; then, with a change of mood, but no answer to the former argument, [asserts] that our nation is the one best equipped to lead the world into a new era of racial love. Earlier, we are told that it is impossible for the Negro not to hate his oppressor and respond to Muhammed's call; but in the rosier last pages, the Negro is extolled for having resisted the temptation to hate."[22] Baldwin also argues that "the Third Reich" makes Christianity obsolete, that the "American dream" has been shattered by "our curious role in Spain," that "belief in Christ is based on an ignorance of 'several elementary historical details,' such as 'that the real architect of the Christian Church was not the disreputable, sunbaked Hebrew who gave it his name but the mercilessly fanatical and self-righteous St. Paul.'"

Asking whether anything a Negro writer says must be taken as "excusable," Wills wonders whether Baldwin did not in fact mean to issue just that challenge: "He says we do not have any ideals. . . . And he proves this by attacking all our so-called beliefs, then standing back and observing that no one defends them. In fact, everyone rushes to defend *him*." Treating Baldwin as if he were any other writer, Wills argues that "somewhere along the line . . . somebody should take Baldwin's charges seriously enough to ask, not whether they are moving, or beautiful, or important, or sincerely meant—they are obviously all these, and there has been enough repetition of the obvious—but whether they are true." Is it really true, for example, that the Negro's sufferings, as Baldwin says, cannot be overstated? *Are* they incomparable?†
Again, is it actually true that Christianity, as he says, has done nothing for the Negro—had nothing to do, for instance, with the abolition of slavery? In *The Fire Next Time*, as Wills

† *National Review* has been, to my knowledge, unique in introducing a note of sanity into discussions of this kind. "Actually the manifestations of racial discrimination are more acute and extreme almost anywhere in the world than they have been in the United States for nearly a hundred years." (Guy Ponce De Leon, "The Myth We Call 'Abroad,'" *National Review*, II, xxvi, p. 16.) Elsewhere, speaking of manifestations of dislike for Negroes in England, France and Germany, *National Review* observed that "the U.S. tends to cripple its diplomacy with the delusion that this is the only country where racial prejudice exists. Perhaps, of all the nations, only Portugal offers more to the Negro in terms of racial complaisance. Could that be why everyone's ganging up on Portugal?" (*National Review*, XV, p. 176.)

points out, the reasons Baldwin gives for rejecting the Christian West "would have served an early Christian as an excuse for dismissing the whole of 'natural' civilization so laboriously built up over the centuries"—after all, the Greeks and Romans had owned slaves. "When a Dachau happens, are we—as Baldwin suggests—to tear up all the Bibles, disband all the police forces, take crowbars to the court buildings and the libraries? . . . Does he think we will be any less liable to these dark exhalations of unreason if we have none of these institutions? Does he think we will recover from them more rapidly, or reduce their frequency, by treating Dachau as the product of the Decalogue?"[23] Among all those who reflected in print upon *The Fire Next Time*, Wills was the only one really to treat Baldwin as a writer deserving of serious attention, and *therefore* of criticism and refutation. The book drew rave reviews from the *New York Times* and the *New York Herald Tribune*, and from the liberal and Left weeklies, and it made the recommended reading list of *Commonweal*, a liberal Catholic journal. Could Baldwin's frustration, Wills wondered, have been more complete?

IV

In effect, the conservatives seem to be asking that the Negroes achieve equality in the same fashion as the other ethnic groups in America. Just as the Irish and the Italians and the Jews, all latecomers, and many at first slum-dwellers, have had their small businesses—their candy stores, and fruit stands, and even pushcarts—but have then gone on to more substantial businesses, to higher education, to the professions, and to at least reasonable social equality, so the Negro could work, save, study and rise. The recommendation may slight some of the serious injustices the Negro has endured: the history of slavery, for example, is generally admitted to have played an important role in weakening the Negroes' family structure. Still, it is possible to achieve some perspective even on this. As Garry Wills points out, "The Western history of black slavery is an instant of time compared with the ages of white servitude we lived through and, finally, purged."[24] The word "slave," as a matter of fact, derives from the word "slav."

It might be pointed out, however, that the conservatives have had nothing to say on the question of what will happen if, for whatever reason, the Negro *fails* to rise in the normal American way. Would they be prepared to put up with the Negro's descent into nihilism or radicalism? On the other hand, to assume that the Negro *would* in fact fail to rise in the normal way—the hidden implication of special legislation for his benefit—would suggest a considerable degree of condescension. The conservatives, in any case, have made us wonder about the implications of an alternative to the traditional American pattern.

Depending as they have on discussion of legal traditions, and of the freedoms associated with the rights of property, the conservative writers have tended to neglect careful analysis of the actual social traditions that have obtained in American society, though, indeed, a recognition of those traditions is at least implicit in their overall position. A number of social scientists, however, have pointed out that the demand for the "integration" of distinctive groups is radically new in American life. The Irish never asked to be entirely merged with the older Protestants, but rather maintained their own resorts, as at Spring Lake, New Jersey, their schools, their neighborhoods, even their local bars. The Jews have not, on the whole, wished to fuse with the Irish or the Italians, and likewise have maintained their distinctive communal institutions. Despite the official egalitarian doctrine of American society, its history has actually been one of quasi-independent groups, with their characteristic customs and organizations, manners and morals—groups blending at the edges, indeed, but maintaining their identities. (Most large cities, indeed, have a section set aside for the mixing of groups—as New York does in Greenwich Village. It is called "bohemian," after a part of Central Europe, which, at least in the view of outsiders, *was* a melting pot. This has not, however, been the American pattern.) Most Americans, for example, would feel that it would certainly be unjust for the N. Y. State Commission Against Discrimination in New York to bring charges against an Italian restaurant that hired only Italians: but if the restaurant has six or more employees, the SCAD can move into the case.

Given their concern with the concreteness of history, the conservatives might have paid more attention to this; interestingly enough, it has been Jewish social scientists who have made the most concrete analysis of the Negroes' demand for integration, perhaps because the Jewish community has always been especially concerned to preserve its own identity. In an important article published in the Jewish magazine *Commentary*, Nathan Glazer points our that previous groups, such as the Irish, the Jews, and the Italians, did "not demand the complete abolition of lines between the communities because they too wanted to maintain communities of their own." Their demands for equality did not embrace dissolution of the group, and they set a good deal of store by "their power to control the character of the social setting in which they lived." The Jewish communities have their synagogues, their schools, and their clubs; Protestant and Catholic communities have their churches, schools, and other characteristic institutions; and each of these communities has its distinctive tone. The various groups within American society have been able to maintain their distinctiveness within a structure of *legal* equality. The force of the Negro demand for integration, Glazer argues, is that "the sub-community, because it either protects privileges or creates inequality, has no right to exist. . . . The Negro now demands entry into a world, a society, that does not exist, except in ideology. In that world there is only one American community, and in that world heritage, ethnicity, religion and race are only incidental and accidental personal characteristics. . . . [If] we do move in this direction, we will have to create communities very different from the kinds in which most of us who have already arrived—Protestants, Catholics, Jews—now live."[25]

Similarly, Oscar Handlin has his doubts about the desirability of mixing "all men so as to minimize the effects of diverse antecedents." "From this point of view," he argues, "all ethnic institutions carry within them the source of discrimination and therefore must go."[26] He points out that the hidden costs of the proposals of the "positive integrationists" are likely to be high: " 'Positive integration' or de facto desegregation sacrifices important values embedded in the neighborhood and in the ethnic institutions within which Americans have, in the past, organized their life. It threatens to reduce the individual to an integer to be shuffled about by authority without reference to his own preference or to the ties of family and other social groupings. There may be circumstances under which this course of action will be unavoidable; but those who advocate it show no awareness that hesitation to hasten the change may have other roots than prejudice."[27] It might be pointed out in this connection, however, that unlike the other groups in American society, the Negroes do not have any distinctive *cultural* values that seem to Negro activists worth preserving. This adds a special difficulty to the attempt to assimilate the Negro to the traditional pattern of American groups. Ironically enough, recent attempts by groups like the Muslims to fabricate a distinctive Negro culture, though weird, parodistic, and doomed, actually have a traditional bearing, and aim at making the Negroes analogous to the other groups in the society.

Under these peculiarly painful circumstances, there exists a real possibility that Negroes will move beyond the attainable in their demands and expectations. Discussing Baldwin's *The Fire Next Time*, Buckley cut through the rhetoric that customarily obfuscates discussion of the Negro problem, and tried to imagine just what it is that Baldwin wants. Concluded Buckley, "He wants the day to come—soon; certainly within his lifetime—when color-consciousness will disappear, when you and I, entering a room, will not have noticed even at the time we leave, who there, if anyone, was black, who was white. Moreover, in pursuing his goal of an end to racial self-consciousness, his instrument is, of all things, racial self-consciousness. He wants a mobilized Negro community which will view all life as Baldwin does, with direct relation to the goal of absolute integration."[28] How, wonders Buckley, could this state of color-blindness and total integration be achieved, even if we were willing to devote to the project all of our legal, even all of our military resources? He points out that in *The Fire Next Time*, Baldwin "cites two typical humiliations: one from his early childhood, when an Irish policeman in downtown Manhattan yelled at him to go back to Harlem 'where the Niggers belong,' another that happened to him only last year at age 38 when a bartender at the Chicago airport refused to serve him a drink, affecting not to be able to tell whether he was over eighteen." How can prejudice of this daily, concrete, personal sort be cured by legislation? asks Buckley. "The Nazis in occupied France had all the laws on their side and all the machine guns on their side, and still they couldn't get the French to treat them like human beings. . . . What shall we do, in the new order, to that policeman and that bartender? Shoot them? It is more to the point to shoot human nature, whence the troubles really come, but there seems to be no practicable way to do that. Pass a law that forbids bartenders from being rude to Negroes, and you have passed a law forbidding human beings from being human beings—such laws are not likely to make for the kind of Society which Negroes—or whites—would want to live in, or to have struggled to achieve." The difference, Buckley argues, is real, visible, and one of the "givens" of life: "If I am born different—whether a Negro like Baldwin, a hunchback like Quasimodo, a beauty like Elizabeth Taylor, or a conservative like myself—I shall be treated 'differently.' . . . So long as the eye remarks the differences between black and white, existential differences, of greater or lesser consequence, but of meaning just the same, will exist."[29]

A refreshing bit of realism, it seems to me: and all the more refreshing because of the oceans of sentimentality and ideology that have inundated discussion of the Negro problem. Earlier, I quoted Richard Rovere as observing, after his *own* study of the writings of the conservative intellectuals, that they were void of ideas, "almost nothing but insults to the intelligence." They were primitive and futile, guilty of "bogus petulance." This does not seem to me a responsible description of the Buckley reflections I have just quoted, or of other conservative writing on the Negro problem.

IV

The Protracted Conflict:
Beginnings of a Dialectical Conservatism

On a cold November day in 1917, the tottering liberal government of Kerensky's Russia, desperately trying to save Petrograd from the Bolsheviks, ordered the drawbridges raised over the River Neva.[1] By this tactic the government hoped to isolate the working-class quarter and prevent its masses from reinforcing the Communists, who were trying to occupy the public buildings, powerhouses, and telegraph offices of the city.

The bridges over the Neva would not stay raised for long. As a cold rain blew in from the Gulf of Finland, the armored cruisers of the Baltic Fleet, whose crews had already gone over to the Bolsheviks, steamed into the river. "The cruisers," wrote Whittaker Chambers, "nosed into the Neva within point-blank range of the bridges. Their slender guns rose with mechanical deliberateness, and as they rose, the span of the bridges slowly dropped again. The masses streamed across into the central city. This was the crisis of the uprising, and one of the decisive moments of history. The upraised guns of the cruisers—one hopefully named the Dawn of Freedom —did not lower. They swung, and lobbed their shells into the Winter Palace, which stood next to the Admiralty on the river bank. Inside, the rump of the government was in its final, dying session. Outside, fierce fighting was going on.

Directing it, was one of history's most grotesque figures, Antonov-Avseenko, the Communist mathematician and tactician, the co-contriver of the coup d'etat, the man with the scarecrow face and shoulder-long hair under the shapeless felt. Antonov rushed toward the guns and the head of the steps. His armed rabble followed him. They stormed the doors. The Winter Palace fell. With it, in that vast snow-afflicted sixth of the earth's surface, fell the absolute control of the destinies of 160 million people."[2]

That this was, as Chambers says, one of the decisive moments of history proceeds from the fact that it coincided with a deep crisis in Western civilization, aggravated, indeed, by the calamity of the First World War, but long in preparation. Without such historic resonance, the fall of the Winter Palace would simply have been another event in a remote and unattractive country; it was a decisive event because it coincided with a world revolutionary situation.

Surely it is impossible to doubt that the fundamental political fact of our time is the existence of a deep moral division—a fissure—within the West. And because all of the ideas that have any significance at all in the world today are Western in origin, that fissure is revealed in the world at large. It has appeared in the various wars and revolutions earlier in our century; it appears, very graphically, in that characteristic phenomenon of our time—the nation divided into two parts, North and South, or East and West, by an armed boundary; it appears in the division of all Western nations into a Right and a Left, both positions proliferating not only political but also moral and even metaphysical positions—all the while glaring at each other, though firing, as yet, only paper bullets.

The Revolution, in the sense in which I use the term here, is a larger thing than Communism. It did not begin in 1917, and today it proliferates far beyond the boundaries of formal

Communist affiliation. The Communist movement, indeed, is only its most current phase, its most acute manifestation. The Revolution, the fissure that has opened in the West, has the deepest historical and psychological roots. Perhaps the best way of understanding its nature would be to return to its beginnings, at the end of the eighteenth century, when Burke, confronting the doctrines of the French *philosophes*, found himself "alarmed into reflection" by what he saw to be a "revolution of doctrine and theoretic dogma"—a revolution whose doctrines and emotions, he thought, would render impossible any stable condition of society, would issue, indeed, in a *permanent* revolution. As Burke says near the beginning of the *Reflections*, in a sentence which reverberates in the mind like the opening bars of a great and dark symphony, the French Revolution was a "great crisis, not of the affairs of France alone, but of all Europe, perhaps of more than Europe."

I think the best way of stating Burke's fundamental objection to the Revolution would be to say that it turned on a definition of *freedom*—that for Burke, freedom was a concrete and historical thing, the actual "freedoms" one enjoyed in an actual society: in his case, English freedoms. What Revolutionary theory proposed, and Revolutionary passions longed for, was something else entirely: a freedom that was abstract and unhistorical—not the rights of Englishmen; not rights under any actual law; but the Rights of Man. But for Burke there was no such thing as an abstract Man, and to posit one, as Rousseau seemed to do in the famous first sentence of *The Social Contract*, was to construct a battering ram against all actual and normal social relationships: "Man is born free," said Rousseau, "but everywhere he is in chains." I am not saying, idiotically, that Rousseau *caused* the Revolution—that is not the role of ideas in relation to historical events—but rather, that in the rhetoric of this famous sentence we may find articulated the longings that were at the heart of the Revolutionary ethos—and that continue, ever more powerfully, to inform its spirit.

Let us meditate upon Rousseau's sentence. In what sense, we might well ask with Burke, was man "born free"? The actual infant of our experience does not *look* free. He seems completely dependent. And the violence of Rousseau's statement is suspicious: everywhere—everywhere!—in chains? And it is suggestive that the *chains* in Rousseau's sentence are concretely imagined, but that the "freedom"—man is "born free"—remains hypothetical, abstract, a mere proposition. What *is* this freedom that Rousseau has in mind? It evidently is not the freedoms to be enjoyed in an actual society —the freedoms Burke has in mind. Rather, it is the hypothetical, indeed *mythical*, freedom of a presocial self. It is, finally, freedom from society—freedom, that is, from history. Traditional thought (and this is the real reason why religion is necessary to any viable conservative politics) envisioned man as achieving radical freedom of this kind only outside of time: in eternity. Obviously, the traditional position is logically consistent and intellectually respectable. But what Revolutionary theory sought, and this is the deep source of its appeal, even as it allies itself, variously, with such forces as nationalism, racism, or "socialism," is the experience of radical freedom, the freedom from conflict, *from history*— but *in* history. And that is why Revolutionary feeling has proved to be so powerful a weapon. Any concrete circumstance standing in the way of that dream of radical freedom —and any concrete circumstance would *have* to stand in the way of that dream of radical freedom—is at best to be regarded as a bothersome and interim thing, merely to be tolerated; and at worst, if it *refuses* to be interim, is necessarily regarded as detestable and intolerable—something to be smashed. The *particular* sort of society desired by the

[130]

revolutionist is always difficult to describe: the principal emotion is *destructive*, of smashing the known—in the name of an indescribable freedom; to smash, actually, the West—in the interest of those on the other side of that armed frontier that divides the world.

II

The presence of this spirit we can detect instantly from revolutionary *manners*, the reflection of revolutionary anger. Beginning close to home, everyone must have noticed that recent protest movements, while differing in aims, resemble one another in appearance and behavior; and it is this resemblance, and its quality—not their specific aims—that is certainly the most important thing about them. Hatred for the ordinary modes of personal dignity is their most conspicuous characteristic; defiance of law is routine—perhaps their *actual* object, emotionally. Even dress has its symbolic quality.* And this temper is common to nuclear protesters, student demonstrators at Berkeley and elsewhere, and, in-

* "In all the news coverage concerning the increased political activity among college students, the costumes or uniforms have been generally set—the students with clean (even if well-worn) shirts, ties, dresses and stockings, are the conservatives, and the ones with scraggly beards and sloppy leotards are the Leftists. Soul-searching on the Left has apparently convinced them that they must scrub up their Image if they are to have a pleasanter effect on the political community. So, in *Maroon*, the student newspaper at the University of Chicago, we read about the preparations for the Turn Toward Peace demonstrations last month in Washington. Gail Paradise, University of Chicago chairman for the appeasement-pacifist project, assembled her picketers and gave them their instructions: 'We are trying to project an image of clean-cut American youth,' she told them ('amid a roar of laughter,' reported the *Maroon*). Girls were told to wear skirts, and the boys were begged to 'please shave or take showers or something.' Take a bath for peace!" *National Review Bulletin*, Vol. XII, No. 11, p. 1.

creasingly, to civil-rights activists.† Their aims become secondary—it is the revolutionary manners of the protest that are important.

As a number of social scientists have pointed out, and as everyone knows instinctively, the maintenance of a civilized society depends not only on the formal institutions of democracy—the ballot, equality before the law, constitutionally guaranteed rights—but also upon some more subtle, less formal things. There must be a general atmosphere of trust among the citizens, even though they may disagree on particular issues; there must be a tradition of political legitimacy, and a tacit agreement to "play by the rules." The strength of any political commitment must not be so great as to result in behavior bringing trust, legitimacy, and the "rules" into question: they are more important than any political "commitment."[3] But the revolutionary manners perfected by the various protest movements in the 1960s are

† With respect to the revolutionary temper of some civil-rights activists, see Rowland Evans and Robert Novak in the *New York Herald Tribune*, March 18, 1965, p. 20: "While successfully forcing an emergency voting rights bill, Martin Luther King surrendered valuable ground to Leftist extremists in their drive for control of the civil rights movement. The sad truth is that Dr. King at times abdicated command of the Selma, Ala., demonstrations to John Lewis and James Forman, the two hot-headed extremists who lead the Student Non-Violent Co-ordinating Committee (usually called SNIC). . . . Unless King breaks with the SNIC extremists, liberal whites may no longer follow his leadership. And even if he does, SNIC can create no end of trouble for the cause of Negro rights. That's because SNIC and its leaders aren't really interested in the right to vote or any attainable goal but in demanding the unattainable as a means of provoking social turmoil. As revolutionaries, they aren't about to stop demonstrating and pitch into the hard task of actually registering voters."

Two days later SNIC members appeared with other civil-rights groups in a sitdown at the Chase Manhattan Bank in New York to protest the bank's loans to South Africa. The forty-eight pickets "were carried away after ignoring an appeal by Inspector Henry A. Yack to move. Among the others arrested was George Wiley, the associate national director of CORE." *New York Times*, March 20, 1965, p. 11.

perfectly adapted to do just that: they are a *calculated* outrage to the community.‡ In the Spring, 1965, issue of *The
Columbia University Forum*, William Peterson, a Professor
of Sociology at Berkeley, described the radical elements on
the campus in these ominous terms: "If the whole of American society is evil," he wrote, "if our alienation from 'the
system,' the 'power structure' is total, as speaker after speaker
blares forth through FSM [Free Speech Movement] loudspeakers, then where one begins to attack this monstrosity is
important only in a tactical sense: the issue shall be one able
to attract the broadest support. . . . How many of the FSM
leaders are 'card-carrying members' of these various parties
and sects I do not know, nor is it especially relevant to an
analysis of the movement. The radical leaders on the Berkeley
campus, like those in Latin American and Asian universities,
are not the less radical for being, in many cases, outside the

‡ See, for example, the following news dispatch about Mario Savio's behavior
in court. "*Berkeley, Calif. March 2* (AP)—More than 400 University of
California students who took part in a sit-in on the Berkeley campus last
December waived jury trials Tuesday. Two others asked for jury trials. Among
the students was Mario Savio, 22 years old, leader of the Free Speech
Movement at Berkeley, and an instigator of the night-long sit-in at Sproul
Hall, the administration building. Mr. Savio was sentenced to two days in
jail for contempt of court by Municipal Judge Rupert Crittenden after the
judge asked him if he realized what it meant to waive trial by jury. 'I
fully understand,' Mr. Savio told the judge, '*the shameless hypocrisy to
which this court has been reduced.*' Mr. Savio repeated the statement word
for word, at the judge's request, and was handed the two days. Tuesday's
trial waivers brought to 666 the students who had taken the same action."
The protest with which Savio had been associated was called the Free Speech
Movement. Subsequent reports from Berkeley disclosed the birth of a "foul
speech movement": "For about ten days, through signs and loudspeakers,
some students have argued that they have a right to utter four-letter words
not ordinarily used in polite conversation. 'The four-letter-word signs and
utterances had a significance beyond their shock impact,' said Mr. Meyerson
[the acting Chancellor of the University]. They also symbolized intolerance
for the rights and feelings of others." *New York Times*, March 10, 1965,
p. 27.

discipline of a formal political party. They are defined not by whether they pay dues to a party, but by their actions, their vocabulary, their way of thinking. The best term to describe them, in my opinion, is Castroite. That some of the leaders make a point of their sympathy with the Castro government is true, but almost beside the point—which is that in crucial respects all of them imitate the Castro movement."

It is one of the inevitable consequences of the world revolutionary situation in which we find ourselves that seemingly disparate movements become inextricably interrelated. Look for a moment beyond the borders of the Western world, to the revolt against Portuguese control of Angola—ostensibly, and certainly in part, nationalist and anti-colonial in nature. Yet students of the situation know very well that the leaders of the revolt, Mario Pinto de Andrade and Holden Roberto, have been intimately involved with Communism. While studying at Lisbon, Paris and Frankfurt, Andrade evidently became a member of the French and the Portuguese Communist parties; he then continued his training in Warsaw and Moscow. Holden Roberto, leader of the terrorist MPA, has long been associated with Soviet, Czech and Belgian Communist groups; and it was his MPA that organized the mass massacre of white settlers on March 15, 1961, so blood-curdlingly described by Bernardo Teixeira in his recent *The Fabric of Terror*. Such is the dynamism of the revolutionary spirit, however, that it sweeps into its orbit persons and movements supposedly devoted to limited and independent goals.

To an increasing degree, unfortunately, the American civil-rights movement has worn a double aspect. In part, it has looked to the alleviation of particular grievances and the attainment of definite political aims, such as the right to vote. It has, that is, operated within the American political consensus. But its more activist elements, with increasing openness, have aligned themselves with the broad movement of world revolution. Outside the American conservative camp, *New York Herald Tribune* columnists Rowland Evans and Robert Novak have been the most candid in attracting attention to this dimension of the Negro movement. For their pains, of course, they have been vilified in the liberal press. In a number of columns published in 1965, Evans and Novak drew attention to the non-civil-rights involvement of the activists. At Pennsylvania State University, for example, the local CORE chapter put on a "peace" rally featuring a film actually prepared by the Communist Viet Cong. As Evans and Novak observed, "A CORE unit crusading against U.S. intervention in Viet Nam might be surprising to conventional politicians who regard the Negro revolution and the Viet Cong as wholly separate. But in recent months, peace and civil rights militants have approached an intersection. . . ." Even the more moderate James Farmer, point out Evans and Novak, is "personally committed to a pull-out from Viet Nam. So are most other civil rights militants." For these militants, the connection between the civil rights and the peace movements is "tied . . . to racist and revolutionary tendencies inside the civil rights movement. Swallowing Communist propaganda whole, many civil rights radicals regard Viet Nam as a classical case of white imperialism against a colored people—identical with the situation in Mississippi and Alabama. Beyond this, the James Formans frankly view not only segregation as a rotten institution in American society but see American society itself as rotten."

In their actual political behavior, as Evans and Novak have shown, these civil-rights figures confirm such an analysis. A member of the Student Nonviolent Coordinating Committee attended the Moscow World Youth Festival in September, 1964, and SNCC workers plan to attend a Communist-sponsored youth rally in Algeria during the summer of 1965. Predictably, members of SNCC were bussed to

Washington to join the fifteen thousand students who picketed the White House to denounce U.S. participation in the
war in Viet Nam. A significant number of civil-rights leaders
have involved themselves with the African phase of the
world revolution. James Farmer, National Director of CORE
—and, as we have observed, a moderate in comparison with
Forman—took a five-week tour through nine African countries and at the end of it urged the United States to get
Portugal to grant independence to Angola—i.e., turn it over
to Andrade and Roberto—and also to cut off all aid to
Tshombe—i.e., to turn the Congo over to the rebels, now
supplied by the Soviet bloc via Cairo and Algiers.[4] Earlier,
other civil-rights activists, such as James Forman and John
Lewis of SNCC, and Robert Parris (ne Moses), familiar to
newspaper readers through his role in Mississippi, paid a visit
to Sekou Touré in Guinea and increasingly have identified
themselves with the leadership of the "emerging new nations."
To cap it all, Parris was a speaker in November, 1964, at the
annual dinner of the *National Guardian,* a publication described by the House Committee on Un-American Activities
as "a virtual official propaganda arm of Soviet Russia."[5] Activities of this sort do not, of course, suggest formal Communist involvement on the part of the individuals concerned;
they do, however, suggest revolutionary involvement, and a
recognition by all parties concerned that they have revolution
as a common denominator. Thus do seemingly disparate political phenomena become interrelated: James Farmer uses
his fame as a proponent of civil rights to promote the African
revolution, in Angola, the Congo,§ and South Africa, while

§ As the revolutionary sensibility is aware, but as the ordinary intelligence
is only beginning to discover, the interrelatedness works the other way too.
As Evans and Novak point out, "the strong U.S. stand in Viet Nam . . .
hurts subversive Communism throughout the [Western hemisphere]. It shows
Latin America that an Uncle Sam willing to risk all in far-off Southeast

Forman, Parris and Lewis use the example of Africa to rad-
icalize the civil-rights movement, Parris going so far as to
participate in a Communist function. Such activities, far more
than the recondite explanations that have been offered, account for the increasing tension between the Negro activists
and those whom they call "white liberals." Sentimentality
cleared away, the "white liberals"—at least some of them—say
with the conservatives, "Rights, Sí!—Revolution, No!"

III

Though some Leftists may feel that they have interests in
common with the Communists, a distinctive feature of the
conservative position is the view that we are at war with
Communism. Whatever their differences on matters of timing and strategy, conservative writers agree that the Communists are engaged in an all-out revolutionary campaign against
the West which, if successful, would mean the end of a
recognizable Western culture. Although, as I have argued, the
revolutionary emotion was generated by the West, its spirit—
so the conservatives argue—is implacably hostile to the civilized values of the West. "On an April day in 1937," Sir
Arnold Lunn wrote, "a British General and I, both on our

Asia won't hesitate to intervene in the Guatemalan jungles or the Colombian
hills, if need be . . . This stiffens the spines of Latin American governments.
'If Johnson had pulled out of Viet Nam,' one Latin-American anti-Communist
told us, 'governments all over the hemisphere would be thinking about
accommodation with the Communists rather than risk a guerilla war.'" On
the other side of the world, in the Congo, a similar effect was felt. Reports
Seymour Freidin: "The hard-nosed American response to Communist tactics in
Viet Nam dealt a shock-wave impact, felt half-way around the world in the
heart of Africa. Primarily and most importantly, it reinforced the resolve of
the moderate African states to resist subversion." (*New York Herald Tribune,*
March 10, 1965.)

way to the [Spanish front lines], entered the cemetery of
Huesca shortly after it had been liberated by the Nationalists.
This is what they had found: Coffins had been broken open—
I photographed the corpse of a small child whose head had
been torn off—and the walls of the cemetery were covered by
obscene drawings. The chapel of Our Lady had been turned
into a bar, and somebody had carefully removed with a dia-
mond the actual face of Our Lady from a stained glass
window. 'You can't call this kind of thing bestial,' said my
companion. 'A beast could not sink so low. There is something in this cemetery which is not of this world.'"[6] A
scholarly dispute goes on, of course, about whether the Communists really dominated the Spanish Republican cause—or,
if they did, at what point they actually achieved such domination. But such a debate is irrelevant. The other elements
in the Republican amalgam *behaved* like Communists—indeed, were frequently more violent and revolutionary. Middle-
class citizens in Republican territory, ironically enough, quite
frequently were relieved to have the Communists in actual
control, for they disciplined the revolutionary violence of the
anarchists, the syndicalists and other such groups. Recognizing the fundamental nature of the issues that had been at
stake in Spain, Antonio Salazar of Portugal said in 1956: "It
was clear to us twenty years ago, when we were confronted
with the Spanish civil war, that what was happening in the
world was a conflict of *civilizations*. To be more precise, it
was plain that Western principles and values were being attacked by alien philosophies. . . .'[7] Thus, "understanding
Communism"—quite contrary to liberal expectations in the
matter—leads to greater hostility towards it.‖

‖ The Spanish civil war was a kind of representative struggle in the world
revolution. It was immediately internationalized, and it split the West. Most
intellectuals supported the Republicans (that was their label), though some
did not: T. S. Eliot, Yeats, Santayana. On the other side, the great cellist

Certainly it is possible, even without bearing arms at the front in one of the many battles in the long drawn-out struggle for the world, to realize that two very different views of human destiny are in contention. From the giganticism of the portraits carried in Communist parades, and the surrealistic rhetoric of Communist speeches, to the antinomian gestures of the revolutionary demonstrators here in the West —the lying-down-in-the-street, the Columbia University students spitting at Madame Nhu, the bombs planned for the Statue of Liberty: gestures from one point of view in the realm of the absurd, but from another point of view in the realm of the totally rational—it is clear that the revolution in its various forms has at its heart a hatred of the manners and modes of the West, as well as of its central tenets.

Conservative theoreticians have articulated some of the fundamental differences between the East and the West. Gerhart Niemeyer, Professor of Political Science at Notre Dame and author of *An Inquiry Into Soviet Mentality* (1956), points out that "from its very beginnings, Marxism-Leninism has conceived the relation between itself and

---

Pablo Casals has exiled himself from Spain, and will not play there; though he will play in Hungary.

Quite rightly, the Left does not regard the Spanish Civil War as over: *all* the newspapers and journals of the Left refer to Franco in quite different tones from those they use in connection with figures (Republicans?) like Tito and Gomulka. Journalists of the Right, like Buckley, tend to think that Franco should have arranged for the transition to a legitimate government some time ago (presumably a constitutional monarchy), but, as for the war itself, they are glad he was there: "General Franco is an authentic national hero," writes Buckley. "It is generally conceded that he above others had the combination of talents, the perseverance, and a sense of the righteousness of his cause that were required to wrest Spain from the hands of the visionaries, ideologues, Marxists, and nihilists that were imposing upon her, in the thirties, a regime so grotesque as to do violence to the Spanish soul, to deny, even, Spain's historical identity." (*Rumbles Left and Right*, p. 49.)

the rest of the world as one of destruction. Communists assumed that the relationship must be so understood on both sides, that this must be the one premise shared between the Soviet system and the outside world. For the purpose of active and complete negation, the Communists recognize a universe of common rationality, a world of mutual 'understanding' and communication. In the subversive business of destroying social institutions, traditional loyalties, integrity of individuals, indigenous authority, etc., the Communists have shown a remarkable sense of tactics and timing. They perceive precisely where groups, individuals, institutions or leaders are vulnerable; how they can be deprived of their moral backbone; how any will to resist can be broken by sheer exhaustion."[8] Any Western institution has a point of vulnerability that can be exploited, as long as the exploiter really denies the value that he is using tactically to exploit it. The principle of "self-determination" can be used to paralyze Western action when what is taking place has nothing whatever to do with the independent choice of a people. The principle of "freedom of speech" can be used when those who invoke it have nothing of the sort ultimately in mind, and the principle can be used to bring a community or a university to heel. Things like "justice" or "nationalism" can be used to obliterate all competing values. The revolutionary strategy is always to use one value to destroy others. This strategy—this implacable hostility—is informed, Niemeyer argues, by a utopian vision of the future, a vision charged with emotions of religious intensity. "In all the gyrations of Communist theory, certain parts have remained untouched, an inviolate dogma. Significantly, this residue is precisely the irrational element, the 'intuition of the future.' This vision, temptingly dressed up as a foolproof 'scientific' theory, has taken a deep and almost subconscious hold on those who have embraced it in the way of a pseudo-religion. It supplies them with a hope, a task, a notion of life's meaning, a criterion of the elect."[9]

Other conservative intellectuals, such as Meyer, Burnham, Molnar, Bozell and Buckley agree with the essentials of Niemeyer's analysis, though not employing his terminology and differing in certain emphases. Like Niemeyer, they view Communism as another civilization, indeed as another religion. In his remarkable book *The Moulding of Communists* (1961), in which he draws on his experience as a member of the upper echelons of the Communist Party, Meyer explains in detail how the "Communist consciousness" is created by training in the Party schools, by "self-criticism," and by ruthless discipline. The Communist, Meyer says, develops an intense sense of identification with "our heroic Chinese comrades," with "our glorious Soviet comrades, moving forward from the successful construction of socialism to the building of Communism." The "compelling power of this sense of grandeur is more than sufficient to make up for the personal difficulties and dangers in which the individual Communist may find himself. The cause is advancing, the chariot of History is rolling inexorably on, and the Communist is seated firmly on that chariot, no matter how uncomfortable his personal position. The leaders of the Soviet Union may control the Party, but the emotional focus toward which the devotion of the Communist personality directs itself remains not the Soviet Union and its leaders, but 'the Party.' Certainly, 'the first duty of Communists is the defense of the Soviet Union'; certainly, 'the Soviet Union is the touchstone of all political questions,' the 'socialist fatherland,' the 'stronghold of world Communism'; but the Soviet Union is subsumed, as it were, under the greater symbol of the Party. The faith triumphant, the Soviet Union, is still but an aspect of the faith. It is the faith, whole and entire, Communism, the Party, which inspires the Communist's universe and is the object of his devotion."[10]¶ An emotionally compelling and internally consistent interpretation of man and history, Communism may appeal to the poverty-stricken, but such an appeal by no means constitutes its real power. "The Communists' program," as Buckley writes, "is capable (at least for a period of time, until the illusion wears off) of being wholly satisfactory, emotionally and intellectually, to large numbers of people. The reason for this is that Communist dogma is eschatologically conceived. . . . Communism offers a view of human history, holds out a millennial vision, indicates the means (revolution) of effecting this millennium."[11]

The failure of the liberals to understand the profound appeal of Communism proceeds, say the conservatives, from the inherent shallowness of their *own* vision of life. The "pragmatic" political analyst or politician, the practitioners of a "politics of compromise"—these exist in a realm far removed from commitment and fanaticism, and from those sicknesses of the soul for which commitment is the only cure.[12] As Thomas Molnar observes in discussing the work of George Kennan, even the most sophisticated liberal scholars simply do not come to grips with the psychological and spiritual needs which actually do move men to faith and action. As a result, Kierkegaard, Dostoievsky and Nietzsche

¶ "We are believers. Not as you are. We do not believe either in God or in men. We manufacture Gods and we transform men. We believe in Order. We will create a universe in our image, without weakness, a universe in which man, rid of the old rags of Christianity, will attain his cosmic grandeur, in the supreme culmination of the species. We are not fighting for a regime, or for power, or for riches. We are the instruments of fate." (The statement of a young Soviet official, quoted on p. 180 of *The Moulding of Communists*.)

"Their [Communists'] primary allegiance was to a revolutionary faith and a vision of man and his material destiny. . . ." (Whittaker Chambers, quoted in *The Moulding of Communists*, p. 204.)

[142]

provide a surer guide to what can be expected in modern history than Kennan's blander analyses. "As a Western liberal brought up in the humanistic tradition," Kennan seems "really *annoyed* that in his own lifetime such subterranean forces as quasi-religious convictions and destructive ideologies have reappeared when universal humanistic values ought to have extirpated them long ago."[13] Thus Kennan and other such neorealists as Walter Lippmann remain baffled by the "ambiguity," as Kennan calls it, "of Soviet policy . . . the combination of the doctrine of coexistence . . . with the most determined effort behind the scenes to destroy the Western governments and the social and political systems supporting them." Kennan at his best, thinks Molnar, is a good exponent of the *Realpolitik* of the nineteenth century, but this, "while it is valid as far as it goes, does not go far enough. It understands that power is the decisive political reality, but not that power in this century has a strong ideological component."[14] In the view of conservative intellectuals like Molnar, it is a fatal error to suppose, as Kennan, and indeed de Gaulle, seem to suppose, that we are facing a Russian or Chinese "regime" in something like the traditional sense, rather than an armed revolutionary doctrine of profound mass appeal.[15]

IV

In a seminal study entitled *Protracted Conflict*, which appeared in 1959, Robert Strausz-Hupé, Director of the Foreign Policy Research Institute of the University of Pennsylvania, writing in collaboration with three other members of the Institute, sets forth a broad analysis of the Cold War upon which virtually all American conservative intellectuals seem to agree. Recognizing that we are in the midst of a world revolution which the Communists frequently are able to direct and exploit, Strausz-Hupé points out that Western strategy has been crippled by its tacit acceptance of *Communist* ground rules.

According to Strausz-Hupé, Communist strategy, backed up by Communist propaganda and political maneuvering, envisions the world as divided into a "war zone" (the non-Communist nations) and a "peace zone" (the Communist bloc). As the Communists wish, the Cold War has been more or less confined to the "war zone," while the "peace zone" has been effectively closed to Western intervention. Operating on the basis of the "containment" policy, the West, as Strausz-Hupé writes, has been "willing to give a round and take a round. If the West won a round as, for example, in Korea and Jordan, it was in defense of the *status quo*. When the Communists won a round as, for example, in Czechoslovakia, China, Indochina and the Middle East [and, we might now add, Cuba], they gained access to ground previously closed to them. At best, the West stood its ground; but the Communists in winning their grounds made a net gain."[16] As all conflict of significance in the Cold War takes place in the "war zone," when a country such as Czechoslovakia or Cuba passes into the "peace zone" it is permanently removed from the conflict. Thus the Western "containment" strategy is at very best a defensive one, and even to maintain the status quo the West must win every round with the Communists.

Viewing the conflict in these terms, Strausz-Hupé is able to make illuminating comments on such things as the role of the U.N. "Almost all the debates in the United Nations from 1948 until 1958 over 'threats to peace,' 'intervention,' 'imperialism,' and 'rights to self-determination' dealt with problems and tensions arising primarily within the non-Communist world and between the Western powers and the colonial areas. The question of Soviet imperialism or violation of the rights of self-determination of peoples has been raised much less frequently and with a noticeable lack of fervor by the majority of U.N. membership."[17] Conservatives are likely to have a more jaundiced view of the U.N.'s possibilities than the liberals, to whose universalism it makes a strong appeal. Again, the liberal is likely to take a strong stand against Spain or South Africa, and even to support revolutionary movements in those countries; but the conservative, giving high priority to the protracted conflict, views them as non-Communist strongholds.

Conservatives share Strausz-Hupé's view that we are at war with the Communists. "The D-Day of World War III," wrote James Burnham in his book *The Struggle for the World*, "is not an event of the future but of the past." In Burnham's opinion, and that of political scientist Anthony T. Bouscaren, the Third World War "began in December 1944 when the International Communist movement launched its attack in Greece."[18] Moreover, unlike much liberal analysis, which views the conflict as an extension of traditional *Russian* imperialist aims, the conservatives have stressed the *Communist* character of the enemy. "No mystical doctrine of an Orthodox Muscovite Third Rome," argues Frank Meyer, "no nationalistic nineteenth-century mystique of Pan-Slavism . . . can enlighten us as to the ideological appeal of Moscow to the rising power-hungry intellectuals of the Arabic world, or can make intelligible the Communist lodgement in Brazil or Guatemala—or, for that matter, in New York or Chicago or Washington. Can one imagine a devotee of the Third Rome penetrating our Department of State, going to jail on a charge of perjury with the devotion of a martyr?"[19]

Of course, to call this conflict World War Three as Burnham does, though it has the advantage of stressing the fact that it *is* a war, has also the disadvantage of suggesting that it is a war of the traditional sort, like the first two, rather than the uniquely revolutionary struggle it really is. Unlike our past antagonists, as *National Review* pointed out in 1956, "the Communists consider overt and general war as a secondary and reserve method—to be initiated only when a favorable outcome is assured by either the small size of the opponent or by his prior internal collapse. In the preferred schedule of Communist conquest, the main burden of the offensive is carried by political warfare and internal subversion. The main armies remain in reserve as a defense, or to be sent to gather the harvest that political warfare has ripened."[20]

Because the conflict is of unprecedented nature, the conservatives have had some difficulty in devising a terminology appropriate to it. The unique is hard to define. "The 'cold' in 'cold war,'" as James Burnham points out, "never did justice to the blood that flowed hotly enough in Korea, Malaysia, the Philippines, Iraq, Algeria and Hungary . . . 'protracted conflict' correctly emphasizes the long-drawn-out time scheme, but in no way suggests the conflict's nature. 'Limited war' is satisfactory if we take it to refer to the qualitative and quantitative restrictions accepted by both opponents on the weapons used in waging the struggle. In this sense the struggle is not an 'all out' or 'general' war. But to call it 'limited' obscures the more important fact that the *objective* of this struggle is *unlimited*. Moreover, there is nothing necessarily permanent about the self-imposed restrictions on the means. These may at any moment be lifted by one or the other opponent."[21]

Whatever the terminological difficulties, conservative writers have had little doubt that the passive "containment" is inadequate. Sometimes, as in a *National Review* editorial on the Berlin Wall, they have used Strausz-Hupé's vocabulary:

Once again the Communists have succeeded in their favorite gambit. The Zone of Peace (their zone) remains always inviolate. They raise a ruckus in the Zone of War (our zone), and put forward a slew of demands. Everyone then calls for "reducing the tensions" by "negotiating a compromise." We negotiate, and we compromise. That is, we grant them half or two-thirds or nine tenths of what they have asked, and we "win" one tenth. Until the next round.[22]

The same analysis was applied in an article James Burnham wrote comparing Communist and Western responses in situations that were in their essentials analogous.[23] Burnham observes that when rebellion broke out in the Peace Zone, in Hungary, the Communists moved with energy and dispatch, while the West did nothing. In the case of Cuba, previously in the War Zone, the Communists again moved decisively, exploiting a volatile situation for their own ends. As a result, Cuba joined Hungary in the Peace Zone. Again, in Tibet, the Communists moved decisively. The contrast between Western and Communist behavior, Burnham observes, "is too complete and too obvious to need detailed statement. We did just next to nothing. We had made no preparations, and had no share in the preliminaries. We did not intervene, directly or indirectly, in mid-crisis. For Hungary the Western leaders made a few platonic speeches; for Tibet, not even that. How are we to explain this total contrast? We do nothing because we are afraid to risk nuclear war. But that cuts both ways. *They* do not hesitate to take the risk—if it really is a risk—and they get away with it. Why should we suppose that the results would be different if *we* were intervening in *their* sphere?"[24] As a result of our passivity, Burnham notes, we are not "containing" the Communists: rather, they are containing us, behind a constantly

contracting perimeter. As *National Review* observed sardonically when Laos became a Communist invasion route into
South Viet Nam: "Having looked and looked and looked
for the New Frontier, we finally spotted it. . . . It's five
hundred miles closer to us than the old frontier."

The alternative to passive containment would not by any
means entail all-out nuclear war, as those who really have
not read the conservative writers so often assert. An alternative policy would envision using political and psychological
warfare on the Communist side of the line. Instead of hoping
for opportunities for such intervention, however, the West
actually fears them. A *National Review* editorial, written just
after the Berlin Wall went up, quotes the *New York Times:*

> The likelihood of an East German uprising, similar to the bloody
> June 17, 1953 revolt, has been worrying the [Western] Allies for
> weeks. . . . The hope among all officials here [in Washington] is
> that the East Germans would not rise. . . . The policy of the
> United States and its allies continues to be that nothing will be done
> to encourage a rebellion in East Germany and nothing will be done
> to assist if one should erupt because of the danger of a military clash
> with Soviet forces.
>
> *New York Times*, Washington dispatch, Aug. 14, 1961

In a similar vein, the *New York Herald Tribune* observed
that "the Kennedy Administration is trying to avoid any
. . . shadow of moral involvement in East Germany." *National Review* went on to observe that "those words perfectly express the bankruptcy of American and Western international policy. The very eventuality that would be the
target and triumphant climax of a rational policy has become transformed into its exact opposite: a 'peril,' a 'danger,' a disaster to be staved off by all possible means."[25]

An alternative policy, *National Review* observes, would
have exploited the enormous Communist vulnerability the
revolts exposed. It would "have planned and moved deliberately and in detail, toward situations where mass actions

of varying intensity and scope within the enemy sphere would be used as strategic weapons. . . . [We] should be able to swing into support of its people others—large masses as well as trained activist units—elsewhere in East Europe and Asia. We should be prepared to furnish guidance, communications, supplies, psychological and political support in every form . . . Khrushchev's attitude would be something very different from his contemptuous dismissal of the 'vigorous protests' that are now the limit of our arsenal. Khrushchev knows as well as any man how realistic a policy of liberation is. 'Liberation'—his style—is *his* policy."[26] East Germany, conservatives agree, is only one place where sanctions short of open warfare would have been effective: each time the situation becomes fluid, they argue, the West should be prepared with boycotts, cancellation of exchange programs, embargoes, resumption of nuclear tests, raids on exposed positions like Cuba, and so on.

V

Because they consider that the Communists are pressing forward in the protracted conflict whenever and wherever they can, conservatives tend to view even apparently conciliatory Communist gestures as mere tactics in the struggle. Most liberals acclaim any step toward disarmament. Writing in *National Review*, however, Strausz-Hupé points out that disarmament agreements thus far have been calculated to put restrictions on those weapons peculiarly important to the West:

The arms race is fraught with terrible dangers; its cessation would be a boon to mankind. But it is difficult to see how partial disarmament—according to Premier Khrushchev, total disarmament will have to be preceded by gradual arms reduction—would diminish

Soviet capabilities for fighting the kind of wars the Communists have actually been fighting since the termination of World War II. These wars were limited; they were fought with conventional weapons and, in some places, with the simplest of conventional weapons.[27]

The large population advantage enjoyed by nations hostile to the West renders Western security dependent in the long run on technological advantages, and perhaps on technological break-throughs. The more rudimentary the weapons employed, the better for the Communists; the more sophisticated the weapons, the less sheer numbers will count. In the concrete terms of the world struggle, therefore, groups that agitate against the development of such sophisticated weapons are working against the interests of the West. Conservatives, in contrast, have consistently pressed for the development of advanced weapons—for nuclear versatility, for experiments directed toward the military use of space. As James Burnham pointed out, we have entered an *unpoliced* agreement with the Soviet Union not to put nuclear weapons in orbit, even though the most advanced strategical projections indicate that "orbital weapon systems will in all probability become strategically decisive in the 1970's. This means that in a certain sense they are already decisive: for the decisions on appropriations, research, development and experimentation that will determine the state of affairs in the 1970's are being made now."[28] In the opinion of Burnham and other conservatives, the West has slowed down in the search for a technological and military break-through— in aerospace, in the development of an anti-missile missile, and so forth—with no assurance that the Communists have done likewise. But they also point out that even advanced technology is not likely, in itself, to help the West unless its leaders realize that they are *at war*, and design a policy on that assumption. We must not forget, Burnham writes, "that from the end of the war until a couple of years ago we had overwhelming superiority in advanced armament over the Soviet Union. This superiority did not prove to be an answer to the Soviet threat. Though lacking both nuclear weapons and strategic airpower, the Soviet Union marched briskly up the path of the world revolution. It was in just those years of our overwhelming arms predominance that Communism conquered China, Tibet, North Korea and North Viet Nam, and consolidated control over the captured nations of East Europe."[29] Clearly weapons development can be only one half of the answer to the West's strategic problem; weapons are useless without a coherent overall strategy that uses the weapons for *political* purposes.

As long as the protracted conflict lasts, conservatives argue, the West must wage unremitting political warfare against the Communists, and like the Communists should view even "negotiations" as a political weapon rather than as a genuine mode of "settling differences." "Communists don't negotiate," observed *National Review* in 1959. "They conduct political warfare. Communists are not diplomats but revolutionaries. What we call a 'conference' or a 'meeting' is for Communists a political warfare operation to be fought by all the relevant means as a battle in the struggle for the world. From the Communist point of view it is of tertiary importance whether any formal 'agreement' comes out as a by-product of a conference. If so, and if it is in their favor, so much the better; if not, they will violate it in any case as soon as that becomes expedient. They seek not 'agreement' but victory. In Communist language, a conference is 'a forum from which to speak to the masses over the heads of their leaders.' "[30]

Under the circumstances, Western representatives should view them the same way. If the Communists press for the seating of East Germany or Red China at the conference table, why should the West not reply: "Yes, Mr. Gromyko,

[151]

we agree: It has year after year been our proposal that these unhappy slaves of tyranny should be given a free voice to choose representatives, a government of their own. We urge that representatives of the Germans now captive beyond the Elbe should be seated at this table. If such representatives of the Germans of the East were here today, instead of those traitorous puppets you dance on your string . . . we might learn why three million Germans have fled to the West from the infamies of those agents of yours whom you now seek to foist on us as German spokesmen. . . . Czechoslovakia and Poland also? Of course: if there were a voice to speak legitimately for Poland and Czechoslovakia, to tell us at last the whole story of the death of Jan Masaryk, of those cattle-train journeys of four million Poles to Arctic slave camps, of the looting of Czech and Polish goods, of the studied Soviet exploitation of the Polish and Czech economies, of the saga of the secret police . . . the whole world would listen."[31] Instead, the West goes to a conference as if it were going to an ordinary conference among nations, bringing with it a set of largely traditional objectives; while the Communists come, of course, with their revolutionary ones.

In contrast to liberals, conservatives take a skeptical view of so-called changes in the Communist world. The famous "de-Stalinization" under Khrushchev was interpreted by Frank Meyer as actually a triumph of Stalinism. Noting three years after Stalin's death that "de-Stalinization" has actually entailed an *increase* of Communist pressure against the non-Communist world, Meyer pointed out that "the Middle East has been breached; the Titoist schism healed; united front connections with the neutralist bloc immensely strengthened; the blockade of trade in strategic materials broken; our position in Western Germany and Japan undermined."** This is a bad harvest, Meyer observed, "for three years of *detente* and the 'lessening of international tension.'"[32] Rather than indicating Communist strength, Meyer argues, the brutal Stalinist policies were actually *defensive*, and a sign of postwar Communist weakness. Because of Communist vulnerability, Stalin took an intransigent position as regards the non-Communist world, and practiced savage repression at home, these courses calculated to consolidate Communist gains made during the war and at the conference table, and to carry out domestic programs necessary for reconstruction after the war. While Stalin's rhetoric and political tactics often were aggressive, his strategy was ultimately defensive. Conversely, post-Stalinist Communist policy, operating in a world where the balance of power has shifted radically, employs a milder rhetoric and tactics that appear less aggressive —"primarily directed toward disarming the enemy"—but projects overall aims that go far beyond Stalin's. The vilification of Stalin by Khrushchev, accordingly, is based upon the triumph of Stalin's policy, a triumph that permitted the revolution to enter a new phase. And the *method* of making the political transition to the new phase is Stalin's as well. Just as Stalin vilified the symbols of earlier policy, such as Trotsky, so he is vilified in his turn. In Meyer's interpretation, Khrushchev's famous speech denouncing Stalin was, in essence, Stalinist. It may be that the post-Stalinist situation is more complicated than Meyer's dialectical analysis takes account of; but Meyer's analysis would nevertheless seem to be truer to the facts of the matter than the usual optimism of

** In Meyer's remarks on Japan and Germany one may detect the operation of an excessive pessimism. He was writing at the time of the massive riots against Eisenhower's visit; yet the stability of Japan, historically considered, is one of the remarkable phenomena of our time; and West Germany does not seem to have been undermined. Pessimism may be one of the rhetorical, and, indeed, political temptations for conservatives to guard against.

the liberals. Meyer wrote, after all, in 1956; and we might well remember that the "moderate" Khrushchev crushed Hungary, built the Berlin Wall, put missiles in Cuba, and tested multi-megaton nuclear bombs.

Liberal optimism about the significance of events inside the Communist bloc seems invulnerable to experience. The *New York Times*, for example, was completely taken in by Mao's "hundred flowers" speech, in which the Chinese ruler observed that the same measures should not be applied against "misguided elements" and against "the enemy," and stressed the "non-antagonistic resolution of contradictions among the people." This the *Times* hailed editorially as a new doctrine, a break with totalitarian conceptions, an endorsement of "democratic freedoms." As Meyer points out, those with a truly profound knowledge of Communist theory and tactics recognized Mao's speech as perfectly orthodox, and indeed a "striking analysis in the Marxist-Leninist tradition."[33] The whole point involves the ambiguity of the term "people" as used in Communist rhetoric. Mao observed that the term means different things in different situations:

The term 'the people' has different meanings . . . in different historical periods. . . . During the Japanese aggression, all those classes, strata and social groups that opposed Japanese aggression belonged to the category of the people, while the Japanese imperialists, Chinese traitors and the pro-Japanese elements belonged to the category of enemies of the people.

During the war of liberation, the United States imperialists and their henchmen, the bureaucrat-capitalists and landlord class, and the Kuomintang reactionaries . . . were the enemies of the people, while all [who] opposed these enemies belonged to the category of the people.

At this stage of building socialism, all [who] approve, support, and work for the cause of socialist construction, belong to the category of the people, while those social forces and groups that resist Socialist revolution . . . are enemies of the people.

In this view, obviously, "the people" are those who go along with the Party line at any given moment, and "the enemy" those who resist it. When the situation changes, so does the definition, and some who were included among the people then find themselves "counterrevolutionaries" and the targets of "ruthless revolutionary action." As a matter of fact, Mao's speech, tactically interpreted, was calculated precisely to expose "contradictions" among the "people" before taking another leap forward—i.e., into widespread collectivization. The Party *wanted* "dissident" opinion expressed, so that potential resisters could be weeded out. "The myth of de-Stalinization," Strausz-Hupé observes, "was exploded by the brutal Soviet repression of the Hungarian uprising. Nevertheless,

only a few months later, Mao Tse-tung managed similarly to beguile Western optimists with his policy of "letting a hundred flowers bloom." This policy, which many Western friends of China welcomed as a tender shoot of "liberalization" served ultimately the purpose of ferreting out potential dissidents. Such flowers as had bloomed—and had bloomed, as we now know, in the artificial climate of Mao's ideological garden—soon withered. Within a year after Mao's dulcet call for diversity-in-unity, the Peking regime established the system of militarized communes which shocked not only Western opinion but also Western Communist ideologists and their fellow-travellers.[34]

Just as de-Stalinization heralded greatly intensified expansionist moves, so Mao's "liberalization" foreshadowed a domestic policy of unprecedented harshness. Nevertheless, as Meyer points out, hope springs eternal in the breast of the *New York Times*—"particularly hope that somewhere, sometime, it can find a Communist who really isn't a Communist. Years ago it was Mao Tse-tung and his agrarian reformers; during the war, Stalin almost qualified; then it was Tito, then Malenkov, then Gomulka." During the "hundred flower" phase, Mao returned to favor again, shortly to give way to Castro. The *Times* can sometimes be counted on for the most rosy view of Communist intentions. The most recent example, as of February, 1965, was Premier Kosygin's visit to Hanoi and Peking at the moment of a climactic Viet Cong attack in the South, timed with raids on American installations. Kosygin's visit, thought the *Times*, had been calculated to wean the North Vietnamese away from the Chinese, and to persuade them to pursue a more moderate course. This was too much for Professor Zbigniew Brzezinski of Columbia University, an expert on Soviet affairs, who sent off a letter to the editor, pointing out that the alternative interpretation was at least as likely. Kosygin had decided that the Chinese policy of limited war and increased risk was paying off, and did not want to be left in the wake of the revolutionary wave.††

†† For a conservative proposal on Viet Nam see William Buckley, "On the Right," February 20, 1965. This would mean urging other Asian countries to send "soldiers to fight in Viet Nam if necessary, and anywhere else the enemy threatens to irrupt." This of course would entail facing down leftist-neutralist opposition at home, hewing clearly to an anti-Communist line; backing the United States in the United Nations and before all the councils of the world —in effect, taking over, and fighting and directing their own fight, with the aid of our tools.

"Otherwise it is quite truly a lost cause, we having permitted the morale of the free Asian community to sink so low. As the result of our ambiguous policies with respect to everything from crossing the Yalu to crossing the Formosan straits, it will be hard to revive that morale: and without it on our side, we almost certainly will not be able to prevail in the end. Bear in mind that in the end the Red Chinese will have an operative atom bomb and a moderately effective delivery system. And will be able to talk about using it against her enemies in quite credible accents. It will not be possible, when that day comes if it comes, for a government in Tokyo, or in Manila, or even in Taiwan, to bind the community together in resistance to Red China.

"An international conference, then, there should definitely be. But not another of the silly kind, the kind proposed by U Thant, which would simply provide cover for the Vietcong as it pursues its goals. A conference rather

Viewed against the developments of the last ten years, the overall performance of the conservatives in foreign policy analysis has been impressive. They have made some mistakes. In 1960, for example, *National Review* sponsored and published as a separate supplement, a collection of essays called *Bear and Dragon*. In it, eight experts on China and Russia, most of them academicians, analyzed Sino-Soviet relations, and concluded that serious disputes between the two countries could not arise. *Bear and Dragon* remains immensely informative about Chinese and Russian history and culture, and about ideological matters; yet what these experts said would not happen, did happen. There has been a division between the Russian and Chinese Communist parties that divides not only the two Communist countries but also their international parties, in country after country throughout the world. Nothing in *Bear and Dragon* gave any hint that this could happen. Still, one may wonder: how significant for the West is this dispute within the Communist camp? It certainly is not obvious that either Russian or Chinese Communism means to "coexist" with the West in the ordinary meaning of that term: at the very best, the debate would seem to be one over modes of extermination. "We have

---

of representatives of the free peoples of Asia. The crisis is primarily their responsibility. They are the ones who will end their lives free or slave.

"The moment is at hand, and perhaps for the last time, when we can view the problem as a regional one involving the future of what is left of free Asia. The time has come to summon our allies or potential allies, notably Japan, the Philippines, Malaysia, Formosa, Thailand and Australia—and tell them exactly how far the United States is prepared to go in helping them safeguard Asian freedom, and on what terms. We should be prepared to go very far indeed. Certainly we should be prepared to bomb the nuclear facilities of Red China. And certainly we should be prepared to use our technical resources to effect defoliation sufficient to expose the main supply routes to the Vietcong. But in return we should insist that the nations of Asia accept their responsibilities: and take the initiative in creating and maintaining an anti-Communist Asian policy."

been told ten thousand times," writes Burnham, "that the issue is peaceful coexistence vs. revolutionary militancy, and there is no doubt that Russian vs. Chinese *rhetoric* bears this out. But the facts do not bear out the rhetoric. Chou En-lai, on African tour, has long and cozy visits with the most reactionary rulers, the King of Morocco and the Emperor of Ethiopia. Mao happily co-exists with de Gaulle, and is ready for any amount of peaceful business with Japan. Moscow, from its corner, gives far more actual support than Peking to the 'wars of national liberation' in Cuba, Algeria, Venezuela, the Congo, Yemen, Angola and Cyprus. Both Peking and Moscow give full political and material support to the armed struggle in Viet Nam, Malaysia, Zanzibar. Neither Moscow nor Peking shows any inclination for general war."[35] In Burnham's view, our fascination with the "split" may serve to advance the revolution: the Russian advocacy of coexistence and the Chinese militancy both work to advance the revolutionary strategy. The militant wing "smites the enemy of the revolution with riots, arson, terror, bombs and bullets," while the peaceful wing lulls him with negotiations, conferences, cultural exchanges, and so forth— the *rhetoric* of "coexistence"—while in fact ("concretely") providing the material support for revolution from Cuba to Algeria and the Congo.

VI

For a great many people, the United Nations Organization is above criticism, is, indeed—in the familiar phrase—"our last best hope for peace." To them, conservative criticism of the U.N. is prima facie evidence of political depravity. The fact that the nations constituting the U.N. are far from united, and that a great many of them are not even nations has made little difference to the relative immunity of the organization from liberal attack, for, at least in aspiration, it appeals to the central liberal beliefs—in "human brotherhood," in the obsolescence of cultural differences, in the rational transcendence of value conflicts. Nevertheless, dissent has been heard, and not only from committed conservatives.

In a book entitled *The United Nations Reconsidered* (1963), Raymond A. Moore, Jr., gathered together a collection of essays and speeches, mainly from Establishment liberals, pointing to the severe limitations of the U.N., and including contributions by Senators Fulbright, Mansfield, Aiken and Jackson, as well as Max Ascoli, the then Earl of Home, James Byrnes, and Harold Macmillan. As M. Stanton Evans observed in his review of the book, a new feature of anti-Communist strategy "is the intellectual popular front—embracing not divergent sectors of the Left, but yoking elements of Left and Right. The participants are cerebral conservatives and unsentimental liberals who believe domestic issues will mean little if the world should be engulfed by Communism."[36]

In his contribution, which previously had appeared in the magazine *Foreign Affairs*, Fulbright argued that because the U.N. had fallen so far short of expectations, the United States should conduct its policy instead through a "concert of free nations." In Fulbright's view, the U.N. General Assembly, dominant in the world organization since 1950, "is a most unwieldy body and one which bears no relationship to the realities of world power." Instead of pursuing the abstract and utopian goals of the U.N., Fulbright thought, the United States should support this concert of free nations taking "its inspiration from the nineteenth-century Concert of Europe, with its common values and accepted rules of the game. . . . A realistic 'concert of free nations' might be expected to consist of an 'inner community' of

[159]

the North Atlantic nations and an 'outer community' embracing much or all of the non-Communist world."[37] Such an organization would at least have a basis in common culture and community of interest, thought Fulbright. A short time later, Senator Henry M. Jackson made even more pointedly similar criticisms of the U.N. in a speech before the National Press Club. Arguing that "the best hope for peace with justice does not lie with the U.N.," he also pointed out that the U.N. "is not a substitute for national policies wisely conceived to uphold our vital interests," and that the U.N. actually often works to inflame rather than relax tensions: "There are too many votes on too many issues in the U.N."[38] James F. Byrnes, Secretary of State under Truman, put his finger on the fatal weakness of the U.N., the irresponsibility of the General Assembly. "The United Nations of today," he pointed out, "is not the organization we sponsored in 1945." The addition of a great many new nations to the General Assembly, combined with the weakening of the Security Council, has completely altered its character. If the United States is to continue its membership, he said, we must enforce "the provision of the charter that prohibits the United Nations from interfering in the domestic affairs of a state. We must also place less reliance upon the United Nations and more reliance upon NATO and other regional organizations of our allies pledged to the independence of free peoples."[39] Others, such as President de Gaulle and England's Douglas Home, have taken an equally critical view. The United Nations "encourages policies that endanger law and order," Home observed. . . . "A large part of the organization which is dedicated to peace openly condones aggression." The U.N. "seldom condemns Russians but constantly assails us. . . . Everyone has seen the chaos in the Congo and everyone knows that it derives from a premature grant of independence to a country whose people were totally unprepared for their new responsibilities. Yet many delegates were instructed by their governments to sponsor and vote for resolutions which could only multiply and magnify that chaos in other places."[40]

Such attacks as these upon the U.N. adumbrate much that the conservatives have had to say on the subject, but the conservative critique has been more consistently sustained and more comprehensive in its analysis. James Burnham agrees with Byrnes, for example, on the irresponsibility of the General Assembly. In 1950, he points out, the United States, confident of its majority in the General Assembly, built up the authority of the General Assembly in order to circumvent the Soviet veto on the Security Council. This "worked" in the case of Korea, permitting the Western response to Communist aggression to masquerade as a U.N. response. More recently, however, as the composition of the General Assembly has changed, its actions have been increasingly disadvantageous to the West. "In the early years the European bloc plus the American bloc plus the Commonwealth members and a few client states gave the West the two-thirds majority required for Assembly action on other than procedural matters." Gradually, however, with the addition of new members and because Soviet pressure on some of the old ones has had its effect, the West's two-thirds majority crumbled. "On many significant issues the West is now in a minority." Burnham admits that a good deal of the talk about "loyalty to the U.N." on the part of the major powers is pure propaganda, and that the U.S., the U.S.S.R. and even India disregard the U.N. when they consider that a serious national interest is in question, but he also argues that "the motley crew of the U.N. Assembly has come to wield a kind of preventive veto over the Western powers, most frequently over the United States, which is more self-victimized than any other nation by diplomatic forms and ideological abstractions."[41]

In another article, Burnham analyzes in more detail the farcical composition of the General Assembly, and provides vivid confirmation of Fulbright's point. First, but perhaps least important, is the fact that votes in the Assembly bear no relationship to population. Africa, with a population of 227,000,000, has thirty-three votes. North America, with a population of 205,000,000, has two votes. More than half of the member nations actually have smaller populations than the state of Maryland. But more significant for the political behavior of the body are the disparities in political, economic, educational and moral development. "The *total* wealth of sixty of the member nations," Burnham points out, "is less than that of the single state of Ohio. Many of these members can be called 'nations' only as a courtesy, since they possess none of the historical, geographic, ethnic, economic or political conditions that give reality to national existence. In many of them fractions of the population up to 99 per cent are illiterate." More than half of them lack the trained administrators necessary for responsible government; in many of them ritual murder, cannibalism, and savagery persist as organic parts of the local culture. Yet, "there come before this Assembly issues of the utmost moment for human civilization. It is absurd, it is literally insane, to submit such issues to the will of a collectivity so constituted."[42]

This Assembly, conservative writers point out, has exhibited an increasingly anti-Western bias, though, to be sure, it has remained surprisingly immune to criticism in the ordinary Western press. Western colonialism in Angola, and, by a stretch of the definition, in South Africa, is the subject of endless vituperation, but the Assembly is silent on the subject of Soviet and Chinese colonialism, and even closes its eyes to colonialism when practiced by Indonesia. "The

U.N.," *National Review* points out, "gets into a terrific sweat about wars in the Gaza strip, Katanga, Angola and outer space. But darned if any UNer can notice those 28,000 Egyptian troops, with plenty of tanks and planes, fighting month after month to shore up a leftist revolution in Yemen that couldn't have stood two weeks on its own feet; or the Soviet military technicians now building themselves a full-length jet runway on Yemeni territory to give Soviet planes a staging point on the way to Africa and Cuba."[43] Similarly, the U.N. was silent on the Chinese take-over in Tibet. Yet if the U.N. remains silent on matters of this kind, or even, as in the case of Sukarno's grab in New Guinea, actively supports the colonialism, it takes an entirely different line with regard to Portugal, Southern Rhodesia and South Africa, and actively supports "infant pseudo-nations" which, as James Burnham writes, though "illiterate, half-savage, unable to manage their own disintegrating affairs, kept from bankruptcy only by the subsidies of the Western powers, set out to destroy the orderly regimes of the southern sector of the continent, to massacre hundreds of thousands of the inhabitants, and, after wrecking law, order, and economic life, to establish black racist rule over a permanent shambles."[44]

Even its own charter does not stand in the way of Assembly action directed against South Africa. "The United Nations," observed a *National Review* editorial, "have abandoned any respect whatever for their own Charter, as witness last week's vote (101–1) to censure South Africa for arresting African citizens on charges of armed revolt. Under pressure, the United States, England, and even France capitulated, joining in the demagogic parade. The Charter of the United Nations prohibits interference in the internal affairs of any nation."[45] The Afro-Asian bloc naturally calls attention to South African *apartheid* ("separation of the races") as evidence of intolerable iniquity; yet the internal policies of many of the member nations of the Afro-Asian bloc are far more repressive than those of South Africa. "As a 'distasteful necessity,'" observed *National Review* in 1963, "the parliament of Ghana the other day slapped an amendment onto the constitution allowing Nkrumah's government to place prisoners under detention for up to another five years after they have already served five-year sentences. Some Ghanaian MP's confessed their repugnance for the act, saying it put them in mind of the things that go on in South Africa. Limit of detention in South Africa: ninety days."[46]

Because the conservatives regard the U.N. General Assembly as irresponsible, and see its activities as on the whole anti-Western, or, at very best, as generally inflammatory, they have proposed that the U.N. be "de-politicalized." While continuing to perform many valuable nonpolitical services, such as handling technical problems of air and sea transport, disease control, radio channel allocation, measurement standards and the like, the U.N. would cease to vote on matters of political substance. This change could be accomplished, in James Burnham's opinion, without Charter revision: if the United States simply announced that *it* would no longer vote on matters of substance, such votes would become meaningless. "Though they would dislike having their U.N.-swollen self-importance scaled down, the new nations would have no choice but to accept the new rule, and most of our Western allies would welcome it."[47]

Some of the most entertaining rhetoric in *National Review* has been provoked by the spectacle of spokesmen for the Afro-Asian "nations" setting up as moral preceptors to the world. Nehru, who waited two weeks to express even the mildest disapproval of the Soviet slaughter of Hungarian freedom-fighters, set the pattern for countless Pecksniffian moral sermons to the West, and few publications have talked more sense on this matter than *National Review*. The following 1963 editorial is quoted in full:

At Addis Abbaba, where the Africans met last week, the talk was largely on the infamies in Birmingham, Alabama against the Negroes. The Prime Minister of Uganda, the Honorable Milton Obote, railed against the "hypocrisy" of Mr. Kennedy in sending greetings to Addis Abbaba even while blood was flowing in Birmingham. Towards the end of his speech, Mr. Obote pledged his own nation, and by implication all the member states he was haranguing, to a war of liberation against the Portuguese colonies, Angola and Mozambique, and the Republic of South Africa. In the last effort to liberate Angola, more black men, in two days, were murdered by other black men, than were lynched in the South in one hundred years.

The United States obviously has its problems, but in our passion for self-punishment, we are losing our perspective. All sins, we are saying, were created equal, and therefore the United States, where never before have so many agitated themselves so much in behalf of so few, grovels at Addis Abbaba, of all places, the oldest and most primitive despotism on earth, quails before a Ugandan whose illiterate population diligently persecutes the Asian minority, hides its face before Kenyans who have just chosen the organizer of the bestial Mau Mau as their national leader—in a continent where melting pots are a literal danger, not a metaphorical blessing.

There are those who believe it is a greater offense if St. Peter tells a white lie than if Herod issues genocidal orders against the infant population, and that therefore Jim Crow is worse in America than Mau Mau in Africa. These are problems that will tax the reflective power of moral theologians, one of whom, incidentally, Obote of Uganda is not. Meanwhile, we should politely decline to be catechized by these paramount chiefs of primitive societies masquerading as parliamentary statesmen. The United States has a vital interest in its own prestige, a fact we officially recognize year after year when we appropriate hundreds of millions of dollars for projects related to projecting our image successfully. We would have been comforted last week, or the week before, to hear even one of our leaders say to the world: "Gentlemen, that we have our problems, we do not deny. But they are *our* problems. Meanwhile, we can boast that in no country in the world can a member of any minority, racial or religious,

[165]

expect to receive simultaneously a greater share of the prevailing prosperity, a greater ration of justice, or a greater solicitude from the well-intentioned majority. We suggest you give priority to your own problems. You do *have* problems, don't you?"[48]

American subservience to the policies and rhetoric of the Afro-Asian bloc has been in considerable degree a result of liberal doctrine. James Burnham says that liberal opinion "has demanded and demands that the advanced Western nations—Britain, France, the Netherlands, Belgium, Portugal— liquidate forthwith all forms of direct and indirect colonial rule, without reference to economic or strategic interests or the readiness of peoples for independence or the question whether independence will in truth benefit or harm them, or to any other factor than the abstract badness of colonialism."[49] Furthermore, "the group, nation or civilization infected by liberal doctrine and values, [is] morally disarmed before those whom the liberal regards as less well off than himself."[50] Yet United States policy is also based on an overall *strategy* the conservative writers consider erroneous. The United States, Erik von Kuehnelt-Leddihn points out, "clearly is out to win the favor of new nations no matter what the cost. Surely the United States is friendlier toward India, which [invaded Goa], than toward tiny Portugal, her victim."[51] As a result of this effort to win the favor of the so-called "third world," a policy in any case unlikely to be crowned with success, the United States has at one time or another violated the national interest of her natural allies: Holland (in New Guinea), Belgium (in Katanga), France (in Algeria), Portugal (in Angola, Mozambique and Goa), and Britain (at Suez, in Cyprus, and in our neutrality with respect to the Malaysia-Indonesia confrontation). James Burnham, indeed, sees disregard of *Western* interests as one aspect of what he calls the "Yalta strategy," and which he contrasts with the "NATO" or "Western" strategy. Yalta strategy envisions "a Soviet-American deal (with Britain tagging along)." It looks toward a "detente and an enlarging agreement with Russia, with the implicit goal of a Russo-American condominium." In Burnham's view, the downgrading of Western European interests in the American policy amalgam is responsible for the splintering of NATO, which in reality is the "structural foundation of Western power and will." For example, Washington "backs revolutionaries against the NATO member, Portugal, while asking Portugal to renew essential accords on strategic bases." Thus, the Yalta strategy is incompatible with the Western strategy, which is expressed in NATO and "implies the defense of the West as a whole *against* the threat of the Soviet Union and the Communist enterprise."[52]

V

The Academy

The literary critic Hugh Kenner, Professor of English at the University of California at Santa Barbara, recently set forth a theory concerning the role played by colleges and universities in American life. "The United States," he said, "is unique among history's great nations in attempting, with considerable success, to operate a civilization without a capital. (Washington isn't a capital like Paris or London; it's where we keep the government.) In place of a capital, from which lines of force radiate like roads, we have a communications network, continent-wide, along which energies pass to and fro. Washington is a plexus on this network, capable of imparting a certain prestigious torque to selected impulses. New York is another. For the rest, it passes mostly through the universities."[1]

Our colleges and universities thus, in Kenner's view, function as a kind of "dispersed capital." Like the capital cities of western Europe, they generate influential ideas and help to circulate them. "It is through the network of professors and alumni—people whose lives have been touched for four years or more by a university—that the shaping ideas travel in America, precisely as they once travelled about Paris: not always definable ideas: a melange of gossip, colorations, judgments, policies, presuppositions, lists of In and Out . . . the academic network is the country's nervous system."[2] The analogy between the academic network and the traditional capital city can be pressed even further. Just as the Parisian or Londoner or Viennese possesses a sharp sense of his difference from the inhabitant of the provinces, so, says Kenner, an "Alabaman and a Montanan who have both been to college (any college) have more in common than a Nebraskan who has and a Nebraskan who hasn't. Precisely so, in eighteenth century England, did the distinction fall between Londoners and the rest. Samuel Johnson went up from Litchfield to London, having done time at Oxford. His present day American counterpart would go to some university and stay there."[3]

To this academic "dispersed capital," *National Review* stands in a peculiar, indeed a unique, relationship. Like other political and literary magazines, it draws upon the academy for its contributors; perhaps draws upon it to an even greater degree than, say, *The Nation* or *New Republic*. Russell Kirk, Hugh Kenner, James Burnham, Garry Wills, Thomas Molnar, Will Herberg, Gerhart Niemeyer, F. D. Wihelmsen and Guy Davenport, all of whom are or have been professors, appear on the masthead; and among the regular contributors of articles and reviews, a high proportion are academic figures. Even Buckley, though not a professor, has always been associated in one way or another with the academy. He emerged as a public figure while editing the student newspaper at Yale; his first book was an examination of the Yale curriculum; for a long time he wrote a regular column in *National Review* called "The Ivory Tower," in which he discussed academic matters; and for a decade or more he has toured the nation's campuses, making speeches and debating. Yet the attitude of *National Review* toward the academy and the climate of opinion it understands to prevail there has been highly critical; in fact, so prominent has this concern been in its pages that *National Review* might validly be thought of as having arisen as a critical voice within the

walls of the academy, and as endeavoring to have its principal effect within that "dispersed capital."

The climate of opinion at the best American colleges
and universities, Buckley has repeatedly argued, is overwhelm-
ingly liberal, even to the point of excluding competing
views. Such exclusion need not, he observes, reflect conscious
effort: "Though liberals do a great deal of talking about
hearing other points of view, it sometimes shocks them to
learn that there *are* other points of view."[4]

The charge, of course, is not a new one, and had been
made brilliantly in Mary McCarthy's *The Groves of Academe*
and Randall Jarrell's *Pictures From an Institution*. Nevertheless, Buckley has supported his contention with some
fascinating statistics. In the fall of 1952, for example, the
Harvard *Crimson* conducted a poll among its readers, asking
them merely which candidate, Stevenson or Eisenhower,
they favored. "The Freshman class (which at the time had
spent only about five weeks at Harvard) voted Republican
3–2. Upperclassmen, by contrast, voted Democratic 5–4.
Graduate students voted Democratic 2–1. The graduate faculty of Harvard voted Democratic 4–1."[5] At about the same
time, he observes ironically, polls taken at Yale asking the
same question "revealed a bitter political division among
the faculty of the Law School, where the vote was Democratic by 14–1. At the Divinity School (another civil war),
it was Democratic by 13–2."[6]

This sort of thing evidently has nothing whatever to do
with intelligence or level of education. Professional groups
such as lawyers, doctors, and engineers tended to vote Republican; the country as a whole elected Eisenhower, by a
large majority. Reflecting upon the Harvard poll, and upon
the student drift to the Left as they go on in college,
Buckley observed: "Let the person who wants to wrestle
with these statistics blurt forth his secret belief that there

[171]

is a correlation between 'level of education' and 'political liberalism.' But if I may, I shall put it in my own way: there is a correlation between the length of time one spends studying at the feet of liberals and the extent to which one comes to share their views."[7] He cited a description by Dr. Philip E. Jacob in *Changing Values in College* of the difference between the Vassar senior and the Vassar freshman:

> The senior more often than the freshman justifies the breaking of rules on occasion, including civil disobedience; questions whether "communism is the most hateful thing in the world today," or whether the American way of life should be preserved unchanged; would prefer to betray country rather than best friend.
>
> The senior goes to church and prays less than the freshman, and is less likely to believe in . . . a life hereafter, and even that there is a God.
>
> The senior is more likely than the freshman to admit to conduct and attitudes contrary to conventional moral taboos concerning drinking, telling the truth, sexual propriety and even theft. She feels people would be happier if sex experience before marriage were taken for granted in both men and women.[8]*

A professional survey sponsored by *National Review* in 1963 tended to bear out such impressionistic observations. The poll was a complicated one. Originally used by the Harvard *Crimson* in 1959, it had been prepared in consultation with David Riesman, a Harvard sociologist, and consisted of

---

* In a similar vein, Buckley could quote Mary McCarthy who wrote in *Holiday*, May, 1951: "A wistful respect for the unorthodox is ingrained in the Vassar mentality. . . . The effect of this training is to make the Vassar student, by the time she has reached her junior year, look back upon her freshman self with pity and amazement. When you talk to her about her life in college, you will find that she sees it as a series of before and after snapshots. 'When I came to Vassar, I thought like Mother and Daddy. I was conservative in my politics.' . . . With few exceptions the trend is from the conservative to the liberal, from the orthodox to the heterodox." (*Up From Liberalism*, p. 67.)

eighty-two detailed inquiries designed to elicit not only the students' current political and religious opinions, but also the directions in which *changes* in their opinions, if any, had occurred. In 1959 the *Crimson* had polled Harvard and Radcliffe. Under the supervision of Professor Ernest van den Haag, of New York University and the New School, *National Review* expanded the sample to include twelve other liberal arts colleges. These had been selected in such a way as to provide maximum social and academic variety: a small-town college, an Ivy League university, a Catholic university, a state-supported university, a fashionable girls' college, a Jewish university, etc.† In its October 8, 1963, issue, *National Review* published the entire questionnaire, and tabulated student answers to it. Analysis of the results showed that of the students polled "nearly seventy per cent report that significant change has taken place in their political beliefs since entering college. In all but two of the colleges tested, that change has been in a liberal direction. The exceptions are state-supported Indiana University and predominantly Catholic Marquette."[9] Among students who had changed their political views, the poll showed, the college program had been the decisive influence. Some of the figures were striking. The typical Williams parent, for example, is richer than the Yale man's, and the Williams parent appears to be even more conservative than the Yale counterpart (Williams parents are about 75 per cent Republican, the heaviest Republican figure for any of the twelve colleges in the poll). Yet nearly a third of the students at Williams apparently

---

† The twelve schools selected were: Sarah Lawrence College, Williams College, Yale University, Marquette University, Boston University, Indiana University, University of South Carolina, Howard University, Reed College, Davidson College, Brandeis University, Stanford University.

are socialists, defined for the purposes of the poll as someone who favors government ownership of the major industries. The Williams students were also heavily in favor of unilateral suspension of atomic tests and admission of Red China to the U.N., approximating the percentages of Reed, Brandeis and Sarah Lawrence on these questions.

Where religious opinions were concerned, the results were much less clear, but some surprising things appeared nevertheless. A "significant minority (more than 40 per cent overall) has experienced an anti-religious rebellion while at college. And of these campus rebellions, majorities at every college except Williams, Brandeis, and Sarah Lawrence rebelled in their freshman year." Students at the three aberrant schools evidently had rebelled before, or had nothing to rebel against. But, in contrast to their influence on student political views, college courses evidently play a minor role in connection with religious belief. More important solvents, the students said, are the "influence of friends" and "independence from parental ideas." The answers to the religious questions were rendered especially confused by the fact that, except at Marquette, students professing "belief in some form of Christianity" rejected such central Christian beliefs as the Incarnation, the Resurrection, and the immortality of the soul.‡ Oddly enough, a solid majority (excluding Reed, totally agnostic or atheistic, according to the poll) expressed belief in a vague "Divine Presence."

No one, to be sure, would argue that it is the task of a secular college to inculcate religious faith, yet these colleges

‡ For the Resurrection, the definition required was historical: "I believe literally in the Gospel account of Jesus' resurrection as an historical event which occurred as concretely as Lincoln's assassination; unless God had miraculously intervened, I believe the event could have been scientifically documented (by a camera placed outside the tomb)."

would seem to be involved in an intellectual failure if their students remain ignorant of essential religious distinctions which are part of our intellectual tradition, quite apart from questions of belief.

II

It seems unlikely that anyone would seriously dispute the conservatives' main contention: that college faculties are politically liberal, much more liberal than either the population at large or other professional groups of comparable education, such as doctors, lawyers or engineers. Indeed, this phenomenon probably falls into the category of things "everybody knows." And for the prevailing liberalism of the academy there are several explanations.

For one thing, the dominant intellectual tradition of the nineteenth century was critical and innovating. Its representative figures were men like Mill, Comte, Darwin and Marx, or, closer to home, William James, and, later on, John Dewey. Though liberalism has an ancient pedigree, it began to be a powerful historical force only toward the end of the eighteenth century, when its central doctrines and attitudes—skepticism, a critical spirit, hedonism in ethics—proved relevant to the main task of the time. By engaging in a critique of traditional society and its philosophic underpinning, liberalism was able to help clear the way so that newer social and economic energies could come into play. The liberal tradition is not our only one, however; from the perspective of the Western tradition as a whole, it even appears parochial, confined in its predominance to a single century; to some intellectuals, indeed to an increasing number, the liberal tradition seems to be at an impasse, and diminishing in relevance.§ Newman, for example, resisted the principal liberal impulses of the nineteenth century, and today he seems to many a more compelling figure than either Mill or Dewey, far more central indeed to the Western tradition as a whole. Yet for all this, we live in the shadow of the nineteenth century; even if its hopes and doctrines seem irrelevant to the actualities of our time, they lead a kind of ghostly life in books and lectures. The degree to which such liberal attitudes do prevail, moreover, may also be due to more transitory conditions—to the fact, for example, that the men who now are the senior professors—the scholars, critics, social scientists, historians and so forth—came of age intellectually in the 1930s and 1940s, when the New Deal and the struggle against fascism endowed liberal ideas with particularly high prestige. Such people feel as a matter of instinct that their enemies are on the right.

In addition, the academic profession has some built-in moral hazards. The man who spends his life with books and ideas can easily develop a peculiar kind of innocence. It may very well not come to his attention that he is entertaining a false notion of human nature, that the world is less easily ordered than his classroom. He is likely to live in a homogeneous community and associate mainly with other professors, for the most part polite and reasonable men. Even though he may be an expert on Machiavelli or have written a book on Cromwell, he would instinctively despise Mao's maxim that political power grows out of the barrel of a

§ See for example the recent book *The Crisis of Political Imagination* (1964) by Glenn Tinder, not a conservative: "In the face of mass [moral] disintegration, however, one is bound to ask whether liberalism is still pertinent to our foremost social problems. . . . In short, liberalism has been a force making for disintegration" (pp. 25–26).

gun. Perhaps too, the academician's idealism, his desire to be a virtuous man—a very powerful desire in the profession, I think; almost as powerful as among the clergy—can be a kind of snare, the desire sliding over into the delusion that virtuous solutions are easily come by: that we should "disarm," or "get out of Viet Nam," or that South Africa should "end apartheid," or that Spain should have a "democratic government like ours." Ironically enough, though such views, if acted upon, would issue either in chaos or a victory for radicalism, the academic people who hold them are themselves almost universally conservative *socially*, in manners and morals. To them the sight of Mario Savio or LeRoi Jones or a Spanish anarchist approaching would be cause for confusion and silent alarm.

Nevertheless, even if the conservatives' main point about the climate of opinion in the academy be granted, the actual situation is more complicated than their rhetoric seems to imply. Buckley, for example, argues that "the great liberal vulnerability rests in the conflict between the symbols under which they operate, all of which abjure indoctrination and welcome dissent, and their method of operation, which all too often is that of unabashed indoctrination and ruthless persecution of conservative dissent."[10] To be sure, outrages do occur, and the conservatives are able to point to their share of horror stories: to the dean at a midwestern university who thought Sidney Hook a "fascist" and kept him from speaking at the campus, to abuses of the power to promote or deny promotion, and so forth. Sidney Hook himself reports in his book *Heresy, Yes—Conspiracy, No* that there is actually a professor somewhere in the land who presents Edmund Burke to his students as a fascist reactionary. Yet these are surely the pathological cases. What "indoctrination" does occur is more likely to be for the most part unintentional and to flow from the fact that the professor does, after all, have opinions. Nor is it to be supposed that academic abuses are limited to the *political* arena. Cases are well known in which literary scholars have blocked the advancement of literary critics, or the other way around. The proponents of different doctrines in philosophy appear to regard one another as charlatans and rogues, and there is little possibility of peace between rival schools of psychoanalytical theory.‖ It is true, of course, that conservatives have been penalized for their views, and one would not wish to understate the case Buckley and the other conservatives have made on this matter; nor to ignore the noisomeness of those professorial protests that sprout overnight like toadstools in the *New York Times* every time we resist the Communists somewhere in the world. Academic liberalism can be a mindless bore. Yet I also know of situations in which liberal departments and administrators have looked around for an able conservative teacher in order to provide a little variety, only to find that none was available. Until recently, indeed, conservative academicians have been in very short supply, for conservatives have tended to let the academic situation go by default, becoming—perhaps because of conservative cultural *normality*—lawyers, businessmen, doctors, and politicians, rather than scholars and intellectuals.

‖ Writing of the 1965 Bernstein controversy at Yale, in which a clash between "analytical" and "speculative" philosophers appeared to be the issue, Fred M. Hechinger remarked in the *New York Times*: "Although academic men often stand in the forefront of the battle for freedom of expression for all views in society at large, they are frequently not nearly as liberal about granting free range of expression to rival opinions or divergent schools of thought within their own domain." (*New York Times*, "News of the Week in Review," March 14, 1956, p. 9.)

III

Conservative writing on the subject of the academy has not confined itself to political criticism. Russell Kirk, who possesses a remarkable sense of the romance of learning and of the academic traditions of the West, has written an excellent book on the community of higher learning called *Academic Freedom*, which appeared in 1955. The role of the academy in Kirk's view is a lofty one, and he defends academic freedom on the ground that it protects the opportunity for contemplation and reflection, "for the highest development of private reason and imagination, the improvement of mind and heart by the apprehension of Truth."[11] Society at large, by its very nature, can bring sanctions to bear against the free expression of one's views, and so it seems vital to Kirk that certain communities be set apart from ordinary society and protected from its sanctions, thus providing the opportunity for free reflection and the cultivation of mind and heart. Such freedom, he considers, though "always valuable beyond price, has today an importance even greater than it possessed in most ages—such an importance for human dignity and right reason as it possessed, in its rudimentary form, in the monasteries founded by Cassiodorus and St. Benedict. The universities of Salerno or Prague, Oxford or St. Andrews, if they experienced seasons of decline, in centuries long gone by, might be reinvigorated by the pulsating life in the society just without their gates, or might pass on their functions to other foundations. But I doubt whether there subsists within our present society, if our surviving centers of intellectual independence should go down to dusty death, the energy and the devotion required for a renewal of the true life of the mind. We live, when all is said, in the Iron Age. If the world is to

[179]

become once more aureate or argentine, every remnant of truly liberal understanding which may yet be found in our academies will be needed for the undertaking."[12] Like Buckley, Kirk has written about the "ritualistic liberalism" of many academicians, yet he evidently hopes that the free exercise of the mind possible within the academy will succeed in transcending liberalism, recovering awareness of "right reason," and regenerating society.¶

It is from this standpoint that he is able to offer some cogent criticism of American academic practice. In an essay which first appeared in *National Review* and then was included in his *Confessions of a Bohemian Tory* (1963), Kirk evoked the atmosphere of St. Andrews, Scotland's oldest university, from which he holds an advanced degree and where he spends most of his summers. He then contrasted it with the atmosphere all too common in America. At St. Andrews "there are a thousand students at the old town itself, and half as many more at Queen's College, across the estuary of Tay. This is the smallest of the British universities,

¶ Both Buckley and Willmoore Kendall have maintained that the doctrine of academic freedom rests on the assumption that outside of the sciences there is no such thing as truth, and that the doctrine is therefore hopelessly relativistic. "Academic freedom is conceived as a permanent instrument of doctrinal egalitarianism; it is always there to remind us that we can never know anything for sure. . . ." (William Buckley, *Rumbles Left and Right* [New York, 1963], p. 137; see also *Up From Liberalism*, pp. 152–53.) This view seems to me mistaken. Academic freedom really represents a kind of institutional forbearance, and perhaps is a department of manners. I have never met a professor who supposed that his own doctrine or interpretation—on the French Revolution, or on a poem by Keats—was not, in fact, true—or that his colleague, who contradicted him, was right *too*. They simply agree to treat their disagreement as decorously as possible, so that the community of which they are members can continue to function. Of course, there are limits: you can't teach alchemy; but even a teacher who has an idiosyncratic interpretation of, say, the French Revolution, may also know a great deal about it, and be recognized as valuable.

and one of the best. Philosophy, classics, and chemistry have been its famous departments in this century. The undergraduates, in their scarlet gowns, stroll among massive ruins: the smashed hulk of the Gothic cathedral; the brown wreck of the castle where Cardinal Beaton was dirked and pickled; the mile-long fortified walls of the vanished priory; the roofless houses by the derelict harbor. The world is not too much with one here; and as Dr. Johnson said when he visited the place, it is admirably suited for study."[13] At St. Andrews, he says, the students have the opportunity for reflection and contemplation, and for the cultivation of truth, to a far greater degree than has "any student in one of the gigantic air-conditioned-nightmare dormitories at certain state universities of ours." The "corruption of many American institutions of higher learning into training-institutes for material success have severed hundreds of thousands of the better minds among our rising generation from even the awareness that a university education is supposed to be a leisurely and contemplative process, not a mere hurried business of bluffing and cheating one's way through innumerable courses, crowned by a sham degree. . . . Little St. Andrews University still turns out graduates of some intellectual power; while Behemoth State University, on the average, turns out the adolescent with the sheepskin, filled only with that smattering of learning which is perilous to himself and society."[14] It is in education on a humane scale that Kirk sees hope, as in the campus planned for the University of California at Santa Cruz, whose colleges, modeled after those at Oxford and Cambridge, will accommodate 250–1000 students each.

Kirk's archetypal Behemoth University is his alma mater, Michigan State, which has undergone fantastic expansion, and actually, he writes, offers courses for credit in flycasting and a four-year program in packaging. "The distinguished scholars on the faculty, however," Kirk writes, "may be numbered on the fingers of one hand."[15] At Michigan State, he reports, "one dormitory complex will lodge four thousand students, when completed. . . . Business-machine methods of registration, testing, and grading have vitiated the old professor-student relationship. Students' numbered identity-cards are replacing even proper names. . . . The aggrandizement of MSU has been paralleled by protests and resignations among the faculty. When a lowering of degree-requirements was pushed through the graduate school last year, Dean Erickson of the College of Education found it necessary to reply to charges of debasement of standards: 'Don't use that phrase!' he entreated. 'Say rather that we are extending the opportunity.'"[16]

IV

Concerned as he is with humane association on a small scale, and with the protection of privacy, Kirk has had some intelligent things to say on the issue of college fraternities, which have already been abolished at a number of institutions and are on the defensive at many others. At the State University of New York, for instance, national fraternities have been banned, and demands have been made for similar action at the University of Colorado. At Amherst, an effort was made during World War II, when most of the fraternity brothers were away in the army, to close the houses permanently, and fraternities are scheduled to disappear at Williams.

The primary charge leveled against them is that they are socially exclusive—that is, that they encourage the hardening of social hierarchies generally, and, more particularly, discriminate against Negroes, Jews, and (in the South) Catholics. Beyond this, they are held to be anti-intellectual in spirit; and it is also charged that their hazing practices are physically dangerous. Now whatever the truth of all these charges, it is indisputable that there are political overtones to the fraternity issue, and that some key principles are at stake. As Kirk points out, "on nearly every college faculty will be found some persons who talk of 'total education,' of how the college ought to remake the personalities of its students . . . of how the college ought to stamp out ancient prejudices and parental notions and creeds outworn. These ideologues commonly have a good deal to do with campus movements to abolish or strictly regulate the fraternities."[17] The attacks on fraternities, as Kirk points out, often flow from a liberal leveling attitude that is hostile to all social distinctions. "The general assumption [of the attackers]," he writes, is "that our society ought to be completely egalitarian, homogeneous, and uniform. I do not propose to enter here into the merits of this doctrine; I merely point out that it never has been the consensus of opinion of the American nation."** Furthermore, he says, the "fraternity is not a laboratory for the experiments of academic social reformers; it is not an annex of the department of sociology, or of the school of religion. It is simply a private club, a place of

** In December, 1962—to cite an example from personal experience—I took part in a discussion of the fraternity question on the TV show "The Open Mind." To a man, the liberals on the panel were anti-fraternity. The most intransigent, not surprisingly, was Harold Taylor, a veteran liberal energumen. Advocating "total education" for a "democratic" America, he concluded: "I don't see any way in which the fraternity system can survive except at hardcore institutions which are not related to the rest of America. . . . I think it will have to be a pretty backward community in which the fraternities flourish. It's just not possible amid the newly developing democratic attitude on these issues." [Taken from the CBS transcript.] Here we see exactly the leveling totalism Kirk refers to, as well as the liberal-Left penchant for converting a value judgment into a historical prediction: in effect, a mode of historical success worship.

[183]

residence, with nearly all the rights and privileges of private associations and homes."[18]

As he argues, college fraternities, far from being obsolete, will probably fill a need even more pressing in the future than in the past. "American college fraternities arose to satisfy the most fundamental of social instincts, the desire for community. . . . And as American colleges increased in enrollment, the need for community among the students became the more real. Our fraternities, some of which are a century and a quarter old, came into existence as social clubs and arrangements for companionable living. In this country, we never had anything very like the English collegiate system, in which the colleges of a university are at once private clubs and teaching bodies. For lack of Magdalen and Christ Church, Pembroke and Merton, our students developed clubs called fraternities, in which a small number of friends, united by some simple bonds of common belief and background, might live together on a humane scale." Dormitories, to which students usually are assigned on a first-come, first-served basis, can scarcely fulfill such a function. Kirk points out that "the fraternity, the college residential club, remains our principal American means for giving students a home in a college town. Fraternities are more important, indeed, than ever before: because the enrollments of most of our universities and colleges are now swollen to bursting-point, and the individual student is lost in a faceless mob of five or ten or even twenty thousand young people. Fraternity life is an important means of redeeming our colleges from the menace of the herd."[19]

Surely Kirk is on firm ground here. It is difficult for a student to feel very much attached to large institutionalized facilities, and though they may be efficient they are likely to deepen his feelings of powerlessness and alienation. Privacy, elegance, a sense of personal proprietorship, the continuing intimacy of small groups, are important and ought to be fostered. Student feelings of powerlessness—and such feelings are ubiquitous—must surely be connected with the fact that few students exercise power over anything. The connection of *privately* exercised power with the traditional values of freedom and dignity has long been a commonplace of Western thought, as in Locke and Burke, and college is as good a place as any to learn about this relationship. As for the charges leveled against fraternities, that they are socially exclusive, anti-intellectual, and sometimes violent—these are to a very large degree anachronistic. What faults fraternities do have would seem to be very clearly outweighed by their virtues.

VI

The Varieties of Conservative Thought

Writing in the Spring, 1964, issue of *Modern Age*, the philosopher Eliseo Vivas warned his fellow conservatives that liberalism, as a comprehensive attitude toward the world, had established itself through the efforts "of some of the best minds of the nineteenth and twentieth centuries," and that its architects included "not only philosophers and political thinkers of the first order, but social scientists, biologists and students of jurisprudence," as well as "a number of first-rate theologians." Vivas' point was that if conservatism "aspires to be for the future what liberalism is and has been for the last few decades, we shall have to go at the job in the way in which the liberals went at it. They put into it not a few years, but decades, of quiet, unsparing, theoretical work, work that was hard, honest, and scholarly. . . . It was only when the foundational work was done that it began to pay off in political, in social, and in legislative terms." Conservatism, he said, "will not prosper and become a strong force in the nation" until its proponents make "contributions as thinkers and scholars" to the foundations of their position.[1]

Vivas is quite right in his description of the immense intellectual effort that has gone into the development of liberalism, and also right in his demand that conservatives make the same kind of effort. On the other hand, his stress on liberal honesty and effort could be misleading. Most scholars and intellectuals are honest and willing to work, but they differ in their assumptions. There is also something else in his tone that is not appropriate, for first-rate scholars, philosophers and historians *have* made genuine beginnings in the effort to raise to awareness the intellectual substance of conservative beliefs, intuitions, and habits of behavior. The task that faces them is a complex one, for conservative impulse, perhaps because of its intimacy with the contradictory actuality of experience, has taken a variety of forms—some of them seemingly incompatible. Philosophical consideration of the conservative position has had to face this fact from the start. Raymond English, Chairman of the Department of Political Science at Kenyon College, has provided a good guide to the various Western conservative positions, and all of them, in varying degrees of prominence, may be found in contemporary American conservatism.

First, according to English, there is *unreflective*, or habitual, conservatism, the resistance of human nature to change in accustomed things. No doubt this emotion is common to all men, but its principal historical exemplars are the peasant, the soldier and the aristocrat, attached to their habits and codes and not accustomed to submit them to analysis. In an old Anglican phrase, each believes in "my station and its duties," and takes criticism of either station or duties as a personal insult.

Professor English then distinguishes among five kinds of *reflective* conservatism—conservative positions consciously held and supported by principle of one kind or another. No doubt these may shade into one another, but his classification is nonetheless useful for analytical purposes:

(1) Economic conservatism, of the sort associated with Senator Taft, Prof. Milton Friedman and Wilhelm Röpke.

(2) Romantic conservatism, meaning love for the past

partly because of its *pastness*, and partly because of such non-liberal values as heroism, variety, and communal loyalty as may be found in it. Burke, Coleridge, and Walter Scott exemplify this mode in various ways, as does Russell Kirk today.

(3) Skeptical or empirical conservatism, embodying a deep distrust of large "solutions" and attachment to a *modus vivendi*. Skeptical conservatives are likely to argue that the "solution" will cause as many difficulties as the "problem" does. This variety is found in Montaigne, Dryden, Hume, Oakeshott, and perhaps in Santayana.

(4) Natural-law conservatism, which deduces principles of behavior from the fact of "human" nature as distinct from natures of other kinds, and on that account resists moral change based on fashion, historical accident, or false analogies between human nature and other kinds. Conservatism of this kind is found in Aristotle, Aquinas, Burke, and, today, in Leo Strauss.

(5) Neo-idealist, historicist conservatism as found in Hegel and codified by conservative neo-Hegelians, and perhaps found today in Eric Voegelin's conception of a "history" of order.

To Professor English's classification we might add still another and less definite category, which may be called "anthropological" conservatism, meaning the attachment— quite "reflective"—to a *particular* culture, and the desire, both aesthetic and moral, to perpetuate it. This form pervades most of the others, and is found, for example, in Willmoore Kendall's defense of a social consensus against the idea of an "open" society.[2]

Obviously, no one can fail to see the difficulty involved in calling all these things "conservative." Historically, the first "reflective" form, as listed above, economic conservatism, was the enemy of romantic and natural-law conservatism, and skeptical conservatism could, at any time, pour its dissolving acids on several of the others. Yet there is another historical fact that cannot be ignored. All of these different positions are to be found on the "conservative" side of the "battle line" dividing contemporary liberals from their conservative opponents. On the actual issues that are now before us, the romantic conservative, the natural-law conservative, the economic conservative, and even the skeptical conservative, find themselves on the same side, though their reasons for being there are different. Skeptical conservatives like Burnham and Van den Haag would oppose the Supreme Court prayer decision, as would natural-law conservatives like Bozell, Stanlis and Bredvold, or, for that matter, economic conservatives, like John Chamberlain and aristocratic individualists like Frank Meyer. On foreign policy, most of them would agree as against the liberals. Such actual agreement among seemingly contradictory positions suggests that they have affinities too, or at least interests in common. As a consequence, conservatives of every variety have been endeavoring to analyze these positions, demonstrate their relationship to one another, and show their relevance to American life.

II

"Conscious conservatism, in the modern sense," wrote Russell Kirk in *The Conservative Mind*, "did not manifest itself until 1790, with the publication of *Reflections on the Revolution in France*." Until then, the "modern issues, though earlier taking substance, were not yet distinct. . . . In any practical sense, Burke is the founder of our conservatism."[3] And Burke, in considerable part through Kirk's advocacy, has played an important role in contemporary American conservative thought. Kirk and such scholars as Peter

Stanlis, C. P. Ives, Louis I. Bredvold, and Ross J. S. Hoffman, have devoted themselves to editing Burke's work, studying his career, and expounding his ideas. Indeed, the scholarly revival of Burke studies has been one of the important intellectual events of our time.

In a general way, it is easy enough to see why Burke should have had such a revival. Confronting the revolutionary doctrines of the Jacobins, in France, but also through their disciples in England, he elaborated a defense of English institutions based on tradition, custom, and natural law. His great passages are well known: "People will not look forward to posterity, who never look backward to their ancestors"; or that in terms of Jacobin doctrine "a king is but a man, a queen is but a woman; a woman is but an animal, and an animal not of the highest order." "Prejudice," Burke said, "renders a man's virtue his habit; and not a series of unconnected acts. Through his prejudice, his duty becomes a part of his nature." "We know," he said, "and what is better, we feel inwardly, that religion is the basis of civil society, and the source of all good and comfort." Everyone remembers, from Burke, that the Jacobins' "attachment to their country itself is only so far as it agrees with some of their fleeting projects; it begins and ends with that scheme of polity which falls in with their momentary opinion." Burke said, in opposition to Locke, that "society is indeed a contract. . . . It is a partnership in all science; a partnership in all art; a partnership in every virtue, and in all perfection. As the ends of such a partnership cannot be obtained in many generations, it becomes a partnership not only between those who are living, but between those who are living, those who are dead, and those who are to be born."

Burke's views, expressed with an eloquence that moved even his opponents, no doubt played an important part in preventing the spread of revolutionary doctrine in England. At

the present time, the West, and the United States in particular, is a kind of *ancien régime* buffeted by a world both
revolutionary and increasingly totalitarian. It is an *ancien régime*, moreover, whose official doctrines—egalitarian, optimistic, universalistic—offer but little resistance to the currents
of revolutionary change. "We are living," Frank Meyer has
pointed out, "in the midst of a revolution which is directed
towards the destruction of Western civilization. Conservatives are by definition defenders of that civilization; and in a
revolutionary age this means that they are, and must be,
counterrevolutionaries."[4] In many ways, our situation thus is
analogous to Burke's, and the uses of his thought are obvious.
"Burke was largely neglected up to 1914," as Peter Stanlis says,
"because the great social issues which he and his contemporaries had debated were obsolete. . . . The modern world
has witnessed the rise of new forms of military despotism and
political totalitarianism, even more brutal than those of Napoleon and the French Jacobins, because reinforced by racial,
nationalist, and economic ideologies, and by the power of science and industry."[5]

Willmoore Kendall, now Chairman of the Department of
Political Science at the University of Dallas, does not belong
to the Burkean school of modern conservatism, and he has
had, as we shall see, some sharply critical things to say about
it, but he concedes that Burke did discern the issues that divide one side from the other in the world revolution—the issues, that is, that divide conservatives on the one hand from
liberals and radicals on the other. In a seminal article, written
in collaboration with Professor George W. Carey of George-
town University, he argues that "not merely in England and
France but all over Europe and the United States as well
[Burke's principles] seem to remain the great divide between
conservatives and progressives." Drawing upon Burke, the authors characterize the issues in this way: 1) relativism versus

principled morality; 2) equality versus hierarchy; 3) rights of man versus historic rights; 4) will of the present generation versus entailed inheritance; 5) redistribution of income versus retention and inheritance; and 6) atheism versus religion. Using these oppositions as tools of analysis, Kendall and Carey turn to the issues of recent decades (division of powers versus plebiscitary democracy, minimum wage laws, expanded social security, property rights, the status of religion) and show that the six Burkean criteria still serve to distinguish conservatives from progressives in the United States.[6]

In Russell Kirk's writings, as in Burke's, the idea of tradition has occupied a central position, and this has given rise to sharp controversy within conservative ranks. As against liberals like Louis Hartz, Arthur Schlesinger, Jr., and Morton Auerbach, who proclaim the genial paradox that the American tradition is antitraditional, Kirk has tried to show that it is not. The American political tradition, he writes in a *National Review* essay, "is rooted in two bodies of opinion and custom: first, the Christian religion; second, the English and colonial historical experience in politics, with its fruits of representative institutions, local government, private rights, and the supremacy of law. We have been governed by a genuine tradition—that is, a body of beliefs passed on from generation to generation, as prescriptions, customs—and not by ideology, or rigid, abstract dogma." In Kirk's view, "Richard Hooker, directly or indirectly, had far more to do with the fundamental opinions of the Founding Fathers than did Locke. Americans have had no difficulty in agreeing with Edmund Burke for the reason that they, like Burke, have formed their opinions of human nature and society on the authority of Christian tradition." If the American moral tradition is Christian, its political wisdom has affirmed the desirability of "filtering democracy through a *variety* [italics added] of representative bodies" and in a "jealous regard for private and local rights." If we abandon this tradition, "replacing our territorial democracy for some neat scheme of central administration, then we may not succeed at all in meeting the problems of modern society. We may succeed only in breaking that continuity of custom and institution upon which rests any decent social order."[7] Kirk's analysis of the American tradition obviously places him athwart the principal liberal tendencies discussed in Chapter II. That he says a "variety" of representative bodies—not a "number"—suggests that he would want them to continue to be selected in different ways rather than on the mathematical and uniformitarian basis of one-man one-vote, recently espoused by the Supreme Court; and his insistence upon the Christian roots of American tradition places him in opposition to liberal secularizing tendencies.

Kirk's attitude toward tradition, furthermore, has informed his continuing assault upon progressive education. "I contend," he writes, "that liberal education is necessarily traditional . . . that an educational system severed from tradition is like a tree severed from its roots. . . . With Chesterton, I happen to believe in 'the democracy of the dead,' the filtered wisdom and decisions of wise men in many generations, which comes down to us as Tradition."[8] The conservative victory over the theory of progressive education, in which Kirk has been one of the leaders, promises to be the first sector of the battle in which the conservatives achieve a decisive victory.

In other matters, Kirk has been able to use Burkean principles to analyze social ills. His essay "York and Social Boredom," for example, which first appeared in *Sewanee Review*, examines the phenomenon of mass boredom, of moral impoverishment, which is characteristic of much of life in the industrialized and modernized town of York, England. Typical of a great many cities in England, York is inhabited by a "population among whom thirty percent of the babies are born out of wedlock, of whom only ten percent go to church, who spend twice as much on drink and tobacco as upon rents and property-taxes, whose acquisitive habits make it impractical to put towels in public lavatories, whose Sunday reading is the rape and seduction items in News of the World."[9] There remains "a powerful remnant of those sober, book-reading, conscientious, old-fashioned folk who dominated Britain throughout the nineteenth century." Nevertheless, "England is indeed the two Nations of which Disraeli wrote; but the two nations are distinguished today not by an economic demarcation, but by a radically different kind of conscience." The masses are "cut off from tradition, social sympathy, and the hope of posterity . . . men and women bored with pleasure, bored with people, bored with life, trying to forget through a few pints of beer or a ticket in the football pool the drab futility of existence." They "have more money than ever before; they are better fed, many of them; they are more regularly schooled. But they seem to be growing worse as human beings." Kirk analyzes the causes of this decline in Burkean terms, finding in Burke a prescription for the good society derived from tradition. "Religious faith," writes Kirk, "is an invaluable aspiration," and along with such faith, three other "passionate human interests" have been served by every viable society in the past: "the perpetuation of [one's] spiritual existence through the life and welfare of . . . children; the honest gratification of acquisitive appetite through accumulation and bequest of property; the comforting assurance that continuity is more probable than change—in other words, men's confidence that they are part of a social and natural order in which they count for more than 'the flies of a summer.' With increasing brutality, the modern age, first under capitalism, then under state socialism, has ignored these longings of simple humanity."

Other scholars have been able to bring Burkean principles to bear in a valuable way when discussing current political issues. In a very important essay included in *The Relevance of Edmund Burke* (1964), a collection of essays by authorities on Burke's work, C. P. Ives of the Baltimore *Sun*, and a sometime contributor to *National Review*, addresses himself to the widespread awareness that "the United States Supreme Court and the rule of law which in theory it exemplifies are going through one of their historic crises."[10] Reflecting upon the composition of the current court, and the controversy that has surrounded so many of its decisions, Ives sardonically cites Burke: "'It is the public justice that holds the community together.' And not in derogation of that statement, but, precisely, to fortify it, he added that 'the judges are, or ought to be, of a *reserved* and retired character, and wholly unconnected with the political world.' What Burke would have thought when justices of the highest court feel compelled to campaign, at least quasi-politically, in defense of their own prior decisions as judges, it is not hard to infer."[11] After discussing a number of recent decisions whose ideological and untraditional character was at variance with everything Burke stood for, Ives goes on, very damagingly, to cite the criticisms that even liberal legal scholars have felt impelled to make of the Court's procedure. By 1949, says Ives, "Thomas Reed Powell was reporting that one who read the then current justices . . . 'gets the impression of a company of independent essay writers rather than of members of an official body.' In 1957, Alexander M. Bickel and Harry H. Wellington find that 'the Court's product has shown an increasing incidence of the sweeping dogmatic statement, of the formulation of results accompanied by little or no effort to support them in reason, in sum, of opinions that do not opine and of *per curiam* orders that quite frankly fail to build the bridge between the authorities they cite and the results they decree.'" In 1959, Professor Henry M. Hart wrote that the votes of the

Court "are influenced more strongly by general predelictions in the area of the law involved than they are by lawyer-like examination of the precise issues presented for decision," and concluded that "the 'failures' he and his colleagues detect 'are threatening to undermine the professional respect of first rate lawyers for the incumbent justices of the Court, and this at the very time when the Court as an institution and the justices who sit on it are especially in need of the bar's confidence and respect."[12]

Demonstrating as it does the prevalence of the view that important decisions of the Court have proceeded from judicial will rather than judicial reason, and that, indeed, the Court has constituted itself a kind of standing Constitutional Convention, Ives's article doubtless will have, as it deserves to have, considerable influence. Only recently, indeed, conservative criticism of the Court has begun to find an echo in the more independent liberal journals. One of the fiercest attacks on the mentality informing much of the Court's behavior appeared, for example, in the *New York Review of Books.* "Since 1950," observed Yosal Rogat, Associate Professor of Political Science at the University of Chicago, "[Justice] Douglas has written twenty books and dozens of articles. Whether we see this list as confirming or as refuting the widespread belief that Supreme Court Justices do not have time to think, it is clear that Douglas rejects the austerity and detachment traditionally imposed upon a judge. Indeed, he has come to think of himself as no mere judge, but a moralist, a political visionary, a universal philosopher. The results are appalling."[13] The banalities of Douglas' style Rogat found to be "part of Douglas' relentless effort to simplify our understanding of the world. In pursuit of this doubtful end, he reduces the most complex legal and political difficulties to a few abstract moral principles, and the sharpest antagonisms to a flabby and homogeneous togetherness." Douglas maintains a "shallow and undiscriminating radicalism," is a "reductionist," and "seems to think that Supreme Court Justices should answer legal questions by *directly* applying their beliefs about the overall needs of the country, or even the world."[14]

With regard to the Court, criticisms that conservative writers have been making consistently for some time have begun to be made with increasing frequency in the liberal world as well.

Russell Kirk's Burkean position is an important one in modern American conservatism, but it is by no means the only prominent one, and it has come under sharp attack from other conservative intellectuals. Writing in *National Review* in 1958, the Reverend Stanley Parry, then Chairman of the Department of Political Science at Notre Dame, claimed to find a shifting of focus in Kirk's writing that had the effect of blurring some important distinctions. How is it possible, Father Parry asked, to espouse a "Burkean defense of existing social institutions as the embodiment of the wisdom of the group," and at the same time write eloquently, as Kirk does, of the marked *deterioration* of those institutions? Since history, argues Parry, "seems to be moving in the direction the progressives prefer, it follows that we must keep a critical eye on history. We must, that is, attempt to change its direction. If, however, we are to evaluate and criticize history, we can hardly appeal to *its* prescriptions."[15] John Chamberlain agrees. Kirk, he says, is really "trying to recover rather than preserve, a sense of 'the great mysterious incorporation of the human race,' held together by custom and immemorial usage. He is not, literally, a 'conservative' in his relations to the predominance of 'what is,' for the things that are worth conserving seem everywhere to be mostly vestigial."[16] Kirk's most intransigent critic, Frank S. Meyer, similarly finds in Kirk's appeal to history no principle capable of resisting undesirable historical developments. "The question is," writes Meyer,

"What do you want to conserve?"[17] Clearly enough, Kirk would not want to "conserve" the conditions he described so well as prevailing in York, England. Meyer also believes that Kirk has insufficient regard for individual freedom, and adduces the stress on community in his writing and his failure to affirm any principle which might be invoked to protect the claims of personal freedom. "The social pattern which emerges from hints and suggestions in his writings (for he never tells us exactly what he wants and certainly never gives any idea of what it would mean in modern circumstances) is shaped by such words as 'Authority,' 'order,' 'community,' 'duty,' 'obedience.' 'Freedom' is a rare word; 'the individual' is anathema. The qualities of this suggested society 'are a mixture of those of eighteenth-century England and medieval Europe.' While admitting that societies so organized have allowed in the past for a good deal of personal freedom, Meyer fears that excessive emphasis on such values as "duty," "obedience," and "authority," given the "increased potentialities of power in our times, could only move inevitably to totalitarianism."[18]*

These criticisms, by conservative intellectuals of good will, have been accumulating for some time now, and one can only regret that Russell Kirk has not seen fit to reply to them in

---

* The settled animosity between Meyer and Kirk is of long standing. In July, 1955, writing in *The Freeman*, Meyer attacked Kirk as, essentially, a collectivist; he argued that nowhere in his thought was there any principle which would oppose state domination of all areas of life. In consequence, Kirk himself has remained implacably hostile to Meyer; and this, I gather, is one reason why Kirk, one of the most frequent contributors to *National Review*, never has consented to appear on the masthead. In the Spring, 1964, issue of *Sewanee Review*, Kirk reviewed Meyer's *In Defense of Freedom* in one and one-half pages of scathing denunciation, accusing Meyer of "believing that the world is governed by little tracts and pamphlets," of being "filled with detestation of all champions of authority," and of wanting to "supplant Marx by Meyer."

any systematic and serious way. Nevertheless, a number of things can be said in behalf of his position.

First of all, the conception of Burke as a thoroughgoing historicist who ratified as right whatever issued from the historical process—a conception upon which Kirk's critics seem to depend—has been rendered obsolete by modern scholarship. According to Peter Stanlis, author of *Edmund Burke and the Natural Law* (1958), the historicist view of Burke has been completely reversed since 1949: "the revelations of Christianity and the ethical norms of the Natural Law jointly form the foundations of his conservative, Christian-humanist philosophy. This is what Burke meant when he said that 'the principles of true politics are those of morality enlarged.'"[19] Thus, Burke did indeed think that the moral law could be discovered in history; as he said, men "attain to the moral reason in their collective experience, they realize and embody it in their stable social relations and organizations." Yet the word "stable" in his sentence is crucial: when the moral law, the law that is in accordance with man's nature, has been embodied in social institutions, those institutions will be "stable," because natural. When they violate that law, they will have to be maintained by coercion. The law thus transcends history, but can be discovered *in* history.

Furthermore, though Burke could appeal more surely to the English *modus vivendi* than Kirk can to the habits and institutions of American society today, Kirk could nevertheless argue that in a real sense America today is "two nations." The regnant ideology, liberalism, is antitraditional, as are its spokesmen, and those spokesmen are highly visible and wield much power. But the American tradition, and the majority of the American people—as Willmoore Kendall argues—are conservative. What percentage of them agrees with the liberal position on school prayers, divorce, abortion, secularization, admission of Communist China to the U.N., oaths of allegiance, the rights of property? This distinction might indeed have been made more explicit in Kirk's work. Still, it is *there*, though partly obscured by his love for the past and his tendency to employ an elegiac tone in evoking it. Kirk doubtless would say that it is the task of conservative intellectuals today, as it was of Burke, to give articulation to the deep conservative feelings of the majority.

Finally, Kirk's appeal to tradition, properly understood, would seem to include a built-in opposition to totalitarianism. The tradition to which he appeals not only honors a source of authority that transcends the state, but also places a high valuation on freedom. Burke himself stresses the importance of the *small* social unit, and of private property, and Kirk identifies that "variety of representative institutions" and "territorial democracy" as central to the American tradition. No doubt we may understand his stress on "order" and "authority" as directed polemically at a liberal rhetoric unconcerned for these things. It may well be true, though, that a good deal of the criticism of Kirk by conservative intellectuals would have been forestalled had he been more explicit, while expounding Burke's views in different historical circumstances, about the relevant distinctions.

III

Willmoore Kendall's essays possess as much stylistic as intellectual interest—for "it is one of the best kept secrets of our age," as Garry Wills has pointed out, "that one of [our] best prose stylists is Willmoore Kendall. The long sentence that argues with itself down one page and around the next did not, we find, go out with William Morris wallpaper. Professor Kendall has given the circumspect Victorian periodicity, which *disciplines* the reader while delighting him, a new lease on life; and this by three means. First, he introduces slang into these staid surroundings. Then, he follows speech rhythms—not the lecturing cadences of a pulpit age, but the lunge of two voices contrapuntally going at each other. Last, he makes fun of his own grammatical arabesques, elaborating them in the most arch fashion. The result is a combination of the colloquial and the baroque that is invariably exciting. His sentences hover somewhere between a ballet and a rumble."[20] Kendall is as much an artist as a political philosopher.

One of the original editors of *National Review,* Kendall nevertheless differs in important ways from other well-known conservatives. His own conservatism, he says, "has no axe to grind for 'aristocracy,'" and, unlike Kirk's, "shies off the vast reaches of argument of Burke's *Reflections on the Revolution in France.*" He will "do no business with Calhoun. Or Babbitt. Or More." Having a good deal of stylistic fun, he distinguishes himself from some of the other conservatives; one must not expect too much, he says, from a "historian doubling in brass (like Russell Kirk); or from a young man, even a very brilliant young man, having his first go at these matters (like Stanton Evans)." Kendall "has sworn no vow of absolute fidelity either to free enterprise *à la* von Mises, or to a certain list of rights *à la* John Chamberlain, or to a certain holy trinity of government functions *à la* (I must mention him again, for he is a great though lovable sinner) Frank Meyer, or to revolving door mistrust of political authority *à la* Frank Chodorov." Kendall's conservatism, he says, is loyal to "the institutions and way of life bequeathed to us by the Philadelphia Convention," and, far from opposing "change," he would welcome it, provided it is in the right direction. Thus, he distinguishes between "'change' directed at the *development and perfection* of our heritage as *that which it is,* and 'change' calculated to transform that heritage into that which it is not." He opposes "not 'change' but change in certain directions" which he condemns "on grounds of inherited principle—inherited principle, however, which [he] values not merely or even primarily because it is inherited, but because it is the product of rational deliberation moving from sound political and moral premises."[21]

Using the *Federalist Papers* and the *Constitution* as the source of principle, much as Kirk uses Burke, Kendall characteristically faces, in a more detailed way than does Kirk, those issues that are in fact and at the moment the subject of active dispute between conservatives and liberals. The "issues that are important for conservatives," he writes, "are those that have been forced upon them by liberals demanding certain 'changes' that would involve the substitution of novel principles for inherited principles."[22] In an important sentence which I have quoted earlier in this book, Kendall argues that a "battle line" divides conservatives from liberals, and that it "stretches from the bottom of the chart of American politics all the way to the top, passing through pretty much every issue that enters into our politics."[23] And he thinks that what is at stake in the overall war is whether the "liberal revolution" will succeed in radically altering the nature of American politics. Nor is his use of the word "revolution" hyperbolic. He considers that if the liberals win on all the issues that are in dispute "the American social order will not bear even a cousinly resemblance to that which is traditional among us." As an example of an issue to which such a statement is relevant, Kendall cites "representative" as contrasted with "plebiscitary" democracy:

First, nothing can be more certain than that the Founders of our Republic bequeathed to us a form of government that was *purely* representative—a form of government in which there was no room, in which moreover there is *to this day* no room, for policy decisions by the electorate—that is for electoral "mandates" emanating from popular majorities. Or rather there is one thing more certain: namely, that the Liberals intend to overthrow that traditional form of government, have a carefully worked-out program for overthrowing it, and labor diligently, year-in-year-out, to seize the strategic points they must seize in order to accomplish its overthrow.[24]

Other issues which, as Kendall puts it, are now "up" include immigration policy (should our policy prevent further inroads upon our cultural homogeneity?); the status of our ethical consensus (are all ethical positions "equal" as far as our public life is concerned, or do we prefer some to others; and if so, are we prepared to make that preference felt?); equality before the law as contrasted to egalitarianism ("The liberals," Kendall says, "attempt to construe the American tradition as an egalitarian tradition, friendly to the kind of levelling whose predictable result would be world wide uniformity." In *The Conservative Affirmation* he remarks that the plan for extensive federal aid to education, providing "equality of educational opportunity everywhere," is a consequence of this principle: "why, ask the liberals, should the education a person receives depend on the accident—accident, mind you—of birth?"); and finally, on the balance of power between the executive and legislative branches of the federal government. In books and essays he has written on all these matters, but perhaps his most original contribution has been made in his analysis of the so-called "open society" and in his description of what he calls the "two majorities" of American politics.

According to Kendall, the "Great Tradition in political philosophy . . . assumes, with Plato and Aristotle and Hobbes and Rousseau, that any viable society has an orthodoxy—a set of fundamental beliefs, implicit in its way of life, that it cannot and should not, and, in any case, will not submit to the vicissitudes of the market place."[25] Accordingly, the conservative, aware of the "orthodoxy" of America, its moral and political consensus, "views with horror the thesis of Mill's 'Essay on Liberty,' according to which a man can hold and publicly defend any opinion, however repugnant to morality, and still be regarded as a good—or even acceptable—citizen. And—to come to the main point—he regards the present clear determination of the American people not to permit the emergence of a Communist minority in their midst—their determination, as I like to put it, to place the price of being a Communist so high that no American is likely to pay it—as a manifestation of good sense that he can only applaud."[26] If by an "open society" liberals mean one that permits, as a matter of principle, the unlimited right to say what you please, "with impunity and without let or hindrance," then Kendall's conservative holds "that American society is *not* such a society, and must not become such a society."[27]

Other conservatives, such as Richard Weaver and F. D. Wilhelmsen, agree with Kendall. Weaver observes that every viable society has a "regime"—his word for what Kendall calls an orthodoxy. As Weaver describes it, a regime is "much more than the sum of the government and the laws." It is these plus beliefs, traditions, customs, habits, and observances, many of which affect the minutiae of daily living. A regime "tells the individual from his early days, through his nurture and education, what is expected of him, how he stands with regard to this person and that, and what kind of social response he can expect from the choices that are open to him." But a regime as a way of life is also a "principle of exclusion. It is a way of rejecting what is inimical or foreign to the group's nature and of retaining what can be assimilated. . . . The difficulty of most people who have been conditioned by 'modern thinking' is [that they] interpret all exclusiveness as having its root in injustice. But this is so far from being true that one can affirm that some degree of exclusiveness is essential to self-identity and self-preservation."[28]

In examining this aspect of the conservative position, we must be careful about what is being said and what is not. Conservatives such as Kendall and Weaver appear to agree that because an "orthodoxy" or "regime" represents an accumulation of human experience, is a *modus vivendi,* and confers many benefits, it is proper for those who participate in it to protect it in a variety of ways—they agree that sanctions against heretics are *not* a violation of true principle even if the position of the heresy eventually becomes incorporated into the orthodoxy. By definition, Kendall argues, there cannot be an orthodoxy without "barriers"; the barriers will be felt by anyone who challenges them; and it is bad theory to deplore this. On the other hand, we should be very careful not to imagine that such conservatives as Kendall and Weaver are in favor of the suppression of all dissent. The argument really focuses on the liberal *principle* of the "open society" as found in the work, say, of Karl Popper: the alternatives are not, Kendall reminds us, the open society and the closed society, but the quite fictitious open society of liberal fancy and the actual consensus society we inherit, operating on what the framers called "the deliberate sense of the community."

In its practical effect, Kendall's argument would mean that if "the deliberate sense of the community" issued in the decision that Communism in America should be proscribed, it would violate no American principle to do so. If "the deliberate sense of the community" decided that a motion picture or a book ought to be banned, it likewise would violate no principle to do so—Justice Black's interpretation of the First Amendment to the contrary notwithstanding. Legal sanctions, however, Kendall considers the least of the means at hand for protecting the orthodoxy. More important are "the so-called social means of coercion (among them are ridicule, ostracism, the boycott and other types of economic pressure)."[29] Kendall thinks that though a society ought to keep "the door open *as wide as possible* to initiatives and proposals by individual citizens," it cannot keep the door wide open, because some initiatives and proposals—those of the Communists, for example—are clearly excluded. They are incompatible with its way of life, with its deepest beliefs about God and man, and finally with the business it is at."[30]

In his consideration of the "open society," first in his columns in *National Review* and then in *The Conservative Affirmation*, Kendall scores, I think, a clear-cut victory over the *principle* he attacks: no society can, no society does, consider all questions "open." Yet it is possible to wonder whether that victory is not in good measure rhetorical. Aside from Karl Popper, how many liberals really consider *all* questions "open"? As sometimes used by liberals, the idea of the "open society" seems really to be a kind of velleity, implying a prejudice in favor of "speaking your mind" that Kendall himself emphatically shares. At other times the idea is used as a weapon against established attitudes the liberal dislikes: some questions are "open" while others, equally problematical, are not.

In any case, it was a valuable exercise for Kendall to take the idea literally—the liberals, after all, put it forward as literal—and destroy it. His discussion of it, furthermore, has the incontestable value of demonstrating that an "orthodoxy," a set of assumptions, constitutes the foundation of every viable society.

Kendall's famous essay on "The Two Majorities in American Politics"[31] is mainly descriptive and analytical, but its motive is clearly to elucidate, and so protect, the conditions which permit the "deliberate sense" of the community to emerge. Kendall begins by noting that the same voters maintain "in Washington, year after year, a President devoted to high principle and enlightenment, and a Congress that gives short shrift to both; that, even at one and the same election, they elect to the White House a man devoted to the application of high principle to most important problems of national policy, and to the Hill men who consistently frustrate him." Kendall points out that an ideological distinction exists between the President and Congress, and argues that it proceeds from the different structure of their "constituencies." The Congress, he says, unlike the executive branch: 1) shows greater sensitivity to internal security; 2) is more alert to "self-interest," that is, "at least where domestic policies are concerned," and tends to equate the national interest "with the totality of the interests of our four-hundred-odd congressional districts"; 3) wants to perpetuate a "discriminatory" immigration policy; 4) is more concerned about the level of the national debt (and *therefore* about the amount of money the federal government spends, and *therefore* about the power it uses); 5) tends to be more willing to spend for "defense" than for "welfare"; and 6) has less animus against Right-wing dictatorships, and tends to act toward them on the basis of expediency rather than ideological commitment to democratic forms of government. The executive branch, for its part, "tends to favor each and every component of the current program (the product of what is generally regarded as enlightened opinion among political scientists at our universities) for transforming the American political system into a plebiscitary political system, capable of producing and carrying through *popular mandates*.[32] As supporting this last "change," Kendall cites the fashionable proposals put forward by people like James MacGregor Burns: eliminate the filibuster, iron out inequalities of representation in Congress, eliminate the seniority principle in Congressional committees, synchronize Congressional elections with Presidential elections in order to reduce ideological discrepancy in the vote, glorify "presidential power" and make the election of the President the central ritual of American politics.[33]

At stake in this tension between champions of the executive and defenders of Congress, Kendall argues, is the large issue of plebiscitary as opposed to representative democracy. The Congress, drawn as it is from a variety of constituencies, is a "stronghold of entrenched minorities."[34] Indeed, the founders of our system deliberately designed Congress to prevent "waves of popular enthusiasm" from transmitting themselves to its floors. Congress is bicameral, its elections are staggered, and it has developed internal procedures that frustrate "majority rule"—such as the filibuster and the seniority principle. The Congress reflects, Kendall concludes, "the anti-democratic, anti-majority rule bias of the Framers, who notoriously distrusted human nature (because of their commitment to certain 'psychological axioms')."[35] The "constituency" of the Congress, moreover, in contrast to the President's constituency, is "to a far greater extent a structured community." In a Congressional election, "the 'heat' can and will go on if there is a powerful community 'value' or interest at stake in the choice among available candidates; so that although the voters vote as nominal 'equals' (one man, one vote) they do so under pressures that are quite unlikely to be brought to bear on their 'equal' voting for President."[36] In a Presidential contest, particular interests are minimized. Both "candidates for the most part merely repeat, as they swing from whistle-stop to whistle-stop and television studio to television studio, the policy platitudes that constitute the table-talk in our faculty clubs. No one, not even the most skilled textual analyst, can tease out of the speeches any dependable clue as to what difference it will make which of the two is elected. . . . And the inevitable result . . . is that what you get out of the presidential election is what amounts to a *unanimous* mandate for the principles *both* candidates have been enunciating, which is to say: the presidential election not only permits the electorate, but virtually obliges it, to overestimate its dedication to the pleasant-sounding maxims that have been poured into its ears."[37]

As between the executive and the legislature, then, the executive is more abstract and hortatory, the legislature more representative of actual interests. The legislature, moreover, because of its structure, is less responsive to momentary majorities. It constitutes a check upon the tides of popular opinion.

Other political scientists have raised considerations that support Kendall's view of the Presidency as ideologically "liberal" in tendency. As Wildavsky and Polsby have pointed out, for example, a Presidential candidate has to campaign for vital votes in states that are closely contested, such as New York, Michigan, and California. Since winning or losing one of these states may hinge on a relatively small number of votes, it is more important for a Presidential candidate to influence votes in those states than in the "one party" states of the South and Southwest that tend to vote "conservative." In consequence, the votes of those states tend to be "over represented" in Presidential politics. In Congress, on the other hand, the "conservative" states tend to be "overrepresented," because of the seniority principle. Moves to strengthen the power of the President, therefore, are really moves to increase the influence of the voters in states where the Presidential vote is closely divided. In fact, such moves are motivated by ideological preference masquerading as structural "reform." "The underlying aim," conclude Wildavsky and Polsby, "is to speed up social changes that they desire by trying to rig the rules of the game more in favor of that political institution,

the presidency, which shares their policy preferences."[38]
Yet whatever the merit of the laws the "reformers" would like
to see enacted, conservatives like Kendall think that moves
toward the "plebiscitary" democracy of the Presidential mandate would ultimately afford little protection for minority
rights, which is precisely why the framers of the Constitution
put so many obstacles in its way.

Clearly, Willmoore Kendall has made a large contribution
to the definition of some of the key issues in our politics, yet
his essays have raised some questions in the minds of other
conservatives. For one thing, he seems strangely optimistic
regarding the outcome of the struggle along his "battle line."
Kendall considers that on most of the important issues the
conservatives have been holding their own, and the liberals,
despite the attention given their views by the communications media, and despite their overrepresentation in the
academic community, have more or less been held in check.
The liberals have *not*, he argues, succeeded in changing the
quotas on immigration; closing "tax loopholes" (which allow
the very rich to get away with paying a mere 40 per cent or
less of their income instead of the 92 per cent they would
otherwise pay); expanding the TVA idea so as to put
government into the electrical power business; abolishing
Congressional investigations; eliminating the filibuster; destroying the seniority system; or nationalizing the railroads
and other industries. Congress, with its inherent conservatism, "pretty consistently gets its way."[39] Other conservatives, including Buckley, have found such optimism "baf-
fling."[40] In their view, Kendall seems to ignore the tendency
of American culture as it currently bears upon American
politics: not only are the conservative champions in Congress mostly old, and one by one fading from the scene,

but they are scorned by "enlightened" opinion.† Kendall's essays raise other problems for conservatives. He can say: "The basic inertia of our politics is a forward Conservative inertia: when American society 'changes' it changes for the most part—as Conservatives wish it to—in the proper direction; that is, in the direction in which it must change in order to become more and more like itself at its best."[41] On the other hand, in speaking of the branch of our government that has effected some changes on key issues as he himself defines them, the Supreme Court, he argues that "the inertia of the Supreme Court is a forward inertia, and always in the direction of the Liberal Revolution."[42] Conceivably, these statements could be reconciled; the country itself *could* move

---

† Professor Kendall does not agree that the 1964 election changed Congress into a liberal ("rubber stamp") institution. Interviewed at Oxford, where he is engaged upon research on Montesquieu, he offered these comments: The 1964 elections certainly strengthened the Left-wing liberal element in Congress, but by no means to the extent that certain commentators would like us to think—and certainly not enough to deprive Congress of its character as a conservative check upon the Executive. As far as the major legislation of the current session is concerned, Congress always "filtered out" the liberal ideology. (See any recent issue of the *New Republic* for evidence of how frustrated the liberals feel about their so-called "triumphs.") The Voting Rights Act? By the time Congress finished with it, it was not at all a mass registration act. The anti-poverty legislation? By the time Congress finished with it, the one thing it was not going to do was make any substantial changes as regards the incidence of poverty; and furthermore, the funds are to be administered by those very city governments the liberals hate so fiercely. Immigration legislation? The bill does not open the gates in an egalitarian way. Entry is tied to skills, to family connections in the U.S., etc. Kendall says that his position on the point at issue will be embarrassed if and when the House votes to abolish HUAC—which the 1964 Congress kept in being, and well-supplied with funds, by overwhelming majority vote. Nor does Kendall think that "reapportionment" is going to alter the composition of Congress in any way "conservatives have to lose sleep over." These contentions are certain to cause debate among conservatives. It might be asked, for example, how *active* HUAC really is. But Kendall's position certainly corrects any temptation that may exist to generalize about the character of the current Congress.

"for the most part" in one direction, while the Supreme Court went in another. To know whether this is actually happening or not would require careful study to determine whether the Court's liberal edicts on school prayers, sale of pornography, law enforcement practices, internal security, and the like, are really effective in practice—i.e., to what extent are they actually ignored? Elsewhere in Kendall, other difficulties crop up: he is both for and against Calhoun's doctrine of concurrent majorities; he can speak of "the over emphasis (as with Russell Kirk, Frank Meyer, and Stanton Evans) on the role of religious belief in Conservatism," yet state flatly that the real issue between liberals and conservatives, finally, is "reason" versus "revelation," and point to liberal immanentization of final meaning as a definitive spiritual error. Yet Kendall's views on the matters continue to develop, and we might even say that the presence of such difficulties in his work reflects the fact that he is thinking closely about an American political reality which itself is highly complex.

IV

Still another position in the spectrum of conservative opinion is occupied by Frank Meyer, who has been associated with *National Review* from the beginning and is currently in charge of the book review section of the magazine. He wrote *The Moulding of Communists* in 1960, a volume in the series of studies on Communism in American Life sponsored by the Fund for the Republic; and, most recently, *In Defense of Freedom* (1962). In the former book, he draws upon his experiences as a Communist Party member to produce a penetrating study of the Communist mentality. *In Defense of Freedom* undertakes to set forth a conservative position at once profound enough to resist the ultimate, and, indeed, religious, challenge of Communism, and, on the other hand, resilient enough to preserve the freedom of the individual in a mass society.

According to Meyer, both modern liberals and such traditionalists as Russell Kirk are victims of a peculiar nineteenth-century intellectual bifurcation. They inherited a fatally divided culture. Such nineteenth-century liberals as Mill, and such nineteenth-century conservatives as de Maistre, tried to defend indispensable truths, but in defending them forgot other important truths. In Meyer's view, nineteenth-century liberalism deserves our gratitude for its defense of individual freedom, but its utilitarian philosophy finally proved unable to sustain the freedom men like Mill valued, because the utilitarian position denied the validity of moral ends firmly based on "the constitution of being."[43] In contrast to conservatives like Kirk and Kendall, Meyer thus admires much of John Stuart Mill, and is sensitive to Mill's own awareness of the dilemmas the utilitarian position faced. For modern Mill scholars, the drama of Mill's thought proceeds from his own awareness of the limitations of his position, in combination with his awareness of the value of his position. Meyer is in harmony with the best current interpretation of Mill in finding that, though he was a defender of individual freedom, his philosophy finally could not sustain the defense, because it was not grounded in ontology, in "the constitution of being." To say that Meyer considers Mill "admirable" would not do justice to the position he holds in Meyer's thought, which is a central one; yet admirable though such liberals as Mill were, Meyer thinks, they nevertheless (to use a phrase, and a very important one, that occurs in various forms in Meyer's writing) were living on the "moral capital" accumulated by beliefs they

had rejected. There was nothing in their philosophy to vali-
date the freedom they valued so much.

The nineteenth-century conservatives, in contrast, were
sound in their fundamental philosophical position. They
recognized, Meyer argues, "the objective existence of values
based upon the unchanging constitution of being as the criterion for moral thought and action."[44] Yet, though these
nineteenth-century conservatives were right in their ontological derivation of values, they "all too frequently forgot about
personal freedom. If only right standards were upheld, they
were willing to accept an authoritarian structure of state and
society. At the very best, they were indifferent to freedom
in the body politic; at the worst, its enemies."[45]

Both conservatives and liberals in the nineteenth century
thus stood for valuable ideas. The liberals defended personal
freedom, the conservatives moral authority. But the philosophical blindness of the liberals was fatal to freedom, while
the political folly of the conservatives made their philosophical truths irrelevant in practice. Students of the nineteenth
century will recognize that Meyer's description is true. He
does not, because he is defining main currents, deal in any
detail with the thought of such men as Newman, Lord Acton,
and, later, Chesterton, who also faced the freedom-authority
dilemma. Yet it is plain that as far as the direction of
nineteenth-century thought is concerned these men were outside the main stream. The nineteenth century, as Mill himself recognized, was "Bentham" and "Coleridge," reason and
authority, skepticism and faith, philosophy and imagination,
statistics and morals, self-interest and love. Modern inter-
preters of the nineteenth century have had to deal with the
dichotomy. F. R. Leavis edited Mill's essays on Bentham and
Coleridge, and he himself attempted to affirm the centrality
of imagination, i.e., literature: he calls it "the common pursuit." Lionel Trilling, whose thought has its roots in the

nineteenth century, rests comfortably in an oxymoron: "the liberal imagination." Facing this same dichotomy, Frank Meyer has tried to bring into some sort of relationship the truths of both positions. It has been his undertaking to show that freedom *and* moral authority are "fundamentally in accord, that they are grounded both in the nature of men and in the very constitution of being."[46]

Other conservatives such as Stanton Evans and Stephen J. Tonsor have faced the same dilemma. Tonsor, for example, Professor of Intellectual History at the University of Michigan, points out in a review highly sympathetic to John Stuart Mill that it is extremely difficult to foster "autonomy, freedom and rationality without fatally wounding organic wholeness and spirituality."[47] Mill sought like Acton and Tocqueville "some combination of the ideas of the Enlightenment with the governing ideas of romanticism and historicism. Mill, for his part, sought in vain for a workable union of the thought of Bentham and the thought of Coleridge."[48] Tonsor seems to doubt that the problem is a soluble one. If the traditionalists are right "in assuming that reason and liberty are suspect and that in his fallen nature man is incapable of either right thinking or right acting," it may also be true that they are right "in asserting that to make liberty an absolute in the face of the metaphysical void which is characteristic of modernity is to drive mankind helplessly and hopelessly into the anti-human ideological pseudo-religions." On the other hand, the claims of authority are none too good. They are "tarnished claims. Authority which violates the conscience and murders the man, whenever it is given the command of the state to preserve a faith or conform a population to the practice of a religion, can hardly claim that either virtue or the creation of a humane culture is its objective." Yet, without providing any solution to the dilemma, Tonsor rejects Mill's "substitution of 'the culture of the feelings' for faith" as "a dangerous and, in the long run, untenable one." Even more untenable, however, is "the stance of modern man, feeling Mill's necessity to believe and to act, but committed to an even less satisfactory epistemology and absolutely devoid of metaphysics."[49]

In his book *In Defense of Freedom* and in his *National Review* articles, Frank Meyer has dealt impressively with this classic dilemma. The "difficulty," he argues, "is that both its major premises are true: on the one hand, freedom *is* essential to the nature of man and neutral to vice and virtue; on the other hand, good ends *are* good ends, and it *is* the duty of man to pursue them. I only deny that in the real situation with which we are dealing these two premises are contradictories. Rather they are axioms true of different though interconnected realms of existence. How can true ends be established elsewhere than in the intellectual, the moral, the spiritual order? Where can the conditions for freedom be established but in the social order, which means —since this is where the determining force centers—in the political order? A good society is possible only when both these conditions are met: when the social and political order guarantees a state of affairs in which men can freely choose; and when the intellectual and moral leaders, the 'creative minority,' have the understanding and imagination to maintain the prestige of tradition and reason, and thus to sustain the intellectual and moral order throughout society. To the degree that either of these conditions is lacking, a society will not be a good society, and the individual men who constitute it will suffer in their humanity."[50] The crux of Meyer's position, a highly controversial one, is that freedom is the *condition* of virtue. The "denial to men of the freedom to accept [virtue] or reject it, *would make virtue meaningless and truth rote*"[51] (italics added).

In Meyer's view, as the title of *In Defense of Freedom*

suggests, freedom is the decisive political virtue: "Political theory and practice, therefore, must be judged by criteria proper to the political order; and the decisive criterion of any political order is the degree to which it establishes the conditions of freedom. On the political and social level this is primary."[52] Such freedom, moreover, is the primary political value, even though intellectually, morally, and spiritually men may arrive at absolutes that are binding.

Meyer's attempt to resolve the paradox of freedom and authority is an impressive one, and a number of conservative intellectuals, such as Stanton Evans and William F. Rickenbacker, agree, in the main, with his position. Perhaps not surprisingly, however, Meyer's position has also come under heavy attack within the conservative camp, and has precipitated an intramural "great debate" in which a number of important issues have emerged.

Brent Bozell's essay "Freedom or Virtue,"[53] for example, attacked Meyer's thesis that the "freedom of the individual person is the 'first principle' in political affairs." If "freedom is the first principle in political affairs," Bozell argued, "virtue is, at best, the second one," whatever one affirms in the moral and spiritual realms. Bozell supports his argument with the example of divorce. (He assumes that Meyer, holding a sacramental view of marriage, would oppose divorce on principle and regard the preservation of marriage as a "virtuous" act. Bozell's argument was meant to apply to any act which he and Meyer could agree upon as "virtuous.") Suppose, Bozell says, that an American, X, has grown tired of his wife. The laws of his state impose no serious obstacle to divorce, and he would suffer no social disapproval should he go ahead and get a divorce. Yet he decides not to do so on the grounds that divorce is "wrong." Suppose again that Y, a Spaniard, has tired of *his* wife. To get a divorce, however, he would have to travel to France; he would face social ostracism; and in Spain the remarriage prospects would be nil. He dismisses the idea of divorce at once. There is a sense, of course, in which the American's decision is more admirable: it was harder to reach, because he was freer. The Spaniard's decision was almost automatic: his circumstances afforded him very little freedom in the matter. Yet can it really be argued, as, in Bozell's view Meyer would argue, that the American's decision was more *virtuous,* more in conformity with man's being? If so, it would follow that "if we are seriously interested in maximizing opportunities" for virtue so defined, we ought to set about discarding all the laws, customs, and traditions that interfere with freedom of choice. "If freedom is the '*first* principle' of the search for virtue, if as Meyer writes at another point, it is 'the *precondition* of a good society,' then by definition there is no superior principle that can be invoked at any stage, against the effort to maximize freedom," and there is no point at which men are entitled to stop sweeping away the traditions and institutions which limit choice and "which every rational society in history has erected to promote a virtuous citizenry." The final meaning of Meyer's position, Bozell argues, is that "virtue must be made as difficult as possible" by maximizing freedom, and that this condition should be brought about in society even while recognizing that "only a few men, if any, can be expected to meet the challenge successfully," and that "the proliferation of unvirtuous acts in the objective order is one of the prices that must be paid for the fulfillment of heroic man." Arguing that such a position has more in common with the existentialist metaphysics of Sartre—the doctrine that man is all potentiality, i.e., all freedom—than with the traditional metaphysic of Christianity, Bozell points out that orthodox Christianity attributes to man a fixed nature to which he must conform in order to be "virtuous." Unlike the rest of creation, man has the power to deviate from the appropriate "pattern of order," to repudiate his nature. But the freedom so to repudiate one's nature scarcely seems to Bozell a blessing. If "individual man is to have any hope of conforming with his nature, he needs all the help he can get. That is why the role of grace is so vital to the Christian view of things, not only supernatural grace, but the natural grace that springs forth from man's constructs: his institutions, his customs, his laws—the ones that have been inspired by his better angel and that remain in time to give nourishment to all of the human race."[54] The commonwealth, in Bozell's view, should attempt to form itself in such a way as to conform to the "divine pattern of order," for then it will be "in a position to help man conform to his nature, which is the meaning of virtue."[55]

It should by no means be supposed that Bozell neglects the need for freedom in the political realm, but his arguments for it are prudential, and focus on "the effects unlimited power is likely to have on those who exercise it, and derivatively on the damage they are likely to do to the commonwealth they govern." For Bozell, the question with regard to the disposition of political power is always: "Will this grant of power, in this instance, for this object, produce a net good for the individual members of the commonwealth?"[56] Unlike Meyer, Bozell therefore considers economic freedom not a good in itself but a prudential measure, usually good indeed, but only contingently so.

Bozell's article evoked a number of replies, the most elaborate of which was by Rickenbacker, who charged, among other things, that Bozell had hypostatized the state and social institutions, whereas, he said, "I have never been personally introduced to 'the state' or to 'social institutions.' I have met only men and women and they have fallen far short of my, and I'm sure of Mr. Bozell's definition of a saint."[57] Bozell overrates, in other words, the amount of "natural grace" that can flow from collections of fallible human beings. Furthermore, Rickenbacker made an important distinction between the coercion exercised by habit, custom, and social sanctions, and that exercised by the state: "*The* vital distinction is that the state has the plain brute power (troops, bayonets, prisons) to enforce its will; whereas social institutions do not have that plain brute power. . . . The merely influential force of accumulated custom may be strong, but it is not commanding. Freedom consists in not being commanded."[58] Thus Rickenbacker, and probably Meyer, would consider a state law against, say, divorce to be coercive, but would not consider social sanctions against it to be an unacceptable limitation on freedom. For his part, Meyer pointed out to Bozell that the position on freedom and virtue set forth in *In Defense of Freedom* corresponds to the actual consensus of contemporary American conservatism, and he implied that Bozell's position is a sort of pipe dream, the result of free-floating speculation, and of little relevance.

A number of things can be said about this debate and the positions that have emerged in it. For one thing, it is part of the attraction and interest of contemporary conservative intellectuals that they are willing to debate first principles. (When was the last time first principles were debated in the pages of the *New Republic* or *The Nation?*) The liberals would seem to have agreed for so long on their assumptions that they have forgotten what they are.

As far as the rival conservative positions are concerned, we may see that the stress in Bozell's writing is religious, whereas his opponents seem more concerned with politics. Thus Bozell, and along with him Weaver, and perhaps Kirk, see the problem faced by the West as primarily religious in nature, and they ascribe the ills of the West to a crisis in faith. Meyer, Stanton Evans and Rickenbacker certainly would agree that the religious aspect is important, but they tend to focus first on the political crisis: the growth of state power and its indifference to individual freedom. The differences in their positions reflect differing diagnoses of our ills.

Yet it is also true that the two positions reflect differing strands of the Western tradition itself, and may even be correlated religiously with Catholicism and Protestantism. The great medieval poem "The Pearl," for example, tells about a child who died before the age of two, but who, because innocent of sin, immediately became a Queen of Heaven. In the poem the child appears in a vision, "arrayed in garments white," "her beauty . . . shining clear," and explains that the innocent, though never tempted—i.e., never having *chosen* virtue—gain salvation *by right*:

> To Grace, if Mercy's aid be lent,
> The guilty may be brought, contrite;
> But one to evil never bent,
> The innocent, is saved by right.[59]

For the author of "The Pearl," freedom thus is *not* necessary to virtue; it is the state of being that matters. The Protestant Milton, in contrast, scorned "a fugitive and cloistered virtue." As he wrote in *Areopagitica*: "He that can apprehend and consider vice with all her baits and seeming pleasures, and yet abstain, and yet distinguish, and yet prefer that which is truly better, he is the true warfaring Christian. I cannot praise a fugitive and cloistered virtue, unexercised and unbreathed, that never sallies out and sees her adversary, but slinks out of the race where that immortal garland is to be run for. . . . That virtue, therefore which is but a youngling in the contemplation of evil, and knows not the utmost that vice promises to her followers, and rejects it, is but a blank virtue, not a pure." This difference, at root a religious difference, is bound to have, as it appears in American conservatism, an effect upon actual political attitudes. Bozell, one assumes, would differ from Meyer on such matters as censorship and laws against vice of various kinds; as far as Spain is concerned, Meyer would certainly be well disposed to it on grounds of *Realpolitik*, as a Cold War ally, but Bozell would find much to admire in such features of Spanish life as laws that foster Christian behavior.

v

At first glance it seems paradoxical that conservatives have failed, on the whole, to endow with imaginative force what, on intellectual grounds, must be counted one of the strongest—most completely and systematically developed, most demonstrably valid—aspects of their position. I mean the economic argument. In other areas they have had important successes. The fight against "progressive" education has ended in a clear conservative victory—the theory lingers on at the teachers colleges, but no one else defends it intellectually any longer. Then too, one may be sure that experience will confirm the validity of the "hard" position on Communism; and surely conservative resistance to secularization and to inroads upon our moral and political traditions will, foreseeably, gain increasing support. Conservative economic arguments, on the other hand, tend to strike the community at large as speculative and problematical.

Some immediate features of the conservative economic position do, perhaps, sometimes become vivid for the general public. There is a widespread, though amorphous, feeling about the virtues of private property that can be mobilized

[223]

intermittently. Similarly, most people do understand that government regulation follows government money.‡ And such things as Dr. John Howard's plan for decentralized aid to colleges would seem capable of arousing wide support —if the barriers erected by liberal control of the communications media can be breached. But the more general conservative economic argument—that economic freedom and freedom of other kinds are inextricably connected—has not become vivid, does not to most people seem relevant to issues of immediate moment.

In part this is because economics is felt to be abstruse and esoteric, the province of specialists. In part, too, it is due to the fact that the modifications and corruptions of the

‡ This in fact becomes more and more patent. In May, 1965 (to choose one example from the many at hand), the *New York Herald Tribune* ran the following news report under the headline "Ending School Bias: The U.S. Big Stick": "In the most significant move since the 1954 Supreme Court decision banning de jure school desegregation, the Federal government yesterday set a deadline of the fall of 1967 for integration of all grades of a publicschool system that wants Federal aid. School faculties and buses also must be integrated. Seeking to accelerate the 'deliberate speed' cited by the high court in a later 1955 decision, the government also declared that there must be a 'substantial good faith start' made next fall: At least four grades of the twelve must be integrated by then—the first elementary, the first junior high and the first and last of high school. At immediate stake for the 17 Southern and border states is more than $867 million in Federal money due them in the fiscal year beginning July 1. This includes almost $565 million scheduled under the new $1.3 billion Federal aid act. Congress has not as yet appropriated funds for the act." Even more ominous is the intention of the federal bureaucracy to take a hand in the rewriting of textbooks. As Evans and Novak reported in the September 15, 1965 *New York Herald Tribune*, the Community Relations Service created by the 1965 Civil Rights Act plans "a systematic effort to contact all publishers and school boards to encourage their publication and adoption of textbooks *conforming to established standards*." [Italics added.] The standards in question have to do with the treatment accorded the Negroes in the textbooks. The federal government thus plans to use its coercive power to control the content of textbooks.

free market frequently do not in fact have immediate and visible effects. The country, after all, is prosperous; and though policy on taxes, interest rates, balance of payments figures, investment rates and the like are admitted to have profound long-term meanings, these meanings tend to be psychologically invisible. And beyond this, intellectuals and opinion makers, as well as the "general public," tend to be bored by economics: it is the "dismal science." The intricacies of philosophy or of psychoanalytic theory they will master; but they think of themselves as involved with higher things than money—with the imagination, with style and pleasure, with morality, with the life of the spirit. And in this feeling, ironically enough, they are thoroughly Western, and even chivalrous. The intellectuals have been interested in economics only when it could be shown to have a dramatic moral consequence. It is an old joke—now, indeed, only a joke of sorts—that during the 1930s poets and novelists were applying themselves to Marx and Engels, were discussing the labor theory of value and were even becoming adept in the remoter features of economic theory. And it is a joke because this is not assumed to be their normal, or proper, activity. In the West, for better or worse, money has been, imaginatively, low in status. Our heroes have been saints and statesmen, soldiers and lovers, poets and philosophers; in the West, the man devoted to the *highest* things has traditionally given up his worldly goods. Indeed, it is one of the ironies that make contemporary life so engaging that intellectuals who hate the West accept this hierarchy of values, and assume that poetry is more important—is "higher"— than finance. But the Western feeling is deeply rooted. In medieval Spain, to choose only one extreme example, the ruling grandees consigned the care of money to non-Western enclaves, to Mohammedans and Jews, and regarded the details of finance as beneath their notice.§ Indeed, we can find some traces of this attitude in our modern social feelings. The "professional" man does not, we notice, actually handle money; he sends a bill, and he is higher socially than the man who does handle it and count it. The "higher" the professional man is, in fact, the less fussy he is about money. Surely it is no accident that the great *imaginative* modern economic thinkers have been rebels against traditional values—Marx pre-eminently, but also, and more mildly, Keynes. It is they who have brought the moral imagination to bear on economics; who, have, in effect, been the great poets of economic theory, linking money and life, money and moral values.||

§ For a fascinating discussion of this see Américo Castro, *The Structure of Spanish History* (Princeton, 1954), pp. 494, 498–99. Castro argues that this attitude on the part of the Christian ruling class has had a profound influence on the course of Spanish history.

|| See Wilhelm Röpke, *Welfare, Freedom and Inflation*: according to Röpke, we do not discover the roots of the inflationary process until we "recognize that inflation and the spirit which nourishes it and accepts it, is merely the monetary aspect of the general decay of law. It requires no special astuteness to realize that the vanishing respect for property is very intimately related to the numbing of respect for money and its value. In fact, laxity about property and laxity about money are very closely bound up together; in both cases, what is firm, durable, earned, secured and designed for continuity gives place to what is fragile, fugitive, fleeting, unsure, and ephemeral. And that is not the kind of foundation on which the free society can long remain standing." In the light of this observation, it is interesting to contemplate J. M. Keynes, a kaleidoscopic figure in economic theory, constantly changing, constantly suggesting, and certainly the source of some sound suggestions; yet also the poet of inflationary economics. See, then, his remarkable essay, "My Early Beliefs": "It seems to me," he says of his moral attitudes at Cambridge, "that this religion of ours [G. E. Moore's philosophy] was a very good one to grow up under. It remains nearer the truth than any other that I know, with less irrelevant extraneous matter and nothing to be ashamed of. . . . It is still my religion under the surface. . . . We repudiated entirely customary morals, conventions and traditional wisdom. We were, that is to say, in the strict sense of the term, immoralists. . . . I remain, and always will remain, an immoralist."

With fatal irony, on the other hand, conservative econo-mists have been made to seem crassly materialistic, con-cerned with nothing but getting and spending.

This situation is preposterous, for the conservative eco-nomic position has deep moral consequences. It may be described, most succinctly, as a *presumption* in favor of the free market. The word *presumption* is important here: their position is not absolute and schematic—they recognize that exceptional circumstances may demand special measures. But the presumption, in their view, is in favor of the free market. In this the conservatives differ sharply from the Left, whose presumptions run all the other way—toward central control and planning from "above."

It seems to me that no one has defined the economic alternatives and demonstrated the basis of the conservative presumption more lucidly than Wilhelm Röpke, a European economist whose prose is as urbane and readable as Gal-braith's. To the extent that an economy is free, he points out, production goes forward at the *command* of the con-sumers, whose desires, reflected in the market, are then re-flected in the decisions of the producers. In the collectivist economy, on the other hand, production goes forward—in varying degrees, depending upon the extent of collectiviza-tion—at the command of the politicians in power: "The decisions as to what will or will not be produced [are] made on the basis of the thoroughly subjective notions of the leaders of the collectivist state; consumer freedom is at an end, and the population must agree to that use of the productive forces of the country which the dominant group in the government of the moment has decided is good. . . . What results is a thoroughgoing economic dictatorship which is inconceivable without a simultaneous political dicta-torship possessed of the necessary means of coercion. . . . *Hence, to fight simultaneously for freedom and for planned*

[227]

economy would be to give evidence of a serious degree of mental confusion"[60] (italics added). Here, with admirable clarity, Röpke defines the connection between economic and political freedom. In actual practice, as he points out, the collectivist state is faced with "the dilemma either of imitating the competitive system, more or less, and basing its production plan on the wishes of the consumers (however ascertained), or of establishing a plan based on other considerations to which the consumers will be compelled to submit."[61] Röpke points out that the collectivist economy aims at replacing the decisions of the market place by "commands from above, and at turning over to a group of government officials the responsibility for decisions respecting the use to be made of the economy's productive resources. The collectivist planned economy thus substitutes a government fiat for the spontaneous reaction mechanism of the market, so that in the interest of clarity it might better be designated as *economy of the bureaucrats* or *command economy*. It is not necessary to list . . . the enormous, even insurmountable difficulties such a system would have to struggle with."[62]

Part of the excitement in reading Röpke's works proceeds from the recognition that while he is as much aware of the discontents that arise from modern civilization as any thinker on the Left, he seems more able to make the necessary intellectual distinctions. Because of the extreme differentiation and division of labor, for example, we experience our economy as "artificial," "impenetrable," its decisions coming from remote sources. And so, since collectivism appears to many to be "the opposite of this economic system, they regard it as a foregone conclusion that it will deliver us from these evils. They fail to realize that a collectivist economic system can no more avoid the evils flowing from exaggerated differentiation than our own."[63] Indeed, as Röpke shows, the collectivist system seems to exacerbate the very problems which its supporters look to it to solve. "Thus we arrive at the height of confusion when the same people who untiringly attack the rationalist, mechanical, and artificial character of our economic system with its industrialization, its proletarianization and urbanization, seek salvation in planned economy and centralized organization, i.e., in an economic structure which will be still more rationalist, still more mechanical, and still more artificial than the existing one."[64] Again, much is said on the Left about the depersonalization of work and the dependent status of the worker in large-scale industry. But, as Röpke says, it is clear that "the techniques of production such as are found in big industry would certainly be taken over by the collectivist state, with the result that the dependence of the worker would actually become even greater since he would no longer be able to choose among different employers."[65] Such features of the free market as advertising and distribution costs have also been attacked as mitigable evils. Yet the "collectivist economic system would also have to reckon with the corresponding costs connected with the setting up of an apparatus for the distribution of goods (including propaganda). The only question would be, then, whether these costs in a collectivist economic system would be lower than under the existing system; and there are enough reasons for assuming that they would be higher."[66] Concludes Röpke: "Phenomena such as costs, prices, profitability, interest, and rent can in no way be construed as devilish inventions of 'capitalism.' On the contrary, they constitute an ingenious and thoroughly intelligible mechanism and serve for the fulfillment of tasks with which any economic system whatever is faced. Together they comprise that apparatus needed to achieve general economic equilibrium for which the collectivist state must find an equivalent, though . . . the probability of its being able to do so is remote."[67]

Röpke is far from supposing that the free market is immune to corruptions, and, unlike some advocates of free enterprise, he insists that government must be strong: but the function he assigns it is not, as in the collectivist system, the regulation of production, but rather the repression of monopoly. "The state can effectively fight monopoly by energetically opposing restrictions of competition and by carefully avoiding economic policies which favor the formation of monopolies. For this, however, it is necessary to have a strong state—impartial and powerful—standing above the melee of economic interests. . . . The state must not only be strong; unmoved by ideologies of whatever brand, it must clearly recognize its task: to defend 'capitalism' against the 'capitalists' " when they are tempted to take comfortable short cuts to profits.[68]

Forcefully, Röpke cites the example of Germany after the economic reform of 1948 as an illustration of the way his principles work in practice. Germany, he points out, provides a unique instance of a country that has operated within a short period of history under both the collectivist (National Socialist) and the free market systems. "It would seem as if one of the world's most important industrial countries deliberately subjected itself to the experiment of demonstrating in succession 1) that collectivism requires not only political unfreedom but leads to disorder, waste, and low living standards, and 2) that the opposite economic system of the market economy is not only a prerequisite for political and economic freedom, but also the road to economic order and to prosperity for all the people as well."[69] Widely termed an "economic miracle," the recovery of Germany after 1948 was, he points out, no miracle at all. "Its success was on the contrary precisely what its architects had expected. The real miracle lay in the fact that in this particular country and in a world still under the spell of inflationism and collectivism, it proved possible politically and socially to return to the economic discipline of the market economy and to monetary discipline." Later, he observes, Japan achieved similar results by using the same principles. England, on the other hand, where both parties are welfarist-socialist in character, seems trapped in a spiral of inflation, excessive production costs, and crippling welfare taxes.¶

Despite all this, the conviction remains firmly entrenched in the intellectual community that the world, including the West, is moving toward "socialism"—and, worse, that this, in a vague way, is a good thing. How odd it is, indeed, to meet intellectuals who espouse the most advanced literary, philosophical, or psychoanalytic doctrines and who at the same time complacently accept the demonstrably obsolete collectivist economic assumptions of thirty years ago. To change this climate of feeling will be difficult, yet to do so is surely one of the principal tasks confronting conservative intellectuals at the present time.

¶ In a recent "Letter from London," *National Review's* correspondent Anthony Lejeune points out that any British family with two children and an income around the national average actually makes a net *profit* when taxes are balanced against welfare benefits. "Such a family, therefore, makes no contribution at all to the defence of the country, to the provision of police and fire services, to the costs of administration; these civic burdens fall entirely on others"—on the traditional middle classes, who are progressively impoverished. "High taxation prevents them from saving: the policies of social justice erase their capital: inflation pushes up the cost of private education." As the costs of the welfare system spiral upward, the middle class themselves progressively come to depend on the government. Gloomily, Lejeune sees the process as irreversible, since both parties foster it. (*National Review*, XVII, p. 418.)

Weirdly enough, some critics have argued that the conservatives' "presumption in favor of the free market" is at odds with Christian and especially with Roman Catholic doctrine. Irving Kristol has written in *The Reporter* of "Mr. Buckley's loyalty to two incompatible ideals"—Catholicism and the free market. "The two," asserts Kristol, "simply do not mix: one cannot believe that it is a duty of society to assist in the salvation of souls, while simultaneously asserting that the individual should have the immitigable right to order his life and his property as he sees fit." But this argument is hopelessly confused, and can be sustained neither logically nor historically. Since when, first of all, has a presumption in favor of the free market implied for the individual "the *immitigable* right to order his life and property as he sees fit"? Surely individual freedom is to exist under law, and entails conformity with the standards of civilized behavior. Just because one *owns* the dynamite one is scarcely free to blow up the police station with it. Furthermore, though it is certainly the duty of society, on a Christian view, to assist in the saving of souls, it is quite clear that that is not the only thing society is set up to do: the sense in which the man who fixes my flat tire is helping to save my soul must be very remote indeed. And if it is the duty of society to help save souls, why in the world should we assume that production at the command of a bureaucrat saves souls more effectively than production at the command of the free market?

Kristol goes on to speak of "Catholic social theory": But when has such theory deliberately chosen a system productive of *less* well-being on the grounds that it is better at saving souls? Feudal economics did not prevail with the support of the Church because it saved souls, but rather because it was the economic arrangement appropriate to its era. It is quite possible to argue, as some have done, that the ideal

Christian life can be lived only in a monastery—or even on a pillar in the desert: but this is hardly *social* theory. Once we admit that one can be a Christian and also live in society, then the question arises of how we can best organize life in society. The argument, obviously, is not between Christianity and the free market, but between two *economic* doctrines; and it turns on the question of which produces the greater well-being and which is the more equitable.

VI

If, as we have seen earlier in this chapter, the political thought of leading conservatives raises metaphysical questions, the work of Frederick D. Wilhelmsen, a frequent contributor to *National Review*, concerns itself directly with them. In his early forties, Wilhelmsen has been a professor of philosophy in this country as well as in Spain, and may be described as a Catholic existentialist. Like other existentialists, he grounds his thought in actual human experience with all its vicissitudes and paradoxes. He believes that the "philosopher who would probe the being of the human person must never forget his history," and he would agree with Eric Voegelin that any valid account of the human condition, indeed any valid political science, must take into account the fact of man's experience of transcendence. If Voegelin's great work, *Order and History*, investigates the various symbolizations of transcendence which have been projected by successive civilizations—and thus, by taking account of all categories of fact, makes the study of politics scientific—Wilhelmsen, in his meditations on being, likewise refuses to ignore the facts of man's actual existence, to which, he finds, no purely naturalistic description is adequate.

"Any attempt to escape [man's] history," writes Wilhelmsen in *The Metaphysics of Love* (1962), "is bound to issue in a philosophy which will be irrelevant . . . because it will fail to illuminate the being of man as we find him in existence. . . . It is *this* human person, the only one who exists, that I am interested in probing in the pages that follow."[70]

What follows is an analysis of man's being which draws upon Tillich, Heidegger, Ortega and other familiar figures, as well as upon some Spanish philosophers less familiar to us, such as Xavier Zubiri. Indeed, it is not the least of the book's merits that it makes us aware of Zubiri, who is considered the finest metaphysician in Spain, but who, though well known in France, has been unaccountably neglected in England and America.

The Metaphysics of Love bristles with ideas, and ranges from an existential analysis of the *Iliad* to some fascinating speculation on the philosophical implications of Spanish syntax, but at its center is an ontological argument with Paul Tillich, who, in Wilhelmsen's view, "sees being principally as a tragedy conquered by self-affirmation, by what he eloquently calls 'the power to be.' "[71] Wilhelmsen argues that "the ontology of Tillich . . . illustrates the division between the Protestant world which has emphasized the tragic sense of life, and the Catholic world which has given the primacy to agape."[72] Wilhelmsen provides a brilliant and sympathetic exposition of Tillich's ontology, and though —finally—he rejects Tillich for the Catholic tradition, he does so with an intellectual grace exceptional among differing philosophers: "If I turn to an analysis of the thought of the Protestant theologian, I do so not principally to take objection to what he holds, but to learn from him. By a singular paradox, those insights of mine which have led me to differ from Tillich would never have been possible had

I not gone to school through the reading of his own system."[73]

Tillich's affirmation, Wilhelmsen points out, arises out of the confrontation with meaninglessness: "By taking anxiety into himself, by affirming the meaning of his own confrontation with meaninglessness, man asserts himself against the void. Such a man, according to Tillich, has the courage to be. Within him, one with the very being he is, is the power to be against the darkness closing round him. 'The source of this affirmation of meaning within meaninglessness,' maintains Tillich, 'is the God of God, the power of being, which works through those who have no name for it, not even the name of God.'"[74] In making such an affirmation "in spite of . . . the negativities of existence," Tillich is in harmony with the spirit of the Reformation. Wilhelmsen quotes the great passage on Dürer from *The Courage to Be:*

It has been rightly said that Albrecht Dürer's engraving, "Knight, Death, and the Devil," is a classic expression of the spirit of the Lutheran Reformation and—it might be added—of Luther's courage of confidence, of his form of the courage to be. A knight in full armor is riding through a valley accompanied by the figure of death on one side, the devil on the other. Fearlessly, concentrated, confident he looks ahead. He is alone but he is not lonely. In his solitude he participates in the power which gives him the courage to affirm himself in spite of the presence of the negativities of existence.

Wilhelmsen finds the same stress on courage and ontological power at the center of Tillich's own work. "It is evident not simply from Tillich's explicit statements, but from the whole temper of his work, that he thinks the Protestant affirmation of being as power, the Protestant experience of 'for thine is the Power and the Glory forever,' is not only one among the many authentic confrontations with existence . . . , but that it represents the supreme articulation by the human

spirit of the very structure and meaning of being itself."[75]
He concludes: "Using a phrase Tillich borrows from Luther
and makes his own, we might say that for him being is not
an *esse*, an 'is' as in Aquinas; being is not an 'as if,' an
als ob as in Vaihinger; being is rather a *trotz*, an 'in spite
of.' But in truth is this the deepest meaning of being, to
be an 'in spite of'?"[76]

Drawing upon Spanish thought as well as scholastic philosophy, Wilhelmsen concludes that it is not. "The shock
of non-being can stir within the mind a questioning as to
why we are at all when every resource within our very
nature cries out its own radical insufficiency and ontological
poverty. When thus shaken to the foundation, the only
alternative to anxiety is gratitude. . . . But when gratitude
is so profound that it reaches within to my very being and
beyond to the whole of being to which I am related, then
gratitude answers Love."[77]

Thus, within "the Catholic world the ecstatic dominates
the tragic because being's power to be against negation, being's courage and fortitude, are experienced as flowing out
of a natural superabundance without being itself. The response to being within Catholic culture is lavish, uneconomic,
in a word—chivalric. This is the deepest secret of the Baroque.
. . . The Protestant of tomorrow will meet the new world
in spite of the anxieties it brings, in spite of the heroism
it demands. He will confront the darkness of outer space
with the courage he has inherited from his fathers of the
Reformation. But we Catholics have an inheritance all our
own—the inheritance of folly. All love is folly because all
love is based on the impossible paradox that a man will
gain his soul only by throwing it away. But the more we are
dwarfed by the stars beyond, the more we shall love them
as creatures of the Triune God. And the more we love them
the more will they be brought low and the more will we

[236]

be exalted above them. We know all these things, but we shall not love because of this knowledge. And this love will be our Catholic courage."[78]

Well, in the considered opinion of our most celebrated liberal political journalists, views of the kind we have been examining in this chapter represent merely "the voice of the *lumpen*-bourgeoisie" (Dwight Macdonald) and "a forced and bogus petulance" and "insults to the intelligence" (Richard Rovere). The Great Dissenter, Irving Howe—now isolating himself once again (no *New Yorker* writer he)—finds James Burnham's writing on foreign affairs "as puerile as a Birchite pamphlet." But why crush such butterflies upon a wheel? The foregoing pages, whether or not they elicit agreement, have shown how fanciful such descriptions of American conservatism have been. On this point there is nothing more to be said. And so I would like to turn to the developing political and cultural situation in which we find ourselves, and make a few concluding observations about the future role of the conservative movement.

VII

The Prospects Before Us

"Serious Leftism," complained Michael Harrington recently in *Partisan Review*, "is not as apocalyptic as one would like." With fair assurance, one can counsel Harrington: Wait.

In an earlier chapter, it was observed that a deep moral division exists within the West, and is reflected in the world at large, as in the nation actually divided by an armed frontier. But even nations not physically divided are divided within themselves. In Italy and France the division has become institutionalized, and large revolutionary parties constitute states within states, their posture that of permanent conflict. Elsewhere the division between Left and Right is less formal, but still very much present—and each successive crisis forced upon us by the world revolutionary movement renders the depth of the division more visible, for the choices presented to us usually seem to be of an either-or character. Under the pressure of choice, liberal opinion itself tends to divide into a Left (surrender) and a Right (resist).

In 1965, for example, the debate within the West over Viet Nam showed how deep the division actually is. Jean Paul Sartre, probably the most forthright as well as the most intelligent Leftist in the West, flamboyantly canceled some scheduled talks at Cornell as a gesture of protest against our Viet Nam policy. Explaining his position in *The Nation*, a Leftist magazine, Sartre made it clear that only the *rate* of anti-Communist surrender in Viet Nam was discussable, not

whether the Communists would be permitted to triumph.*
In a similar vein, Simone de Beauvoir records how she *rejoiced* over the defeat of the French at Dienbienphu by the Communists under General Giap, and provides a vivid example of the moral civil war in the West: "The people I passed in the street [in Paris] imagined that a great misfortune had just befallen their country and mine. If they had had any inkling of how pleased I was, they would have thought I deserved to be stood up against a wall and shot." As Sartre himself put it in his famous "Reply to Albert Camus," "it will be incumbent upon whoever pursues the concrete ends of men to choose his friends, since, in a society torn by civil war, it is not possible to assume the ends of all."

Within the United States itself, a great many people (especially in the intellectual community) made Sartre's choice on the Viet Nam issue. In pointing this out, I do not wish to be misunderstood: I do not refer to those who questioned American intervention on tactical grounds, or felt that we were overextending our commitments—admissible, though it seems to me dubious, positions—but to those who presented their position in "moral" terms: who claimed that our resistance to the Communist take-over was in some

---

* "Washington declares that it is waiting for some sign of good will on the part of North Vietnam. Translated, this means: We are waiting for North Vietnam to concede defeat, to beg us to stop bombarding it *and to promise to give no further aid to the Vietcong.* [Italics added.] Clearly this means the Americans are for extending the war. So let's understand them. That is of first importance. And having understood them, we must take a stand ourselves. That is just what I have done." N. B.: Sartre defines *defeat* for North Viet Nam as cessation of aid to the insurgent army in the *South.* He also, in the same article, calls for "democratic elections" in the South, but makes no demand for such elections in the North. His position is completely consistent: he has made it clear elsewhere that he considers Marxism *the* philosophy of our age—"the humus of every particular thought and the horizon of all culture." Sartre, of course, is vehemently pro-Castro, supported the Left in Spain, condemned successful resistance to Communism in Greece and Turkey, etc.

way "immoral," and who condemned the use of force by
the West while remaining silent on its use by the Communists. These people—professors, clergymen, writers and
artists—in effect made Sartre's choice; though *he* at least was
forthright, and refused to use that peculiarly hollow rhetoric
which is the trademark of the American intellectual Left.
The most unpleasant thing about these American Leftists,
indeed, was the fact that while willing to hand over fifteen
million people—several million of them Christians—to Communist rule, they assumed attitudes of *moral superiority*.
But then Christians, as everyone knows, constitute the one
minority in whose persecution—in East Europe, in Asia, in
Africa—neither the press nor the political Left is very much
interested.

Until the 1930s the United States was largely free from
a hard revolutionary Left on the European model. Our later
and milder industrial revolution, our broad cultural agreement, our muted class conflicts, relative affluence, and freedom from invasion, our religious tradition and distrust of the
great secular ideologies—all of these historical factors helped
to insulate America from the forces of revolution. In this
respect America, even more than England, has been special
—or, from the point of view of the world situation today,
retrograde. Yet no modern nation can hope to remain permanently insulated against the passions generated by an
intense phase of the world revolution, and revolutionary tensions are now appearing within the United States. Significantly enough, in explaining his Viet Nam stand in *The
Nation* article I have quoted, Sartre observed that he was
refusing to visit this country even though he "had noted the
development in the United States of an active minority,
whose views I sympathized with, which has been participating side by side with Negroes in the struggle against racial
discrimination." For surely the most portentous American

political development of the past year has been the merging of civil-rights and "peace" groups. This is a delicate matter to discuss, and most comment has steered clear of it. It has been dealt with at some length, however, in a previous chapter, and virtually every day's paper presents new evidence of it. For example, among the fifteen thousand students (15,000!) who picketed the White House this year to denounce American intervention in Viet Nam, civil-rights groups were prominent.† And even Martin Luther King has come out against our intervention in Viet Nam.

In March, 1965, under the complacent headline "The Stu-

---

† Among the statements put out by groups participating in the march were the following: "[The President's speech at Johns Hopkins] will go down in history as one of the most cynical in our century. [It] ties 'negotiation' to the continuation of the following crimes: MASS MURDERS . . . , OPEN AGGRESSION . . . , VIOLATION OF COUNTLESS INTERNATIONAL AGREEMENTS . . . , DECEIT . . . , FRAUD . . . , VIOLATION OF THE U. S. CONSTITUTION. . . . We support the just and reasonable demands made by the Premier of the Democratic Republic of Vietnam, i.e., Ho Chi Minh, in response to Johnson's peace hoax."—*Youth Against War & Fascism.*

"We hereby declare our conscientious refusal to co-operate with the United States Government in the prosecution of the war in Vietnam. We encourage those who can conscientiously do so to refuse to serve in the armed forces and to ask for discharge if they are already in. Those of us who are subject to the draft ourselves declare our own intention to refuse to serve. We urge others to refuse and refuse ourselves to take part in the manufacture or transportation of military equipment, or to work in the fields of military research and weapons development. We shall encourage the development of other non-violent acts, including acts which involve civil disobedience, in order to stop the flow of American soldiers and munitions to Vietnam."—[Sponsored by] *The Catholic Worker, Committee for Nonviolent Action, Student Peace Union, War Resisters League,* and individual signers including Kay Boyle, Dorothy Day, W. H. Ferry, Erich Fromm, Paul Goodman, Linus Pauling, Bayard Rustin, Harvey Swados.

"We voted for Johnson and peace, but got the 'mad-bomber's' foreign policy. Our war games of torture and murder . . . are directed against the Vietnamese people who are fighting a civil war of independence. These can be matched in history only by the experiments of Nazi doctors and extermination centers. U.S. operations in Vietnam are the modern day Guernicas and Auschwitzes." *NYC Dubois Clubs.* (All quoted in *National Review,* XVII, xvii, p. 358.)

dent Left: Spurring Reform," the *New York Times* took account of another important political development—the proliferation of Left revolutionary groups on the American campus. The major ones, said the *Times*, are Students for a Democratic Society, the W.E.B. DuBois Clubs of America, the Northern Student Movement, and the Student Non-Violent Coordinating Committee. The political climate in these groups is openly revolutionary, and their aims, the *Times* makes clear, go far beyond such prosaic goals as voting rights and job opportunities. "The whole society," said a representative spokesman, "is run and compounded on lies." Though most spokesmen for this "new Left" appeared to be motivated chiefly by resentment against their own society, and to have only the vaguest notion of the sort of society they would like, some were more specific. In the opinion of Bettina Apthecker, DuBois Club leader in California, and daughter of the well-known Communist theoretician, "at present, the Socialist world, even with all its problems, is moving closer than any other countries toward the sort of society I think should exist. In the Soviet Union, it has almost been achieved."‡

I think it is safe to say that we are in for trouble. Within the United States, radical resentment of this character will be energized by the prestige of revolutionary movements abroad, and it seems likely that American politics during the next decade, under pressure from the Left, will depart from its usual "consensual" character. What the radical Left has in mind, obviously, is the proliferation of those social infra-structures (student groups, intellectuals' committees, university organizations, women's groups, labor agitational

---

‡ Ironically enough, while approving of most things in the Soviet Union, Miss Apthecker figured prominently in the Berkeley *Free Speech* agitation. To take such ironies seriously, however, may be characteristic of the bourgeois consciousness.

groups, Negro activist organizations) without which effective revolutionary action would be impossible. Outside the United States the process has gone very much further, though in doing so it has also generated a more knowing and determined resistance. We may recall the anti-NATO demonstrations against General Ridgway in Paris in 1951, the rioting in Latin America against Nixon in 1959, the anti-Eisenhower riots in Tokyo in 1960, the violent and slanderous protests against the visit of the Greek Queen to London in 1963. The picketing of the White House over Viet Nam—fifteen thousand students very professionally organized and bussed to the capital—may be regarded as only a kind of dress rehearsal for the real thing.

I do not think it has been pointed out that this resurgence of revolutionary anger in America was foreshadowed by a shift that occurred in the mood of the literary and intellectual world during the late 1950s, and that thrust to the center of the stage the literary flacks and intellectual voyeurs of revolution. I do not mean to suggest anything so foolish as that this shift in mood *caused* the resurgence of radical anger, but rather that literary intellectuals, for a variety of reasons, were attracted to revolutionary feeling—and were eager to intensify it and render it more glamorous, and anxious to find a social basis for it. As Michael Harrington says, ingenuously enough, "a good deal of the recent activity on the Left has centered on the search for a new proletariat." Translated, this means: the revolutionary anger is *there*, in the mind of the Leftist—but it requires a respectable pretext to exhibit itself in action (riots, sit-ins, teach-ins, etc.).§ Of course, the whole thing has happened before. In Daniel

§ The desperate search for a proletariat sometimes has a comic aspect, as when C. Wright Mills, inspired by student riots in Tokyo, Seoul and Ankara, projected a Youth Class in whose name the revolution might be carried out.

Aaron's *Writers on the Left* (1962), a study of the Left-wing and Communist literary movement of the twenties and thirties, we find that for most of the Leftist writers the Depression did not so much cause the anger as provide a pretext for the expression of something that was already there —a pervasive contempt for the United States, a fierce and snobbish anger. "Americans I would permit to serve me," wrote Kay Boyle in 1928, *before* the Depression, "to conduct me rapidly and competently wherever I was going, but not for one moment to impose their achievements on what was going on in my mind and soul." This year, thirty-seven years later, she is signing petitions against the administration's policy in Viet Nam. What has changed? The hatred is the reality; the political event is the pretext.

Naturally, the following remarks are only a footnote to politics, but still it ought to be recorded that, beginning in the late 1950s, a number of writers of a very particular character were thrust forward, "puffed," one after another— in New York. Installed in that great coiled horn (to use a figure of Hugh Kenner's), unremarkable cicadas, once they had found the right wave length, began booming like bullfrogs. They were not potent as writers, but they provided clues to the mood of culturally powerful circles. Thus, we had the Beat season, the Norman O. Brown season, the Norman Mailer season, the Paul Goodman, Leslie Fiedler, C. P. Snow, and James Baldwin seasons. None of these writers was especially significant in a literary way: Mailer, Snow, and Baldwin, for example, remained of only passing interest as novelists. Their vogue was political, and was understood to be so.‖

‖ Clement Greenberg, for example, confided to me that a conscious effort had been made, for political reasons, to inflate Mailer as a novelist. I am not certain how literally he meant me to understand this remark—such things can be the product of a mood, but appear intentional in retrospect. Never-

What these suddenly fashionable writers had in common, of course, was an irritable rejection of America and of the West: 1) America is a nightmare—secede from it (the Beats); 2) America is a vast fraud, and none of its jobs are worth having; Jack Kennedy looks like a Catholic who's afraid of masturbating (Paul Goodman); 3) America ruins your sex life and its culture is literally carcinogenic (Norman Mailer); 4) America, as its literature shows is incapable of mature sexuality and drives one toward a homosexual death-wish (Leslie Fiedler); 5) America is guilty of psychological mass-murder (a new political category), and is (you guessed it!) sexually deficient, *and* all of its values have to be changed —*only it's too late!* (James Baldwin); 6) unless either America or Russia gives up the atom bomb the world is doomed— and, after all, the Russians can't be expected to give theirs up; and besides, you can live as comfortably in Russia as anywhere else (C. P. Snow)¶; 7) life in society, any society, is impossibly painful—so we should toss it off and return to the polymorphous sexuality of infants: back then, we were

theless, the shift to the Left required, among other things, symposia on the 1930s at Columbia University and elsewhere, meant to convey the idea that Leftist political commitment is admirable and exciting ("those were the days . . ."). Norman Podhoretz, a faithful servant of the *Zeitgeist*, wrote a long essay puffing Mailer and switched to Ban-the-Bomb politics, all the while calling for a "new utopianism." We also saw the refurbishing of such ancient Leftist writers as Maxwell Geismar, as well as the emergence of such figures as Susan Sontag, a sort of Joan Baez of—of all places—the Columbia University Religion Department.

¶ As everyone now knows, something uncalled for happened to the Snow season (1961–62), and he himself felt like a man who had been thrown overboard. Dr. Leavis said No. Even as Snow was touring the campuses as a pundit, even as he was being puffed by *Commentary*, the book clubs, and Lionel Trilling, the Snow season—almost, one sensed, in the middle of a symposium—ended.

happy and not aggressive—i.e., man is born free, but everywhere he is in chains (Norman O. Brown).**

This sort of thing has been highly fashionable in literary-
intellectual circles during the past decade. To this has the
Revolution come. Alas, Bakunin! Alas, Marx! But then this
was its intellectual destiny. Its political destiny is another
matter, and what presents itself as a farce may end as a
tragedy.

II

I wrote of the tendency of liberal opinion to fragment into
a Left and a Right under the pressure of actual choices.
Because the choices pressed upon us are frequently of an
either-or character, a "third" position becomes, increasingly,
illusory. Should the Communists be resisted in Greece, or
should they not be? Should they be allowed to take over in
Cuba or not? In Venezuela? In Viet Nam? Only when this
question is answered in the negative does discussion become
relevant on the anti-Communist side about possible courses of
action. But there is no "third" answer to the question. Once
again the example of Sartre is useful, this time in his symbolic break with Camus. "While Sartre believed in the truth
of socialism," writes Simone de Beauvoir, "Camus became
a more and more resolute champion of bourgeois values;
The Rebel was his statement of solidarity with them. A

** Other voices joined the chorus—indeed a kind of grotesque anthology
could be compiled. At a conference in 1960 on "American Writing Today,"
James Baldwin, Philip Roth and John Cheever offered us their insights:
"There is no structure in American life today and there are no human beings" (Baldwin); "life in the United States in 1960 is Hell . . . [The] only
possible position for a writer now is negation" (Cheever); America "stupefies,
it sickens, it infuriates" (Roth).

neutralist position between the two blocs had become impossible; Sartre therefore drew nearer to the U.S.S.R.; Camus hated the Russians, *and although he did not like the United States, he went over, practically speaking, to the American side.*" (Italics added.) As both Sartre and Camus understood, and Camus, of course, was very far to the Left, the aggressive nature of the revolutionary enterprise ruled out any "third" position.

Turning from this symbolic dispute among intellectuals to the choices that actually present themselves to policymakers, we see the same dichotomy emerge. Thus, in both the Dominican Republic and Viet Nam, a liberal Democratic administration—faced with a choice between Communist take-over and resistance—adopted in its entirety the "extremist" foreign policy it had denounced during the 1964 Presidential election campaign. It adopted this policy with broad popular support, and with the support of conservative congressmen—but it came under violent attack from its own liberal intellectual supporters. This situation may be taken as paradigmatic: there *is* no distinctively liberal mode of resistance, and when a liberal policy-maker does choose to resist he merely adopts the policies of his conservative opponents.

Odd as the notion may seem at first, the political circumstance in which liberalism finds itself may be illuminated by comparing it in key respects with the religious dilemma faced by John Henry Newman in the middle of the nineteenth century. We might even view it as the *secularization* of that religious dilemma. Newman, attempting to pursue a "middle way" between Protestantism and Roman Catholicism, came to understand that the Anglican "middle way" in actuality contained no principle upon which, as he said, churchmen could take their stand. The supposed "middle way" was simply the uneasy meeting place of contradictory tendencies, and in practice more hospitable to "liberalization" —even to skepticism and rationalism—than to doctrinal strictness. In the famous controversy over the Jerusalem bishopric, Newman saw the Anglican Church willing to overlook its own fundamental doctrines: it "actually was courting an intercommunion with Protestant Prussia and the heresy of the Orientals. The Anglican Church might have the apostolical succession, as had the monophysites: but such acts as were in progress led me to the gravest suspicion, not that it would soon cease to be a church, but that it had never been a church at all." In Newman's view, the "middle way" was hospitable to positions quite contradictory to its own supposed nature.

Moving into the political arena, we may see that liberalism also presents itself as a "middle way," but that under pressure from the hard Left it tends to fragment—part moving in the direction of Sartre, another part moving toward the Right. The suspicion that arises about liberalism therefore is a deep one, and goes beyond the question of whether its characteristic attitudes—its universalism, its minimizing of privacy, its faith in progress, its secularism—are *relevant* to our real problems, to widespread anomie and alienation, to the breakdown of community, to the attenuation of moral sanctions. Clearly, liberalism is not relevant.

The deeper question, suggested by the evocation of Newman's dilemma, is whether liberalism (despite the familiarity of its attitudes) has *ever* existed as a position, except in a derivative way. Is it, really, only a criticism of one thing, and a tendency toward another—but, in itself, nothing? Upon examination, even such classic and valuable liberal positions as Mill's on the virtues of "discussion" would appear to assume a prior agreement on fundamentals among those participating in the discussion. What is there really to discuss with a man whose assumptions and goals are totally different from one's own—who denies, to choose the extreme case, one's right to exist? Or what would be the value of a political discussion with Sartre, who has already made a considered choice that is thoroughly consistent with his assumptions? No "information" would change his position. He was perfectly right, and quite unsentimental, in refusing to come to the United States. Among those who enjoy a broad agreement on their interests and goals, the sort of discussion Mill had in mind is useful indeed, and certainly can be a mode of illumination. But because Mill's position in this matter seems to depend upon broad prior agreement—in point of fact, on the existence of a common civilization—and because there is nothing in his position capable of generating or sustaining such a civilization, his position comes to seem merely an attractive, indeed a desirable, derivative.

To point to the derivative nature of liberalism and its tendency to fragment under the pressure of actual choices is to suggest, as well, the proper role of conservatism as an intellectual movement in the decades ahead. As liberalism disintegrates, part will become, as K. R. Minogue puts it, increasingly "visionary"—will move toward the far Left. But another part will move to the Right. We have seen the division open over foreign policy. It is certain to do so over domestic policy, and it is part of the logic of the situation that the hard Left will strike first not at Republicans and conservatives but at that complacent agency of our uneasy consensus, the Democratic Party—perhaps through some divisive dispute over the Mississippi Freedom Democratic Party. Because, under a variety of revolutionary pressures, liberalism will fragment, it is extremely important that a coherent and articulate conservative position be available in America. For reasons set forth in the opening chapter of this book, the conservative position, latent though it is in our civilization, has only recently begun to receive significant articulation. The tone of the literary world continues to be set by *soi-disant* Marxists and intellectual revolutionaries; the communications media and the Academy continue to be far more open to the Left than to the Right. As a result, it is, as Whittaker Chambers once wrote, "almost impossible to communicate anything outside the stimulus and tone range of the bonging [liberal] bell." Nevertheless, as we have seen in this book, the effort is being made. And surely, the cause is not hopeless. England stood out against the revolutionary frenzy in 1789—and in so doing performed a great service for civilization. With sufficient determination and intelligence, we can do the same thing today.

To this conservative effort, *National Review* has made a most important contribution. Not only has it provided a demonstration for the community at large that a coherent conservative case can be put forward with wit, style, and intellectual force—and even discovered a satirist of original genius in Kreuttner—but it has, within the conservative movement itself, acted as an agent of education and intellectual refinement. By bringing together the different conservative spokesmen, it has forced them to take serious account of one another, and, in consequence, to refine and deepen their own positions. Russell Kirk's writings, for example, have shown an increasing appreciation of the role of economics, and he has thus added to and complicated his traditionalist position. Frank Meyer, on the other hand, has modified some of his earlier positions to take account of the claims of continuity and community. Furthermore, as the only conservative journal with a substantial circulation, it has been able to perform intellectual services which, policies aside, are good in themselves. The book review section, for example, has maintained a consistently high quality and discovered some striking new reviewers—such as Wills, Davenport, and Didion; but its particular strength lies in the fact that it calls attention to authors who are usually greeted with silence or perfunctory dismissal in even the abler liberal journals. It is in *National Review* that one can find an intelligent account of new books by, say, Eric Voegelin, Christopher Dawson, Charles Williams or F. D. Wilhelmsen. An entire area of intellectual concern is thus rescued from an entirely intentional neglect.

To be sure, *National Review* has made some omissions. One would like to see in a conservative magazine, surely, a continuous concern for the conservation of the American countryside: all this should not have been left to Rachel Carson and Stewart Udall. Conservatives will also have to devote more thought to such things as city planning and the problems implicit in automation. Frank S. Meyer, speaking at the first national meeting of the Philadelphia Society—an organization of conservative intellectuals—pointed out how far conservative thought has come during the last few years, but also how much remains to be done—in historical scholarship, in ethical thought, in metaphysics, in political theory.

Everything cannot be done at once, and though a great deal does remain to be done, the conservatives have succeeded in bringing a sense of alternative possibility into our political and cultural life. The last ten years, indeed, have seen a dramatic change in the prospects of intellectual conservatism. In 1954 its voices were few and scattered, its books for the most part still unwritten. Today there is something like a conservative intellectual Establishment. *National Review* has played a vital role in bringing about this transformation. There most certainly is an alternative to the revolutionary Left and to a dissolving liberalism—an alternative that is in harmony with our traditions and with the best that is in our actual civilization.

Footnotes

PREFACE and CHAPTER I

1. *Commonweal* (Dec. 11, 1964), p. 373.
2. Fall, 1964, p. 593.
3. Kenneth R. Minogue, *The Liberal Mind* (London, 1963).
4. *National Review*, II, xxv, p. 12.
5. Frank S. Meyer, "Principles and Heresies," *National Review*, II, xiii, p. 17.
6. "Principles and Heresies," *National Review*, XV, p. 386.
7. "Notes Towards a Definition of Conservatism" in *What Is Conservatism?*, ed. Frank S. Meyer (New York, 1964), p. 214.
8. "The New Journalism: '*National Review*'," *National Review*, III, p. 328.
9. "Trivia as Trivia," *National Review*, XVII, p. 287.
10. *National Review*, VI, p. 55.
11. "A New Look at a Controversial Committee," *National Review*, XII, p. 15.
12. *Up From Liberalism* (New York, 1959), p. 4.
13. See "Scrambled Eggheads on the Right," *Commentary* (April, 1956), pp. 367–73.
14. *The Progressive* (July, 1956), pp. 13–16.
15. *Commentary* (March, 1965).

CHAPTER II

1. *Suicide of the West*, p. 143.
2. "The Asphalt Bungle," *New York Herald Tribune* (Jan. 3, 1965).
3. "Notes on the Other America," *National Review*, I, xxii, p. 8.
4. "Report From the Publisher," *National Review*, xi, p. 8.
5. *Suicide of the West*, pp. 143–44.
6. *Ibid.*, p. 37.

7. *Rationalism in Politics* (New York, 1962), p. 21.
8. Kenneth R. Minogue, *The Liberal Mind* (London, 1963), p. 3.
9. *Ibid.*
10. Michael Oakeshott, *Rationalism in Politics*, p. 5.
11. *Ibid.*
12. "South African Fortnight," *National Review*, XIV, pp. 17–23.
13. *Rationalism in Politics*, p. 3.
14. *Suicide of the West*, p. 182.
15. *National Review*, XI, p. 184.
16. Quoted in *Suicide of the West*, p. 67.
17. *Ibid.*, p. 50.
18. *The New Science of Politics*, p. 129.
19. *Ibid.*, p. 131.
20. "To Magnify the West," *National Review*, XII, pp. 285–87.
21. *Autobiography*, Chapter V.
22. *The United States in the World Arena*, pp. 463–64.
23. "What Is Conservatism?", *The Conservative Affirmation*, pp. 7–8.
24. "To Make the Crooked Straight," *National Review*, VII, p. 490.
25. "Easy Conclusion," *National Review*, I, ii, p. 29.
26. "Religion and Public Life," *National Review*, XV, p. 61.
27. *Ibid.*
28. *Ibid.*
29. *Ibid.*, p. 104.
30. *Ibid.*
31. "Lowest Common Denominator," *National Review*, VI, p. 655.
32. *National Review*, XIII, p. 125.
33. *Ibid.*, IV, p. 482.
34. *Ibid.*, V, pp. 6–7.
35. "Chop Down That Tree," *National Review*, XIII, p. 504.
36. *National Review*, III, p. 78.
37. *Ibid.*, XIII, *Bulletin* No. 11, p. 1.
38. See *Ibid.*, IV, pp. 78–79.
39. "Empty Churches," *National Review*, XI, p. 88.
40. "Letter From London," *National Review*, I, xv, p. 16.
41. "Letter From the Continent," *National Review*, II, v, p. 17.
42. *Ibid.*, ii, p. 13.
43. *Ibid.*
44. *The Liberal Mind*, p. 2.
45. *Suicide of the West*, p. 84.
46. *What's Wrong With the World* (London, 1910), pp. 52–54.
47. *Ibid.*
48. *National Review*, VI, p. 572.
49. *Ibid.*, IV, p. 244.
50. *Ibid.*, XV, pp. 427–38.

51. "What Time Is It?", *National Review*, VI, p. 180.
52. "Americanism," *The Idler and His Works* (New York, 1957), pp. 37–40.
53. *National Review*, I, p. 10.
54. *Ibid.*, p. 15.
55. *Ibid.*, p. 42.
56. *National Review*, II, p. 7.
57. *The Liberal Mind*, p. 2.
58. "Does ADA Run the New Frontier?", *National Review*, XIV, pp. 359–60.
59. *Suicide of the West*, pp. 84–85.
60. *Ibid.*, p. 84, note 6.
61. *Ibid.*, pp. 178–79.
62. Quoted by Yosal Rogat in *New York Review of Books* (Oct. 22, 1964), p. 6.
63. *Commentary* (December, 1964), p. 68.
64. *Suicide of the West*, p. 85.
65. Jacques Barzun, *The House of Intellect* (New York, 1959), pp. 28–29.
66. *Ibid.*, p. 29.
67. "Principles and Heresies," *National Review*, XIV, p. 197.
68. *Ibid.*
69. *Suicide of the West*, p. 79.
70. "The Liberal Line," *National Review*, IV, p. 191.
71. *What's Wrong With the World* (New York, 1956), p. 44.
72. See Michael Oakeshott, "The Political Economy of Freedom," *Rationalism in Politics*, p. 39.
73. "The Eclipse of Property," *National Review*, II, xxv, p. 25.
74. *Ibid.*, VI, p. 2.
75. *Ibid.*, II, xxii, p. 11.
76. *In Defense of Freedom* (Chicago, 1962), p. 91.
77. *Rationalism in Politics*, p. 6.
78. *Suicide of the West*, p. 81.
79. *Ibid.*, p. 82.
80. "On the Right," January 12, 1965 (syndicated column).
81. "Radicals on the Right," *Partisan Review* (Fall, 1964), pp. 564–65.
82. *National Review*, XI, p. 404.
83. See *Ibid.*, XIII, p. 419; also *ibid.*, XIV, p. 8.
84. *Ibid.*, XIII, p. 20.
85. James Burnham, *Suicide of the West*, pp. 170–71.
86. *The Liberal Mind*, p. 6.
87. *Ibid.*, p. 8.
88. *Ibid.*, p. 9.
89. *Ibid.*

90. *Ibid.*, p. 11.
91. *Suicide of the West*, p. 70.
92. *Ibid.*, p. 170.
93. *National Review*, VIII, p. 43.
94. *Ibid.*, II, xviii, p. 13. See also *ibid.*, VIII, *Bulletin* 8, p. 1; *ibid.*, VI, p. 357.
95. *Ibid.*, III, p. 564.
96. *Ibid.*, XIV, *Bulletin* 13, p. 2.
97. *Ibid.*, IV, p. 483.
98. *Ibid.*, III, p. 25.
99. *Ibid.*, IV, p. 87.
100. *Ibid.*, VII, p. 229.
101. *Ibid.*, XIII, p. 420.
102. *Ibid.*, XII, *Bulletin* 7, p. 2.
103. *New York Herald Tribune Book Review* (Dec. 10, 1964), p. 1.
104. *Commentary* (January, 1965).
105. *New York Herald Tribune Book Week* (Jan. 24, 1965), p. 17.
106. *New York Herald Tribune Magazine* (March 21, 1956), p. 17.
107. *Up From Liberalism* (New York, 1959), p. 156.

CHAPTER III

1. See Nathan Glazer and Daniel Patrick Moynihan, *Beyond the Melting Pot* (Cambridge, 1963), pp. 30–33.
2. *Ibid.*, p. 31.
3. *Ibid.*, pp. 51–52.
4. *Ibid.*, pp. 43–44.
5. Garry Wills, "Who Will Overcome?", *National Review*, XVI, p. 820.
6. *Ibid.*, p. 818; John Chamberlain, "The Man Next to You," *National Review*, II, xvii, p. 18.
7. Michael Oakeshott, "The Political Economy of Freedom," *Rationalism in Politics* (New York, 1962), p. 43.
8. *National Review*, VII, p. 292.
9. *Ibid.*, p. 127.
10. *Ibid.*, p. 321.
11. *Ibid.*
12. *Ibid.*, IV, p. 579.
13. *Ibid.*, XII, p. 123.
14. *Ibid.*, II, xxxi, p. 5.
15. *Ibid.*, IV, p. 196.

16. *Ibid.*, XII, p. 123.
17. *Ibid.*, I, xvii, p. 6.
18. *Ibid.*, VIII, p. 193.
19. See *Ibid.*, I, xxii, p. 4.
20. R. H. S. Crossman, "Radicals on the Right," *Partisan Review* (Fall, 1964), pp. 564–65.
21. *National Review*, XVII, p. 180.
22. Garry Wills, "What Color Is God?", *National Review*, XIV, p. 408.
23. *Ibid.*
24. *Ibid.*, p. 411.
25. Nathan Glazer, "Negroes and Jews: The New Challenge to Pluralism," *Commentary* (December, 1964), pp. 29–35.
26. Oscar Handlin, *The Fire Bell in the Night* (Boston, 1964), p. 58.
27. *Ibid.*, p. 57.
28. "The Call to Color Blindness," *National Review*, XIV, p. 488.
29. *Ibid.*

CHAPTER IV

1. The following account depends upon Whittaker Chambers' essay "Morningside," in *Cold Friday* (New York, 1964), pp. 89–144.
2. *Ibid.*, pp. 108–09.
3. See, for example, John M. Cuddihy's review of *The Civic Culture* by Gabriel Almond and Sidney Verba (Princeton, 1964), in *The Burke Newsletter* (Spring, 1965), pp. 449–52.
4. See *New York Herald Tribune* (Feb. 10, 1965); also *National Review Bulletin* (Feb. 16, 1965), p. 3.
5. See report by the Committee on Un-American Activities, House of Representatives, U. S. Congress, entitled: "Trial by Treason—The National Committee to Secure Justice for the Rosenbergs and Morton Sobell" (August 25, 1956), p. 12.
6. "Spanish Ordeal," *National Review*, XI, p. 91.
7. "Speech to the Portuguese Legion," *National Review*, II, xxxii, p. 8.
8. Gerhart Niemeyer, "Are Communists Rational?", *National Review*, III, i, p. 16.
9. *Ibid.*, p. 15.
10. Frank S. Meyer, *The Moulding of Communists* (New York, 1961), pp. 126, 154–55.
11. William Buckley, *Up From Liberalism* (New York, 1959), p. 115.
12. See, for example, E. A. Mowrer's review of Thomas Molnar's *The Two*

Faces of American Foreign Policy (New York, 1963) in *National Review*, XIV, p. 29.

13. Thomas Molnar, "All-Too-Hasty Wisdom," *National Review*, XI, p. 20.
14. *Ibid.*, p. 21.
15. See, for example, the *National Review* editorial in VIII, p. 285.
16. Robert Strausz-Hupé, William R. Kintner, James E. Dougherty and Alvin J. Cottrell, *Protracted Conflict* (New York, 1959), p. 21.
17. *Ibid.*, pp. 86–87.
18. "Can Anyone Strike Back?", *National Review*, I, xv, p. 19.
19. "Nature of the Enemy?", *National Review*, III, p. 283.
20. *National Review*, I, xvi, p. 6.
21. James Burnham, "What Kind of War?", *National Review*, VIII, p. 228.
22. *National Review*, XI, p. 222.
23. See "Hungary, Tibet and the Caribbean," *National Review*, VII, p. 203.
24. *Ibid.*
25. *National Review*, XI, p. 111.
26. *Ibid.*, p. 112.
27. Robert Strausz-Hupé, "Soviet War Doctrine," *National Review*, VII, p. 430.
28. "The Battle for Aerospace," *National Review*, XV, p. 346.
29. "The Answer to Sputniks," *National Review*, IV, p. 542.
30. *National Review*, VII, p. 69.
31. *Ibid.*, p. 70.
32. "Communism Remains Communism," *National Review*, II, p. 10.
33. "The Times Finds Another Nice Communist," *National Review*, IV, p. 41.
34. Robert Strausz-Hupé, *et al.*, *Protracted Conflict* (New York, 1959), p. 71.
35. "Dialectic of the Split," *National Review*, XVII, p. 274.
36. M. Stanton Evans, "Collective Insecurity," *National Review*, XVI, p. 201.
37. Sen. William Fulbright, "For a Concert of Free Nations," *Foreign Affairs* (Oct. 1961), pp. 16–17.
38. James Burnham, "What to Do About the U.N.," *National Review*, XII, p. 284.
39. *Ibid.*
40. *National Review*, XII, p. 8.
41. James Burnham, "Arithmetic of the United Nations," *National Review*, VIII, p. 99.
42. James Burnham, "Emancipation Proclamation," *National Review*, XIII, p. 348.
43. *National Review*, XV, p. 88.

44. James Burnham, "Mr. Kennedy Goes to War," *National Review*, XV, p. 59.
45. *National Review*, XV, Bulletin 17, p. 2.
46. *National Review*, XV, p. 466.
47. James Burnham, "What to Do About the U.N.," *National Review*, XII, p. 284.
48. *National Review*, XIV, Bulletin 23, p. 1.
49. James Burnham, *Suicide of the West* (New York, 1964), p. 199.
50. *Ibid.*, p. 197.
51. Erik von Kuehnelt-Leddihn, "Growing Disillusionment with the U.S.," *National Review*, XIII, p. 265.
52. See both "The Yalta Strategy," *National Review*, XV, p. 237; and "Does Johnson Have a Foreign Policy?", *National Review*, XVI, p. 190.

CHAPTER V

1. Hugh Kenner in "A Program for a Goldwater Administration," *National Review*, XVI, p. 598.
2. *Ibid.*
3. *Ibid.*
4. William Buckley, "The Ivory Tower," *National Review*, I, viii, p. 24.
5. William Buckley, *Up From Liberalism* (New York, 1959), p. 66; see also Buckley, "The Ivory Tower," *National Review*, I, viii, p. 24.
6. "The Ivory Tower," *National Review*, I, viii, p. 24.
7. *Up From Liberalism*, p. 66.
8. *Ibid.*, p. 67.
9. *National Review*, XV, p. 281.
10. William Buckley, "The Ivory Tower," *National Review*, I, viii, p. 24.
11. Russell Kirk, *Academic Freedom* (Chicago, 1955), p. 27.
12. *Ibid.*, pp. 28–29.
13. Russell Kirk, "St. Andrews," *National Review*, II, xiv, p. 18.
14. *Ibid.*
15. Russell Kirk, "Behold Behemoth," *National Review*, I, xi, p. 24.
16. *Ibid.*
17. Russell Kirk, "In Defense of Fraternities: Part II," *National Review*, III, p. 479.
18. Russell Kirk, "Knox College and Fraternities," *National Review*, V, p. 401.
19. Russell Kirk, "In Defense of Fraternities: Part I," *National Review*, III, p. 453.

CHAPTER VI

1. *Modern Age* (Spring, 1964), pp. 119–33.
2. See Raymond English' review of Michael Oakeshott's *Rationalism in Politics* in *The Burke Newsletter* (Winter, 1964), pp. 295–98.
3. *The Conservative Mind* (Chicago, 1953), pp. 5–6.
4. *National Review*, V, p. 17.
5. "Edmund Burke and the Twentieth Century," *The Relevance of Edmund Burke* (New York, 1964), p. 45.
6. Willmoore Kendall and George Carey, "Towards a Definition of Conservative," *The Journal of Politics* (May, 1964), pp. 406–22.
7. *National Review*, V, pp. 133–35.
8. "Is Tradition Anti-Intellectual?", *National Review*, I, xvii, p. 24.
9. "York and Social Boredom," *Sewanee Review* (Autumn, 1953), pp. 664–81.
10. C. P. Ives, "Edmund Burke and the Legal Order," *The Relevance of Edmund Burke* (New York, 1964), p. 59.
11. *The Relevance of Edmund Burke*, p. 60.
12. *Ibid.*, pp. 67–70.
13. Yosal Rogat, "Mr. Justice Pangloss," *New York Review of Books* (Oct. 22, 1964), pp. 5–7.
14. *Ibid.*, p. 6.
15. "Dilemma of Conservatism," *National Review*, V, pp. 185–86.
16. "A Conservatism of Reflection," *National Review*, XVI, pp. 198–99.
17. "Collectivism Revisited," *The Freeman* (July, 1955).
18. *Ibid.*
19. Peter J. Stanlis, "Edmund Burke in the Twentieth Century," *The Relevance of Edmund Burke* (New York, 1964), p. 50.
20. Review of *The Conservative Affirmation* in *Modern Age* (Fall, 1963), pp. 438–42.
21. See the Preface to *The Conservative Affirmation* (Chicago, 1963).
22. Preface to *The Conservative Affirmation*, pp. 10–11.
23. "What Is Conservatism?", *The Conservative Affirmation*, p. 8.
24. *Ibid.*, p. 16.
25. "Three on the Line," *National Review*, IV, pp. 179–81.
26. *Ibid.*, p. 181.
27. *Ibid.*
28. "The Regime of the South," *National Review*, VI, p. 587.
29. "Do We Want an Open Society?", *National Review*, VI, pp. 481–93.
30. *Ibid.*, p. 493.

31. In *The Conservative Affirmation*.
32. *Ibid.*, pp. 22–24; Kendall's list has been condensed somewhat here.
33. *The Conservative Affirmation*, pp. 24–25.
34. *Ibid.*, p. 34.
35. *Ibid.*, p. 35.
36. *Ibid.*, p. 44.
37. *Ibid.*, p. 47.
38. Aaron B. Wildavsky and Nelson W. Polsby, *Presidential Elections* (New York, 1964), p. 149.
39. "The Two Majorities in American Politics," *The Conservative Affirmation*, p. 29.
40. "Hang on to Your Hats," *National Review*, XIV, pp. 322–24.
41. "Three on the Line," *National Review*, IV, p. 180.
42. "American Conservatism and the 'Prayer' Decisions," *Modern Age* (Summer, 1964), pp. 245–59.
43. *In Defense of Freedom* (Chicago, 1962), pp. 1–2.
44. *Ibid.*, p. 3.
45. *Ibid.*
46. *Ibid.*, p. 6.
47. "To Educate the Present," *National Review*, XIII, pp. 396–98.
48. *Ibid.*, p. 397.
49. *Ibid.*, p. 398.
50. *In Defense of Freedom*, pp. 68–69.
51. *Ibid.*, p. 70.
52. *Ibid.*
53. *National Review*, XIV, pp. 184 ff.
54. *Ibid.*, p. 184.
55. *Ibid.*
56. *Ibid.*, p. 185.
57. "Freedom, Virtue and the State," *National Review*, XV, p. 193.
58. *Ibid.*
59. *The Pearl*, trans. by Stanley Perkins Chase (New York, 1932), p. 58.
60. *Economics of the Free Society* (Chicago, 1963), pp. 239–40.
61. *Ibid.*, p. 239.
62. *Ibid.*, p. 240.
63. *Ibid.*, p. 233.
64. *Ibid.*
65. *Ibid.*, p. 234.
66. *Ibid.*
67. *Ibid.*
68. *Ibid.*, pp. 236–37.
69. *Ibid.*, pp. 246–47.
70. Frederick D. Wilhelmsen, *The Metaphysics of Love* (New York, 1962), pp. 14–15.

71. *Ibid.*, p. 97.
72. *Ibid.*
73. *Ibid.*
74. *Ibid.*, p. 98.
75. *Ibid.*, p. 118.
76. *Ibid.*, p. 124.
77. *Ibid.*, p. 145.
78. *Ibid.*, p. 155.

H6